Pr

"Kamikaze Kangaroos did not disappoint in the slightest. It's bloody brilliant! In fact, I think it could be the best one yet. It still maintains all of the calamitous Tony James Slater situations that we have come to expect from him, and, of course, laughs by the bucket-load. But this book also has a level of emotion and sensitivity that sets it apart from his other books. Who knew Tony could write so sensitively and thoughtfully about love and loss? He even made me cry! It's almost as though he has - dare I say it - GROWN UP since his last book. Nah, who am I kidding? He's still a child at heart."

— George Mahood,
bestselling author of *Free Country*

I have honestly never read such a funny book. I laughed all the way through. Congratulations to Tony Slater for a wonderful read.

— *Moonshine Mumma*

This book is a light-hearted story of a three young people travelling and working their way around Australia. I found this story to be very entertaining and humorous and I even learnt a few interesting things about Australia and the Australian way of life. The chapters were just the right length for me to be able to read one whenever I had a 10 or 20 minutes to spare. I would definitely recommend this book, it's a pleasant way to relax and doesn't tax your brain.

— Peter F.
Amazon Top 1000 Reviewer

Tony is a master storyteller and he draws you in, taking you on a grand sweeping adventure. I've loved all his books but this one is his best. He lives the life that some of us perhaps wished we'd lived (or at least a little bit). I felt as though I was the fourth member of the travelling party as they journeyed around Australia. As always he does a masterful job of describing the situations but he does an even better job of introducing us to his other travelling companions. It's funny and touching and a great trip. I was very disappointed when I reached the end. More please author!

— Martin Crosbie,
Bestselling author of *My Temporary Life*

Praise for *'That Bear Ate My Pants!'* by Tony James Slater

"I laughed all through the book until the end, where I became sad to have to say goodbye. I enjoyed myself that much."

— *Night Owl Reviews*

"…not only well-written and entertaining but downright hilarious. I have not laughed so hard while reading in quite a while. And when I mean laugh, I mean I laughed so hard I was screaming. Warning, do not read this book while on the toilet."

— *Indie Eclective*

"Tony Slater is very gifted at writing comically, and laughter accompanied every page I read at the account of his daily routine looking after animals, birds and reptiles of all shapes and sizes and degrees of ferocity. Despite the tomfoolery of the writing, Tony never forgets the seriousness of the work carried out by the rescue centre, he never forgets to inform us of the beauty and uniqueness of Ecuador, and more importantly, never forgets to reveal not only how much the animals came to mean to him in the short time he was there, but also how much the whole experience touched him. This is one I will read again if I ever need cheering up. It's a guaranteed tonic."

— *Kath 'n' Kindle Book Reviews*

I bought it on the spot just for the title. It is truly the most hilarious book I have ever read, and I've read some good ones. It was a "In-Starbucks-laughing-so-hard-the-tears-came-and-I was concerned I was going to pee myself" kind of reading experience."

— *TravelingCrone.com*

"I can completely imagine Tony standing and enthusiastically delivering each chapter to a wide-eyed audience whilst they think inside their heads *'This guy is a little bit mental'*."

— *BookC*nt*

By
Tony James Slater

Various THINGS
@t **Different** *Times*

ISBN-13: 978-1514131091
ISBN-10: 1514131099

Copyright © Tony James Slater 2015

All rights reserved. No part of this publication may be reproduced, stored in a retrieval system or transmitted, in any form or by any other means without the prior written permission of the author, nor be otherwise circulated in any form of binding or cover other than that in which it is published and without a similar condition being imposed on the purchaser.

Although this is a work of non-fiction, some names have been changed by the author.

An e-book edition of this title is also available.

This first paperback edition was printed by CreateSpace.

Cover Design by **Various Things At Different Times**
Formatted for paperback by **Heather Adkins**

Please visit the author's website for a selection of photographs that accompany this book:

www.TonyJamesSlater.com

Other books by Tony James Slater:

That Bear Ate My Pants!
Don't Need The Whole Dog!
Kamikaze Kangaroos!

Three down, one in hand, and one still to go.
I'm slowly filling this page…
Might be a while before I need to start a new one, though.

CAN I KISS HER YET?

Contents

(Here we go again...)

The Story So Far...1
Homeward Bound..4
The House That Gramp Built...8
Incoming..13
Ways And Means..18
Where To I Do?...23
The Gift That Keeps On Giving...28
When Is A Castle Not A Castle?..34
Tony's End?..39
Boring...44
Cock Chop Post Op..49
Bargain Hunters..53
Destination: Jordan..58
Amman By Day...63
Dinner...68
Floaters..73
Road To Ruin..79
Foreign Food...83
All It's Cracked Up To Be..88
Petrafied...93
Stalling Tactics..98
Getting The Hump..102
Exodus..107
Paperwork..112
Always A Bridesmaid...117
Mere Formalities...123
A Beginning And An End..128
Bare-Faced Cheek...132
Understanding..137
Full House..142
Nocturnal Activities...147
Last Minute Preparations..151
Official Vibes...156
Tying The Knot...162

Contents
(cont.)

Freedom Of Speech	169
Dirty Dancing	174
More Booty	178
Off To A Flying Start	183
The Honeymoon In Spain	189
Departure	190
A Grand Adventure	195
Supply And Demand	200
Bureaucracy	205
Expenses	211
Getting Off	216
Adapting	221
Life Under Canvas	225
The Difference A Plug Makes	231
Posh Nosh	236
Functions Of The Body	240
Strange Folk	245
Training Day	251
Abridged	255
Variation On A Theme	260
Homes And Castles	266
Being Mum And Dad	271
School Daze	276
Friends And Family	281
Towards The Wall	286
A Long Hard Walk Along A Wall	290
Unreadiness	296
Hitting The Wall	300
Back To The Wall	305
Wall's End	309
The End Of An Era	315
Asia's Best Attraction	321
Where The Heart Is	327
Holiday	332
Crossroads	337

For Dennis Slater
1927–2011

The Story So Far...

Well then. Where to begin?

How about an introduction?

Hi there! My name is Tony James Slater.

And I'm an idiot.

It's okay though – I've accepted it.

Sometimes people hear me introduce myself like this, and they say things like, "No, of course you're not!"

And then I do something particularly stupid – like trying to lever an electrical plug out of its socket with a fork – and they say, "Ah! Okay. I stand corrected."

It's wonderfully liberating, being an idiot, whilst at the same time being oddly restrictive. For example, no-one will employ me anymore; probably because they've read my previous books, and they realise that their insurance isn't up to it.

Over the last ten years or so I've been travelling the world in search of adventure. I'd like to think I've been fairly successful, but that would be a lie.

What really happened was adventure snuck up on me while I was looking the other way, put a bag over my head, and spent the next ten years kicking me around the place like a punctured football.

Adventure can, on occasion, be a bit of a bastard.

But it wasn't all bad. I met the girl of my dreams… as well as being shot at, bitten by a crocodile, clawed by a jaguar, attacked by monkeys, dangled by a water buffalo, drugged, robbed, embarrassed on national TV…

And let's not count sinking a yacht, snowboarding off a cliff, getting chased by horny kangaroos and being washed off the side of Australia's national monument. Honestly, I was starting to think there wasn't much left the world could throw at me.

Not *really*.

I was wrong, of course.
But then, I usually am.
It kind of goes with the territory, being an idiot.

So for those of you who don't really know me yet, let me do a recap.

I trained as an actor, and spent several years chasing the dream of international fame and fortune. Then I made an unfortunate discovery: I loved acting, but, sadly, I was crap at it.

In a panicked reaction I set out to travel the world – hoping not so much as to find myself, but to lose him. I donned my rucksack, kissed my dog goodbye, and set out to explore this incredible planet.

I got as far as France.

Turns out, I'm crap at that, too.

But you know what? I had a great time. So much so that my next trip was to Ecuador, where I volunteered in an animal refuge – and got bitten. A lot. Even though I spent most of my time bleeding from a bewildering variety of injuries, I loved almost every minute of it.

And that was when I knew for sure that this was what I wanted to do.

Travel the world. Seek adventure in strange places. Have fun.
And, ideally, try to bleed a little less.
I'm still working on that last one.

So, what else would you like to know? Physically, I'm the same size as most people. I'm taller in boots, or when I've recently been electrocuted. I am extremely clumsy, and yet I have no fear – it has been pointed out to me that this is perhaps not the best combination of attributes. My eye-colour is hazel. My hair colour is dark brown. My hair style is: other. Personality-wise, I've never grown up; people say that about men all the time, but I still play with Lego. Cooking anything more complex than beans on toast brings me out in a cold sweat, so when my fiancé is away I live almost exclusively on corn flakes. And I have the world's worst sense of humour – unless you count my Dad. He knows more than twenty bad jokes just about eggs, and he cracks them without warning.

More than anything, I am someone who loves to *try*. I'm always looking for new experiences, am willing to push the boundaries of comfort, taste and common sense in the hope that somewhere, amidst all the limitless possibilities of this world, I will finally achieve my ultimate goal; I will be *cool*.

It hasn't happened yet.

Luckily, as my adventures progressed from Ecuador to Thailand to Australia, I met a girl who liked me just the way I was.

Well, mostly.

She wanted me to shower and shave more often, and to stop doing such stupid things. I figured that two out of three wasn't bad, and evidently she agreed; when I proposed to her, near her home in Perth, Australia, she said yes.

And with that little piece of happiness, I do believe we are up to date! I might have glossed over a few bits and pieces – like my stint in the army, my brief career as a professional diver and the time I walked almost a thousand miles just to get to McDonald's – but nothing important.

So! The scene is set. The curtain is lifting. Shall we begin?

Okay then.

Enter, stage left: an idiot.

Homeward Bound

Long haul flights.

You'd think I'd get used to them. But there's something so physically debilitating, so torturous, about sitting cramped in one position for twenty-four hours straight, that I always arrive feeling like I've been run over by a train.

Maybe it's the free booze. I mean, I can't resist anything for free – from someone's abandoned French fries to samples of perfume and lipstick.

I looked and smelled *divine* when I boarded the plane.

But somewhere between the getting on and the getting off, things tend to go a bit pear-shaped. Within the weird, messed-up time stream that is a day-long international flight, there's time to go through the whole process of getting drunk, feeling like shit, being violently ill, sleeping it off and waking up hung-over – at least three times in quick succession.

I know, because I've done it.

I've spent hours in the toilet, trying to figure out the most comfortable way of being sick in a confined space – because you can't just adopt the familiar position, kneeling in front of the loo, clutching the rim of the bowl and hurling your stomach contents straight down the pan. NO! You can't – because there isn't room for your ass. You either have to develop a far more intimate relationship with the toilet than you're used to – which isn't great when you consider how many hairy, sweaty bum cheeks have sat straining on it in since take-off – or you learn how to project your vomit accurately whilst standing up. In turbulence.

It's an art I wouldn't say I've mastered, but one that (unfortunately) I've had plenty of practice at.

Not this time.

Without my girlfriend Roo here to look after me, I determined to stay mostly sober; okay, a bit sober. Alright, so I determined not to get completely hammered. Or, not too quickly, anyway.

Free booze!
My anxious mood wasn't helping to bolster my resolve.

Plus, alcohol cost a fortune in Australia. I couldn't remember the last time I'd been drunk. *And Roo will never know…*

Strictly speaking, she was my fiancé now. Booking separate flights to England seemed like a strange way to celebrate an engagement, but I was coming home at top speed due to a family crisis. Roo would be following in a few short weeks, when the cost of flights had halved. Predictably we were both broke, which wouldn't have been such an issue except we were supposed to be getting married this year.

I'd have to put a bit of thought into that at some point.

But first, I had an ailing grandfather to attend to.

And a long-haul flight to survive.

I ordered one of those miniature bottles of white wine, and flipped through the in-flight magazine. This alerted me to two problems that can arise when flying with an Asian airline:

1. The food was Asian.
2. The entertainment was Asian.

Now I don't want to sound racist, but as an English-speaking Westerner this did sort of limit my options.

Fully one-third of the movies on offer were in the 'Asian Film' category.

Another third were dubbed 'Hong Kong Cinema', which to my uncultured senses seemed remarkably similar. The rest of the options slanted heavily towards drama, with an international – nay, *Oriental*, flavour – just what you need when you want to avoid drinking heavily. No action. No sci-fi. No ass-kicking (at least, not in English).

Maybe they changed the rules after I re-enacted key scenes from The Matrix Reloaded on the flight back from New Zealand. Or maybe whoever chooses movies for Cathay Pacific has really, really lousy taste.

Faced with such delightful options as 'My Week With Marilyn', 'The Ides of March', 'The Help', and 'War Horse' – titles just dripping with promise of scantily-clad female assassins, pithy dialogue and CG explosions – I gave in. The inner geek took over and I watched a whole season of future-tech TV shows narrated by Stephen Hawking.

Whilst drinking.

And then came the food.

I love plane food. I had six scheduled meals across two interconnecting flights, and each meal came with two options. And, presumably because this was an Asian carrier, one of those options was always seafood.

To which I can only say: UGH!?

Who the hell eats seafood on a plane? If you're looking for a way to increase the chance of being sick, go right ahead. But seafood – especially for breakfast – just doesn't do it for me.

Sitting right at the back of the plane I could hear the orders being taken all the way down from the toilets. "Chicken, please." "Chicken." "I'll have... ah... the chicken."

Sure enough, by the time the stewardess got to me, the chicken was all gone. It was either seafood pie with mushy peas, or the vegetarian option. Which was probably the mushy peas minus the pie.

"I'll have the chicken," I told the stewardess again.

"Ah, sorry, no have chicken,"

"Please. You have to find some chicken."

"Ah, I can look, in the back?"

"Yes please! I can't eat seafood. Find chicken!"

Thank God she did, rushing back a few minutes later waving a tray. "One left, I find!"

The chicken was delicious, and was enough to tide me over until the next meal: prawns, in... I dunno, whatever the hell you eat prawns in – seawater probably – or beef. Straight away I heard the panicked calls start for beef...

I often wonder about this sort of thing. You're running a jet full of 500 passengers. Do you pack 250 chicken and 250 squid medley? Really? Or do you think, 'Hm, more people seemed to opt for the chicken and rice, rather than the fish tentacles in slime. In fact, this has been the case on every flight for the last ten years. Maybe this time I'll take more chicken and less octopus...'

Obviously, that thought process has never taken place.

Dinner was a spicy seafood soup. I ate a biscuit.

As half the world's oceans rolled by beneath me, I started thinking about what the coming year would have in store for me. There were several small tasks I had to accomplish whilst back in the motherland – the best part of which was actually visiting my mother. And my father. And my sister. And a mixed bag of friends and relatives, most of whom I'd had no contact with since leaving for Thailand nearly four years earlier.

After that, my 'To Do' list contained the following (in no particular order):

Organise a wedding.
Get married.

Help my sister get married.
Publish my book.
Choose a career.
Map out the rest of my life.
Emigrate to Australia.
That was about it for now; as I said, only a few jobs.
It's surprising how nervous I was, thinking about it.

But every now and then, life throws you these little curve-balls, and you suddenly end up flying halfway around the world on a moment's notice, to do something you really don't want to do.

I never dared say it aloud – admitting a fear being tantamount to making it truth – but I had a horrible feeling that I wasn't flying home for a wedding.

I was flying home for a funeral.

The House That Gramp Built

When I got home, I found the story wasn't quite as grim as I'd feared.

The long version is, my eighty-three-year-old Granddad had driven into Scarborough to pay his road tax, only to discover that the post office he normally used had closed down. Wandering around the town centre looking for another one, he'd become hot and tired. Eventually, after asking everywhere he could think of, he'd decided to give up for the day. Only, he couldn't find his car! He'd checked the usual parking places, and then expanded the search to the surrounding streets. He just couldn't remember if he'd found a spot easily or if he'd had to take more drastic measures. Walking around in circles for several hours in the hot sun, he'd become disorientated and dehydrated. Eventually, despairing, having reached the point of mental and physical exhaustion, he was picked up by a taxi driver and driven home.

It was early evening by this point. He'd got back to the house, and made it as far as the kitchen before he collapsed. He'd had the presence of mind to call my parents in Somerset, telling them (in typical Yorkshire fashion) that he "felt a bit funny". Upon hearing which, my parents shit bricks, called an ambulance, and Gramp was rushed into hospital with multiple organ failure.

He survived. Barely.

His liver and kidneys had shut down, but were coaxed back to life by the ER doctors. My parents arrived the next morning, having driven the length of the country overnight to be at his bedside. En route they'd called me, which is why I was currently on a plane to England; thankfully, by the time I arrived on the scene the immediate danger had passed.

The short version is that he was diagnosed with Alzheimer's.

It was advanced, and degenerating rapidly.

So Granddad might not have long after all.

He was facing a fairly difficult recovery from the ordeal his body had been through, and now we had to consider his safety – from himself more than anything, as his mind began to lose its grip on his surroundings. He couldn't be left alone anymore – not at the opposite end of England, at any rate. He'd always been fiercely independent, even after my Nan passed away fifteen years previously. He had his life in Scarborough, his house, his friends and his beloved bowling club.

Unfortunately, our job was to plan for his future, and that meant boxing up everything that could be boxed, and importing Granddad lock, stock and barrel, to a new life in Somerset.

It was going to be an epic mission, sifting through a lifetime of possessions and reducing the contents of a large three-bedroomed house to what would fit in the small flat we'd seen for sale at the end of our road.

"I won't miss the stairs," he joked, making light of the situation.

And no wonder he wouldn't miss them – the doctors considered it a miracle he was walking at all. "His right knee has crumbled to powder," one told us, "we couldn't even replace it, there's nothing left to attach to!"

It was with heavy hearts all round that we set to, packing up the house in Scarborough and half a century of accumulated belongings. Every nook and cranny of the house was filled with paraphernalia, collections of old tins, toys, coins, stamps, musical instruments, craft supplies, model railways, gadgets and memorabilia.

He'd been there almost his entire adult life, buying this house before it had been built. He'd stood with his wife Grace and my Dad, then aged four, in the field that was to become his back garden, and said, "I'll take it."

Over fifty years he'd seen it all – his first car, the invention of television; my sister Gill and I had been seriously jealous of his computer when he got it, as the cassette-player was *attached*. When Amstrad came out with a purpose-built word processor, Gramp had bought one to help my Nan keep the family accounts. I'd spent endless hours slaving over that thing, tucked away in a corner of the back bedroom trying to get my homework essays done before we left. Of course, they were completely unreadable by any machine other than the one they were written on – for starters, the discs were twice as thick, with a metal protector that flicked closed over the delicate bits with the force of a guillotine. Anything I typed had to be printed out on the chattering dot-matrix, often as the rest of my family sat in the car waiting to drive home. But it was much better than writing it all out by hand – we didn't own a computer capable of word processing (or a printer) for almost a decade afterwards.

I had more memories of that house than I could count.

Like the delight of my first shower – another luxury item that Granddad had managed to acquire several years before us. We pestered Dad after that, Gill and I, and were rewarded with one of those rubber hose thingummies that could be stuck onto the hot and cold bath taps. Not quite the same as Gramp's stylish electric shower, with its pull-cord on the ceiling that turned the water piping hot. He'd installed the thing himself of course, just as he'd demolished the wall between the toilet and the washroom to create a big family-sized bathroom. Having been an electrician for much of his life there wasn't much he couldn't fix, and like most of his generation he was very resourceful. He'd bought the house long before he'd dreamed of owning a car, so Dad had been pressed into service as a teenager, helping him pour the concrete slab for a new garage. Between them the pair had built greenhouses and sheds, fences and patios, along with most of the furniture in the house.

He'd even installed central heating, shortly after it became fashionable.

For me, the house had been a refuge. I used to liken it to Rivendell in *The Lord of the Rings* (my favourite book as a child). It was a place of rest and recovery, where I was surrounded by love and generosity and happiness; a place of free-flowing and delicious food and drink, of fun and games where I could do anything I wanted. And more than anything, it was a place of safety from the world outside.

I mentioned in a previous book that I suffered quite badly with bullying at school, so I won't go into it here. Suffice to say that, whilst my immediate family kept me sane and alive on a day-to-day basis, a trip to Scarborough was like finding a paradise oasis amidst the parched desert of real life.

The thought of never coming here again was bringing me to tears every few minutes. The house had existed virtually unchanged my entire life; every ornament I wrapped triggered memories, some dating back to when I'd first set eyes on whatever it was. A cuckoo clock that had chimed the hour – and the half hour, and the quarter hour – every single day until I'd had to spend the night on the sofa. The bloody thing had woken me up so many times I'd thrown a knife at it. The clock still bore the scar, and it hadn't chimed since – for which I was both eternally grateful, and a little bit embarrassed. What can I say? When I was fourteen, I was still convinced I could be a ninja when I grew up.

To be honest, I still am.

If I was having a tough time letting go, then poor old Granddad must really be struggling. He didn't show it though, sitting there at the dining table, presiding over the packing process with the same cheekiness he used when presiding over a game of Scrabble.

"Are we keeping this?" Mum would say, holding up an object of indeterminate origin.

"No, course not," Gramp replied, "that thing's long past being useful. It's nearly as old as you!"

De-dum tssh.

The whole time he made only one request; that we keep the contents of his glass cabinet, his most precious and treasured ornaments, exactly the same in the new house as it was here. Mum took to this task with deadly earnest, sketching out the cabinet shelf by shelf, marking the positions of every item and preparing numbered sticky labels for all of them. At which point Gill noticed what she was doing, and said, "Why don't you just take a photo?"

I was secretly amazed at how well Gramp was taking this move. He had the stoicism of a generation that had survived the Second World War, and the practicality of outlook that went with it. He'd endured bombs and rationing, being part of the Army of Occupation in Germany, and in more recent times had seen the loss of Grace, his wife of almost fifty years. This latest blow, his diagnosis of Alzheimer's Disease and the loss, to a large degree, of his independence, was one he seemed to be taking in his stride. Certainly, he was coping better than I was, at least in front of us. He'd always been quite a private man though, and I had no idea what was really going through his head as he lay alone in bed at night.

To my mind, there were two ways of looking at it: as the beginning of a closer relationship, where we could visit him every day – or as the end of an era.

On the one hand, he'd be gaining regular company and the chance to play a much more direct role in the life of his family. He'd be free from the burden of worry that comes with living alone, particularly as an elderly person, and would even be able to expand his horizons, accompanying us on everything from shopping trips to holidays. On the other hand, he was losing far more than just a house; more than the dust-laden piles of memories stacked like photo albums in every corner of the place. There was a good chance that, after leaving, he'd never see Scarborough again – or any of the friends he left there.

There was a sad counterpoint to this argument, however. By surviving to eighty-three Granddad had inadvertently outlasted most of the people he knew.

At one point he'd been going to a funeral every other week.

"There's not many of us left now," he often said when discussing his bowling club, "and I could go at any minute!"

We took him round to say goodbye to his next-door neighbour, a spritely old lady Gill and I have always known as Aunty Pat. She's a marvel: ninety-four years old and sharp as a Stanley knife, she still sends a letter to my family every Christmas. The last one was five pages long, front and back, and she has better handwriting than I do.

Aunty Pat would be the only real reason for taking Gramp back to Scarborough at some point in the future – she'd miss him terribly, she said, and we knew she'd be there waiting for us if we returned.

Much to the chagrin of her sixty-year-old stepson, who technically owns her house, but isn't allowed to touch it while she's still living there.

I'm fairly sure she'll outlive him.

Hell, at this rate she'll probably outlive me!

Incoming

As the day of Roo's arrival in England dawned cold and clear, I was watching it – the dawn, I mean – from the back seat of my parents' car. They'd generously offered to drive the hundred and forty miles from Somerset to Heathrow Airport, so that the whole family could welcome my bride-to-be to our glorious country.

I'd originally intended on making quite a scene, but time and budgetary constraints had reduced my efforts to a cardboard sign and a big box of chocolates.

"You taking your phone?" Dad had asked me, on the way out.

"Dad, the only three people on the planet who know that number are going to be in the airport."

"Oh. Fair enough," he said.

I spent the journey in a state of nervous excitement. I hadn't seen Roo in almost a month; that was the longest we'd been apart since we first met, and though we'd been keeping in touch on Skype I still had those butterflies in my stomach when I thought about seeing her again.

The last time I'd seen her, I'd proposed to her. I'd stood on what turned out to be a storm drain cover and offered her a cheap ring I'd bought on eBay, and by some undreamt of miracle, she'd said yes.

I really, *really* hoped she hadn't changed her mind.

The airport was crowded, which didn't surprise me. What did surprise me was that, as the crowd thickened, then diminished, then swelled again ready for the next batch of arrivals, Roo was nowhere to be seen.

Her flight had been on the ground for an hour, but that was understandable.

Then it had been on the ground for two hours, and still there was no sign of her.

Towards the end of the third hour, still waiting fruitlessly with my box of chocolates, I was starting to panic. Okay, so I'd been panicking since ten minutes before she was due, but this was something else. This was real.

Something was wrong.

"And it's definitely Heathrow she was coming in to?" Dad asked, for the thirtieth time.

I just stared at him, admiring his composure.

Because I was freaking out.

And then my phone rang. I jumped about three feet into the air, because not only was I not expecting it, I honestly thought I'd left the damn thing at home.

I was kind of glad of it now, though. Even if it was bright pink and rather dainty.

I fished it out and flipped it open, my hands trembling so much I nearly dropped it. "Roo?" I asked, a mix of hope and desperation in my voice.

But it was a stern, male voice that answered. "Is that Mr Slater?"

"Ah, yes, yes it is."

"This is UK Border Security, Mr Slater. I have a Krista Reynen here, who claims she is your fiancé."

"Yes! Yes, she is my fiancé. Is she okay?"

"That's what we're trying to decide. Mr Slater, you do realise that she is not allowed to get married on a tourist visa."

"I...? Oh. No, I didn't realise that..."

"And that she's not allowed to enter the UK for the purpose of getting married while she is holding a tourist visa."

"Ahh..."

"And that she doesn't have enough money to support herself as a tourist in the UK."

"Oh! No, that's okay! I'm going to support her."

"Uh-huh. And what is your profession?"

"Well, I'm..." And this is when my heart remembered to beat, and started making up for lost time. Suddenly everything was very wrong. I had a bad feeling about this... "I'm an..."

The words died on my tongue. I still proudly proclaimed that I was an actor to anyone who cared to listen, but the truth was I'd had more days of work cleaning public toilets recently than I had acting.

If there was ever a time to lie about that, it was now.

But there's one question which always follows the statement, "I'm an actor."

It's the question all wannabe actors dread.

It's 'What have you been in?'

And in my case – as in so many others – the answer would be

'nothing'.

I had to think very carefully here. I was playing a dangerous game, and suddenly the stakes were astronomically high. If I couldn't convince this man that I could viably support her, Roo could be refused entry to England.

Which meant they'd be putting her on the first plane back to Australia.

And sending her the bill.

It would be even tougher to get married if we were a thousand pounds poorer and ten thousand miles apart.

Think carefully, Tony! Choose your next words as though your life depended on them...

"I'm, err... I'm a writer."

There. That should do it!

"A writer? Really! Who do you write for?"

"Myself."

"Uh-huh. And what do you write?"

"Travel books."

"And do you have any books published?"

"Not... um, not yet."

"So what do you do for a living?"

I was at a loss. Should I start trying to explain medical research to him? How I was testing experimental medicines on my body to fund my exploits? Probably not a good idea.

Quick. Least suspicious lie. Astronaut? Explorer? Pro-Snowboarder?

I cast my mind back to the last job I'd actually been paid for doing in this country. It was quite some time ago.

"I'm doing temp work for an agency," I told him, "mostly data entry."

Was it my imagination? Or could I sense a hint of triumph in his, "Uh-huh."

"Do you have any savings?"

"Ah... not really..."

"Uh-huh. What I'm trying to establish, Mr Slater, is how you are going to afford to support your 'fiancé' if we decide to let her into the country. And I have to be honest with you – it's not looking good."

"But... but... we're going to live with my parents! They'll help to support us. They're here now, if you want to speak to them?"

I felt like a terrible coward for trying to draw them into it, but I was running out of cards to play. In fact, I had precisely two; Dad, whose mild-mannered exterior houses a logic so infallible he could convince an Eskimo that snow falls upwards; and Mum, who despite being only five feet tall, was quite capable of bursting into this guy's office and choking the bastard into submission with her bare hands.

I think she acquired that trait whilst raising me.

But The Voice was back. "No need to involve your parents, Mr Slater, this is about your fiancé and you. I need proof that she can afford to stay in this country without trying to work, or I won't be able to let her in."

Irrationally, I laughed at him. The idea was just so preposterous that I only narrowly avoided telling him so. An Australian? Coming to the UK to work, in the middle of the worst recession in living memory? When their economy is booming, their minimum wage is more than triple what ours is, and they have to walk around with a sign saying 'I have a job' to stop people accosting them in the streets and offering them one?

The Voice, however, did not appreciate the absurdity of his comment.

"I'm not joking with you, Mr Slater, this is not a laughing matter."

Shit! This wasn't going well.

"No sir, of course not," I told him. I applied heavy emphasis to the 'sir' to make sure he knew that he was the boss. Small people on power trips tend to like this, and I was already picturing this man as a pedantic, rules-obsessed jobsworth. Making friends wasn't going to get me out of this one – only money. Of which I had almost none.

If only we hadn't spent Roo's…

"Inheritance!" I blurted.

"Sorry, what was that?"

"Roo, ah, Krista, has an inheritance. Her mother passed on last year, and she has a sizable inheritance in the bank."

"Really?" He sounded sceptical. "How much?"

"I'm not sure. But it is substantial. Tens of thousands of dollars, I believe."

"Right."

And he hung up without another word.

I glanced around in panic, and shook the phone to see if any more sound would come out of it. There was nothing. No clue as to what would happen next.

What have I done?

Five anxious minutes later, the doors to the Arrivals terminal swished open once more – and Roo slipped through them. Her tiny frame was bowed under an enormous blue backpack, which nearly caught in the doors as she stopped to scan the empty hall before her.

Her long, wavy hair had been dyed purple, I noticed – something that probably hadn't helped at Immigration.

She looked scared, exhausted, and close to tears.

Her smile, when she saw me, was like the sun peeking out from behind the clouds. I grinned back, and self-consciously let the 'WELCOME TO ENGLAND!' sign dangle illegibly behind me.

"My love! I'm so sorry! Are you okay?" I asked.

Roo shed her backpack and collapsed into my arms. She was still shaking, from fear, or fatigue – probably both.

"I thought they were going to send me home," she cried, shaking more dramatically now as the sobs she'd been stifling broke free. "The man left me on my own in his little room, and he didn't come back for hours! I think he went on his lunch break and forgot about me."

"It's all okay though, you're safe now," I told her.

"I didn't think... I didn't think they'd let me see you."

I hugged her tight while she calmed down, and my parents stood either side of us, shuffling awkwardly from foot to foot. When I finally released her, they both gave her a hug.

"So great to see you again," Mum told her.

"Uh, welcome to England," muttered Dad, sounding unconvinced.

It was not quite the greeting I'd had planned.

I was glad I hadn't hired a marching band.

Ways and Means

We were okay.

Roo had been admitted to the country, for the full six months permitted on a tourist visa. She still wasn't allowed to get married, but we'd cross that bridge when we came to it. There were quite a few details that still had to be ironed out about the wedding; mostly small things, like where it was going to be, and what it would be like. And, you know, all that sort of stuff.

Okay, I'll be honest: I hadn't done a single piece of preparation yet. I'd read somewhere that women like to be involved in this sort of thing, and I didn't want to spoil it for her...

So we had a fair bit of planning to do.

The decision to get married on my birthday was an easy one. For starters, it was far enough away, in July; also it was a Thursday, which I hoped would make it possible to book a venue without giving two years' notice. It was in the summer holidays, so any guests that had children wouldn't need to take them out of school, and we had a fighting chance of getting nice weather – and there were fringe benefits too.

There'd been a theme developing over the last few years of travelling, wherein the most exciting thing I got for my birthday was a donut. My parents, bless them, have always sent me some money, wherever I am in the world. It almost always arrives just in time to pay off an unexpected car bill, or if I'm really lucky, I get to spend it on food. Having our anniversary on my birthday was a clever ruse to make sure that, from now on, I would always get to celebrate it in style – and it would also make it impossible for me to forget. Pretty much a win-win scenario!

With the date established, we felt we were making good headway.
And the next item on the agenda?
Simple!
I had to earn the money for our wedding budget.

Because Roo was most definitely not allowed to.

Now, what most sensible people would do in this situation is get a job. However, I'm not known for an overabundance of common sense. I already had a perfectly good opportunity to raise the funds I needed; an email had come in from a medical research company, offering me the chance to take part in the longest, and most profitable medical experiment I had ever heard of.

For me, this was a no-brainer, so with four grand on the table, I set off for London. I didn't know it at the time, but this would be the last medical trial I would ever participate in.

The screening went well, and I found myself invited to take part in the study. On my first night in hospital I lay in bed, fantasising about the kind of wedding I could create with four thousand pounds. True, it wasn't a large budget, but I have a bit of a creative flair. I was sure I could pull this off, and some hasty calculations on the back of my consent form suggested that £4,000 would be the perfect amount.

Ha! I've already spent every penny I'm going to earn here, I thought. *Bloody hell, it had better work out!*

I had no reason to believe it wouldn't; it always had in the past.

Well, mostly.

"I hope I pass the blood pressure test tomorrow," said the bloke laying in the bed next to me.

"Of course you will," I told him, "why wouldn't you?"

"It's meant to be a really hard one to pass. They sent half the first group home for failing it."

"What?" This was news to me, and not the happy kind.

All of a sudden my mind was filled with portents of impending doom. I'd never been kicked off a medical trial before. If it happened now… well, I wouldn't be getting married. Simple as that. Our entire wedding budget was coming from this trial, and without it we had nothing. I'd never seen one this big, for this much cash – it could be years before another came along.

I worked myself up so much that when my evening blood pressure test came along, I failed it.

I mentioned this to the doctor at my check-up, and explained my fears. "You'll be fine," he told me, but that wasn't quite the level of reassurance I'd been after.

The next morning, I resolved myself to be calm. As tests were administered to the guys in the first couple of beds, I played meditation music on my MP3 player and practiced breathing slowly.

Then the guy in the first bed was given the bad news: he swore, and started packing his bag for the journey home.

The guy in the second bed was only a few minutes behind him.

By the time they got around to me, I was positively shaking. I'd done dozens of medical trials, and passed hundreds, possibly thousands, of blood pressure tests.

Only this time, for no reason I could control, I was a nervous wreck.

And I failed.

I pleaded with the nurses for a re-test, which they gave me.

And I failed that as well.

I can't believe it, I thought. *That's it – it's over. The money... the wedding. I can't believe I screwed this one up. Roo is going to be devastated.*

Then the doctor I'd spoken to last night popped his head around the door frame. "Oh, that guy's okay," he said, pointing at me.

"He's failed the test," the nurse pointed out.

"That's alright, I spoke to him last night about it. Keep him on the trial."

And they did.

If there is a God out there, he was on my side that morning. Though personally I'd have preferred it if he'd sent a lightening bolt to fry the bastard in bed number three, who's scaremongering had made me panic in the first place.

Despite his alleged fears, he'd passed the test with flying colours.

Damn him.

I won't bore you with the rest of the details of that trial, as I've written about this sort of thing before. Suffice to say it was long and uncomfortable, and I spent a lot of time on the toilet.

I've never had a 'serious' side effect from a medical trial, but minor ones, like headaches or nausea, are par for the course. This one resulted in explosive diarrhoea, which was a bit of a shock. Especially as, after a few days on the drugs, it started to feel like I was shitting battery acid. There were eighteen guys on that trial. Every couple of minutes one of us would leap out of bed and sprint to the toilet, which was close enough to our ward for us all to hear the inevitable sound effects. All of us were farting uncontrollably; the ward smelled like... well, like pretty much every hostel dormitory I've ever stayed in.

The toilet trips dominated our world. It was not uncommon to walk in on a group of guys discussing their bowel movements in explicit detail. I didn't even blink when one of them greeted me with, "Hey Tony, how's your arse?"

"Not too bad today," I reported.

"Yeah? I've got really bad ring-sting," he informed me.

Ring sting. Trust me, it's a thing. Hopefully you'll never have to experience this, but it's the result of repeated, excessive wiping, turning that most tender portion of your anatomy into a red, raw mess.

It is also my word of the week, so I challenge you to try and incorporate 'Ring sting' into casual conversation with someone. Go on – live a little!

Eventually my heart rate returned to normal and I managed to pass the rest of my blood pressure tests. I have a very low resting heart rate, which used to result in me setting off the cardiac arrest alarms every time I fell asleep. This time we weren't monitored overnight though – we just had lots, and lots, of blood pressure tests. By the end of the trial I'd almost forgotten about my little glitch at the start – until we had to come back for our final check-up. It hadn't occurred to me until that point, but if I failed my tests now they would assume that it was a side-effect of the trial, and would keep monitoring me until I passed one. This meant they wouldn't consider my participation to be completed – and they wouldn't release the money…

Stress hormones flooded my system, and I failed the test again.

Three times in a row.

In the end I explained to them, pleaded with them, and they agreed to write it off as a blip. I'd narrowly avoided being called back for a potentially endless succession of tests, each one of which would be preceded by a week of worrying and a five-hour car/bus/tube train journey that I'd have spent working myself up into a right state.

Whew!

Yet again, someone up there was looking out for me.

And perhaps they still are, as there was a serious side-effect of this trial after all. My crazy brain has developed an uncontrollable panic reaction to blood pressure tests, with the direct result that I haven't passed one since.

And that means that this trial, whilst being my biggest payday to date, was also my last.

I always try to look at things from a positive perspective, but it was tough to shrug off the loss of my primary source of income. In the end, all I could think was that maybe it was Fate; any trial could have gone wrong at any time, and I'd missed being on the most infamous trial of my era when I missed my flight home from Thailand. Some of those patients had ended up in intensive care; some had died. Maybe it was time to stop playing the lottery with my body, and start looking for a more sustainable, long-term form of finances.

Like a proper job?

Hahahahahaha! No, not likely.

But I was going to have to do something. I could now afford to get married, but not much more; by the time this wedding was over, I'd be broke again.

And my days of selling my body to medical science were over.

Perhaps it was time to finish that book I'd been writing…

So I did that. Two weeks in hospital with nothing else to do, gave me all the opportunity I needed. I'd spent six years writing about the bear that ate my pants – now, after all this time, I finally had a manuscript. It was still a little rough around the edges, but I was confident it would be well received. I hadn't read anything like it on the market; it was all true, every single, ridiculous word; and it was, at the very least, worth a chuckle.

All I had to do now was sell the damn thing, and I'd be a millionaire!

I mean, that's how publishing works, right?

Right…?

Where To I Do?

Once you start planning a wedding, you suddenly discover that there are literally hundreds of things you have to think about. More to the point, there are hundreds of things you have to *buy*. Once you start adding them all up, it leads inevitably to the question: *is it really worth it?*

But when you've asked someone to marry you, and they've said yes, it's remarkably difficult to go back to them a couple of months later and suggest that it's a bit too much effort. So there was no choice; each item on The List had to be considered, researched and discussed – and a final verdict returned in the form of a cost in pounds sterling.

Neither of us wanted a church wedding. Roo's family isn't religious at all, and after years of experimentation I've settled on a rather eclectic belief system of my own, which I think of as 'spiritual'. With some of my family being staunch Catholics, and the unknown quantity of Roo's Dutch relatives, we didn't want to risk offending anyone, so we decided to have a simple outdoor ceremony referencing the spirituality of nature.

Or, what the Catholics would probably call 'pagan'.

Or 'blasphemy', if we were really lucky.

It took all of five minutes on the internet to discover that outdoor weddings aren't legal in the UK; not for us the excitement of a service on the beach, or exchanging vows whilst scuba diving. Although I doubt Blackpool Beach or the North Sea is anyone's first choice for their ceremony. No, it turns out that a wedding in England has to be conducted in a licensed premises – and that means a building of some sort, even if it's only a garden shed. And the building has to be approved by the council – so the garden shed was out.

Talking about themes, we both had ideas that meshed quite conveniently. Roo's idea of a fairy-tale wedding involved actual fairies, drawn straight from the likes of *FernGully*. I wanted to be a knight, although I drew the line at shining armour – it's kind of hard to hug people when you're clad head-to-toe in steel. We settled on a loose medieval/fairy wedding, with nature and the outdoors featuring prominently. We decided not to ask the guests to theme their outfits too much, as the last thing we wanted was a fancy-dress wedding; I had horrific visions of Uncle John turning up as Friar Tuck, jesters leaping around in the background and that inevitable bloke who thinks it'll be hilarious to come dressed as a tavern wench. I love to laugh and muck about, but this day would be kind of significant. I wanted a tasteful affair which we could look back on in years to come (and show photos of) without being embarrassed. More importantly, I wanted these things for Roo, so we started spreading the word that, whilst it was a medieval-themed wedding, Robin Hood, Henry VIII and the Loch Ness Monster need not apply.

A few days later I discovered our dream wedding venue. I knew instantly that this was the one; a medieval farmhouse in Devon, set amidst four-hundred acres of forest. They had everything; the legal part could be taken care of in their 16th century thatched cider barn, followed by a more meaningful ceremony in a clearing beneath an ancient oak tree. They even had their own stone circle! I requested a brochure straight away, and marvelled at how they'd thought of every detail, from accommodating the wedding guests in the farmhouse to providing a nuptial tepee for the bride and groom.

I also marvelled at the cost. Our dream wedding venue was destined to remain just that, as hiring the place would consume our entire £4,000 budget twice over. And that was before we bothered with such trivial matters as food and clothing. So... back to the drawing board.

It wasn't long before I was feeling despondent. I'd ordered a stack of brochures and received online quotes from every place I liked the look of. None of them were even close to our price range, and our budget wasn't about to get any bigger. It made me seriously consider opening a wedding venue. I mean, there can't be that much work involved – a bit of advertising perhaps, and employing a good cleaner. But these places, impressive as they were, couldn't really be worth £6,000 a pop? Jeez! If they could squeeze in two weddings a week for half the year, they'd make over three-hundred grand! That'd go a long way towards paying the mortgage.

Alas, our paltry wedding budget wasn't the kind of sum to be buying property with. Although judging by the prices I was being quoted, most other couples' was. The TV shows Roo was glued to as part of her 'research' often featured weddings with budgets in the tens of thousands – and all to be blown on one unimaginably extravagant day. Twenty-four hours later, it would all be over, leaving the happy couple as happy and hung-over as if they'd spent a good night on the town – only poorer by the price of a decent sports car. Don't get me wrong – I'm a romantic at heart, and I'm a firm believer that true love is priceless. But I'd still rather get married in a shack and drive a Lotus.

With every new venue I found struggling to outbid the last, it was looking like we needed a Plan B.

And luckily enough, Plan B's are where I excel.

We wanted a forest. That was the important part, as it would set the tone for the entire event. But there are quite a few forests knocking about, and almost all of them are cheaper than six grand a day. Hell, some of them can be bought for six grand. This meant separating the legal and the spiritual ceremonies, but that helped us out as well. It meant we could bag the cheapest, naffest registry office ceremony as no-one would be there but us, and then invite the multitudes to what we considered to be the real wedding.

So we toured some forests. Actually, we toured a lot of forests, but forests have something that doesn't get described very often in wedding brochures; mud. Sometimes they have vast trees and secluded groves, and sometimes they have car parks, but rarely do the two coincide. And when they do, they are usually divided by about a mile and a half of mud. And insects.

Suddenly I was thinking about wheelchairs. And other kinds of chairs; of tables and altars and flowers and the poor buggers who were going to have to lug all this stuff into the middle of the forest.

And the other thing that forests have in abundance is tourists. Especially on days when the weather is nice enough to get married...

We did some great hikes though, whilst exploring the options. The top choice for a while was the Neroche Project, a stretch of nature reserve which had a decent car park and wasn't too far from my parents' house. I spent a couple of weeks bouncing emails back and forth with various government departments until I found the person who had to power to say yea or nay to my plan. He'd never been asked before, and thought it was a wonderful idea. "Will you need permits for toilets?" he asked.

And that was where it all fell down.

Because I have a bit of an issue in that regard; I need to pee more than most people. Five times more than most people, to be honest. And there would be old people and children at the wedding, which meant dirty hands and faces and knees, and straight away I knew I didn't want my wedding to be remembered as the one where Great Aunt Ethel got herself wedged in a Portaloo. I couldn't imagine my guests lining up in their finery to pee in a plastic phone box, and the more I thought about it the dafter it seemed. The real, wild woodland of my dream was far too wild for something as civilized as a modern wedding. I could cope without electricity, though the lack of shelter in case of rain would be a worry, but the lack of adequate toilet facilities, coupled with the logistical nightmare of dragging furniture, décor and people of all ages through miles of soggy woodland, spelled the end of this particular avenue.

So.

Time was getting on.

We needed something new.

We needed a Plan C.

And C, as it happens, stands for Castle.

Taunton Castle sits in the middle of the town, yet is surprisingly quiet most of the time. Part of it has become an enormous hotel called, for the sake of originality, The Castle Hotel. The castle proper, however, is the real deal; ancient, crumbling stonework, a cobbled yard surrounded by thick Norman walls filled with mysterious rooms, and surrounded again by a swathe of grassy grounds that used to be a moat.

It was perfect. We could get married inside it, or outside on the grass with the castle as a backdrop. Photographers, if we could afford them, would love the place, and it would be the ideal setting for an olde-worlde style ceremony.

I wasted no time, emailing the council, English Heritage, the National Trust – anyone who could tell me what I needed to know.

Finally I was put in touch with a curator of sorts, who was responsible for running the place. I sent him an impassioned email, all but begging for the honour of being the first couple in recent times to say their vows in Taunton Castle.

"I don't see why not," came his reply. "I think it's a wonderful idea! We wouldn't charge you anything, but donations to the castle upkeep fund would be welcome of course."

It was a miracle.

I responded by providing him with all the details we had so far, emphasising Roo's love of castles (strangely enough, they don't have them in Australia) and my own deep reverence for their hallowed architecture. He replied with a single sentence; "That all sounds fine – as long as the renovations are finished by then."

Later that day, Roo and I took a trip to the Taunton Castle.

The whole area was fenced off. Builders' vans filled the car park opposite, and the sounds of heavy equipment at work could be heard from within. I could hardly believe my eyes – I'd been standing on the exact same spot less than a week ago, and the castle had been empty. Closed, as it pretty much always was, but undisturbed; now it was in the throes of a full-scale restoration, with an end date that gave me serious cause for concern. 'Opening This Summer', it said on the gate.

"You are absolutely shitting me," I said when I read it.

Slap bang in the middle of summer was our wedding date.

And if there's one thing that can be guaranteed to overrun, it's a government-sponsored renovation. Of a castle.

"We're screwed," said Roo.

"I'm starting to think there's a higher power at work here," I told her.

"Me too," she agreed, "and I don't think it likes us."

It was a fairly quiet drive home.

The Gift That Keeps On Giving

A few days later, Roo had her 25th birthday.

I know! I'm a lucky, lucky man. So what if I went to university when she was twelve? They say that girls mature faster than boys anyway. And I've always been exceptionally immature, even for a boy. (I'm counting that as a good thing, you'll notice.)

Roo was used to celebrating birthdays with her twin sister Sonja, and several times during our travels she'd made the pilgrimage back to Perth for it. This time was different. She'd chosen to spend her birthday in England with me, because having it in Australia would have meant us being apart for two full months.

Neither of us could handle that.

But it did make me hyper-aware of how important this day was for her. She'd be far from her friends, surrounded by my family instead of her own, so I had to pull out all the stops to make sure she was happy.

I wanted to give her something really special, something she would remember. The trouble was, anything I spent on gifts now would have to come directly out of our wedding budget. I already knew we'd be stretched thin on that front.

I knew there would be something out there for her, something affordable yet perfect – so I trusted to Fate, as I often do, and Fate was in a rewarding mood.

The idea came to me as I lay in bed, curled around her like a cat with a kitten, and it was all I could do to keep from yelling out in triumph.

I'd done it! I'd found something that would make her happy – absurdly so, I was sure – and it wouldn't require a bank loan or a trip to the jewellers.

I realised then that I'd never have to worry about this sort of thing again. Roo had always been delightfully low-maintenance, and she valued experience over expensive possessions. Which is probably for the best, or she'd never have been interested in me.

Buying her pressie was simplicity itself. Back when I was trying to propose to her, and was frantically searching for a ring (with remarkably similar criteria – priceless, unforgettable, and cheap) – I'd sneakily opened a second eBay account.

And they say romance is dead!

Now though, this provided the perfect avenue for me to acquire a largish box without her noticing. I wrapped it at midnight, not because of any mystical significance but because Roo likes to go to bed early, and this is literally the only waking time we don't spend together.

On the morning of her birthday, I think I was more excited than she was.

I took her breakfast in bed, then led her downstairs in search of her present.

She saw the size of the box and got excited.

"Oh! What is it?" she hadn't known what to expect, but there was no chance she'd guess what was inside.

She tore at the paper, pausing to roll her eyes at the ineptitude of my wrapping technique. I'd wrapped a perfectly square cardboard box; how in God's name did it end up looking like a coat-hanger?

Must be a thumbs thing.

And then Roo was through the wrapping, and was confused for a few seconds by what she was looking at. Then she shrieked, almost ripping the lid off the box to get inside it. She held up a small, translucent piece of plastic – a pipe, about the same size and shape as a toilet roll tube – and her bottom lip began to tremble.

"Oh Tony! It's not possible... is it?"

"It is, my love."

"No *way!*"

"Yes way."

"You mean I can have... I can get..."

"Yup."

"*A hamster!*"

And she hugged me and burst into tears.

Before I get inundated with complaints, let me assure you that there wasn't a hamster in that box. I believe selling them on eBay is also frowned upon. What I'd bought, and what Roo had discovered, was a modular plastic cage system known as Rotastak. This one was designed to resemble a space station, which as we all know is a common natural environment for rodents.

Since she first discovered they existed, Roo had loved hamsters.

She loved all animals, especially small, cute ones, but growing up in Australia had denied her the chance to own any. All their native animals are protected, and thus illegal to keep as pets, and foreign animals (like rabbits) pose a serious threat to their ecosystem. She'd had a guinea pig, and spent years working in a Koala sanctuary, but she'd never even seen a hamster before coming to England.

It had taken her less than a week to become obsessed.

Her birthday surprise was completed with a trip to the pet shop. Roo picked a honey-coloured Syrian hamster which she named Violet Crumble (after the Australian version of a Crunchie bar). When she put her hand into the tank, Violet came straight over and climbed onto it, which we took as a good sign.

"I can feel her little hairy toes on my hand!" Roo exclaimed, sounding for all the world like a ten-year-old girl.

The manager of the pet shop was bemused.

"She's never been that excited to feel my hairy toes," I quipped.

I'm not sure if that made us seem less weird, or more.

Roo was determined to raise a 'free range' hamster. I pointed out that, although we'd be able to charge more for her meat, there really wasn't that much to start with. Roo ignored me, of course. Her idea was to give Violet the run of the house, at least under supervision, so she set about making the whole place hamster-proof. This was easier said than done; hamsters, it turns out, are master climbers. Violet quickly learned the art of stairs. She'd take a run-up and fling herself at the riser, embedding her tiny claws in the carpet. Then she'd do a pull-up, hauling herself over the edge and onto the next step. Then she attacked the next one – before the day was over, she'd figured out how to get up and down the entire staircase.

Which presented problems of its own, of course. Rodent-proofing the ground floor of our house had been difficult enough. It's possible we were the only family in the country who had to install a hamster stair-gate.

Initially, Violet slept in her space station on the desk opposite our bed. She didn't stay there though. The main advantage of the Rotastak system is also its curse. It is infinitely adaptable – and infinitely *expandable*. Within a week, Roo had bought two more sets, tripling the size of Violet's accommodation. Soon after that she began trawling eBay looking for deals, buying spare connectors and housing pods and feeding stations… and then. Then she found a woman selling a job lot of second hand Rotastak, who lived nearby. No-one else had bid, as it was a collection-only auction and my parents' house is quite remote. Roo bid, and won, and we arranged to meet the lady in a lay-by just off the motorway.

We'd been driving Gramp's tiny blue Nissan Micra recently, what with him not being able to use it any more. Well, I say 'we' were driving it, in fact Roo was driving it, as I still didn't have a license.

Our contact arrived in a Range Rover, and after exchanging pleasantries she jerked a thumb at the Micra. "That your car?"

"It is," said Roo, proudly.

"Riiight. Only, I don't think you're going to get it all in." She opened the back of her car, and the whole thing was stuffed with brightly coloured pipes. She had ten times – no, fifty times the Rotastak that we had. She was very nearly right – we only managed to get it all into the Micra by burying me in it.

That evening, Violet's cage grew somewhat.

It took Roo an entire weekend to clean all the plastic pieces she'd bought, and as she laid the last batch out to dry on the bathroom floor she came to a conclusion.

"There's too much here for Violet," she admitted.

I have to say, I was happy to hear that.

"So," she continued, "what I think we need is another hamster. That should fill most of the other pieces."

It wasn't *exactly* the same conclusion I'd imagined.

A few days later we were back at the pet shop.

Roo had being doing some research, and wanted a dwarf hamster for a bit of variety. In the tank were a mob of the little critters, tussling and rolling over each other – and one tiny, runty little albino hamster sat alone in the corner.

"That one!" Ro said immediately.

I sighed.

"You know, dwarf hamsters are quite social creatures," the manager said. "You might be better off with a pair of them, so they've got some company."

I gave the guy my best 'you bastard!' glance.

"TWO MORE HAMSTERS?" Roo was quivering with excitement.

I sighed again.

"Tony, we could breed them!"

We didn't breed them. Thank God.

We did build a series of cages – a complex, rather – that dominated half our bedroom. It spiralled up from the floor and spilled onto two different tables. I drew the line at giving over bed-space, so this prompted a radical redesign that required cardboard boxes, gaffer tape, and yet more Rotastak parts sourced from eBay. She was buying and selling the stuff like a dealer, even turning a profit here and there, but her greatest enjoyment still came from the free-range play sessions. Violet's greatest enjoyment also came from those sessions – specifically one where she darted off Roo's knee, wormed her way down the side of an armrest and became lost inside the sofa. After a few hours of waiting for her to come out, followed by a strenuous hour playing tilt-the-sofa, we had no choice but to cut the back off the damn thing. Violet was sitting in there quite contentedly, delighted with the adventure she'd had. My parents were somewhat less pleased when they came home, but as I told them, pet owners do have to put up with a little damage from time to time.

They understood, having been long-term dog and cat owners in the past, but I think they were slightly alarmed by the scale of the damage in proportion to the size of the hamster.

"It could have been worse," I said. I don't think this reassured them very much.

Although Roo loved Violet Crumble most of all, my personal favourite was the larger of the two dwarf hamsters. In contrast to the tiny, timid albino we'd called 'Licky', his brother 'Hedgehog' was so fat he was completely spherical. He was grey, with a dark strip running down his back and big bulging eyes. Licky was manic, obviously schizophrenic, probably a genius, whereas Hedgehog was big, dumb and furry. Kind of like me.

Maybe that's why we got so well.

At least, I thought we were getting on well. That's why I offered to hold him, when we took him to the vet to have his claws clipped. They'd grown long and curved, possibly because he just sat around all day while the others were scurrying around their domains.

I bravely took the hamster into my hand, resisting the urge to coo and speak in baby language to him because the vet was actually quite pretty. And, um, I never did that sort of thing anyway. Ahem.

Hedgehog wasn't the least bit bothered.

Until the vet started in with the nail clippers.

Then he became a very small, very cute, ball of psychotic fury.

His little claws, bless him, were too small to do much damage, but the teeth on a hamster are actually quite substantial. Well, I know that, now.

Hedgehog bit right through my finger and refused to let go for the entire operation. By the time his nails were clipped I'd leaked a puddle of blood all over the table, the floor, my shoes...

The vet was very understanding, between giggles.

That night, Roo was kind enough to report on my situation via the medium of Facebook. She let the whole world know that I'd been in an accident, that I'd been seriously wounded, and that I was recovering. Mostly.

"But you were so good, holding him, even though you were bleeding all over the place. You didn't hurt him at all. You're so compassionate. That's why I love you. And that's why I'm going to marry you."

"Ah. Well, thanks for that, love."

"And because you're the only person I know who can be convincingly mauled by a dwarf hamster."

When Is A Castle Not A Castle?

Over the next few weeks we made several trips back to watch the progress of the castle renovations. Which was kind of demoralising because there wasn't any. The signs and the fencing remained, but nothing moved beyond it; we still heard the occasional sound of hammering from within, but I was starting to suspect it was a tape-recording they'd made to fool the public. I understand that a fairly delicate approach has to be taken when refurbishing a nine-hundred-year-old building, but the creaking wheels of English Heritage sounded remarkably like the death-knell for all my hopes and dreams.

However. Next-door to the castle proper was one of Taunton's finest hotels – called, appropriately enough, The Castle Hotel. I'd never been in because I couldn't dream of affording to stay there. Room rates were in the hundreds of pounds per night and the tiny car park was like a millionaire's private garage; I walked past the place several times a week, and the cheapest car I ever saw there was a Porsche. Crucially though, the hotel actually incorporated parts of the ancient castle, and was built on ground that had once been enclosed within the moat. One obvious remnant from this era was a huge gothic gate-house with medieval archways through which a pedestrianized road passed; it had always been one of my favourite parts of Taunton, but I'd never given much thought to the hotel towering above it. Now that I looked at it, the building matched the castle fairly well. Ivy spider-webbed across the stonework, dominating a crenelated tower which may well have been constructed as part of the castle's outer fortifications.

So I called the place, and asked if they did weddings.

Idiot! Of course they did weddings. They even had a person whose entire job was to arrange weddings, so Roo and I put on the clothes we normally saved for job interviews, took a series of deep breaths, and went in.

"Just don't touch anything," she whispered as we crossed the threshold.

We met our contact as she descended the grand staircase; old, impressive, and highly-polished. So was the staircase.

First, she took us into what she called the Music Room. To all intents and purposes it was a ballroom, but that label must have fallen out of fashion. It was a nice big room, with pale cream walls and a pair of ornate chandeliers hanging from the double-height ceiling – not exactly our dream wedding venue, but we were starting to get desperate. It had a vaguely historical feel, and would look quite nice when filled with white-clothed tables. Crucially, it was licensed for weddings, so any ceremony we performed here would be legal. I'd been considering taking care of the legalities in a separate ceremony, allowing us to do something outlandish like getting married in the castle courtyard – but there would be no need for that here. One point in the hotel's favour.

I could easily envisage us standing on that grand staircase for photographs; it really looked the part, as did the lobby of the hotel, with decorative wooden benches that could have been rescued from a medieval monastery.

"And then, for the reception, you move through to The Brazz!"

She said it with such enthusiasm it was hard not to get caught up in it. We followed her down a short flight of stairs, carpeted in a rich red with gold fleur-de-lys pattern. We passed through a stone archway, a tantalising reminder of the building's architectural origins, and arrived at a set of wooden double doors.

She pushed them open, and we stepped through – into a different world.

It was so... blue.

Royal blue. Wall-to-wall carpets, bar stools, the upholstery in the booths, *everything*.

I was speechless.

All traces of castle had been banished in favour of gleaming chrome railings, funky light fittings and modern art on the walls. It was a trendy modern bistro – the kind of place where up-and-coming bankers with too much cash and an appreciation of fine wines would meet their clients for brunch, before heading off to play a round of golf.

Our guide was rattling off accolades for the place – apparently BRAZZ was short for *Brasserie* – but I'd already stopped listening. I didn't care how *exclusive* a venue it was. I wasn't sure what their selling point for weddings was supposed to be. Come to the romantic, ancient castle, marvel at thousand-year-old ivy-clad stonework... and then get married in a wine bar? They had a fish-tank, for God's sake. Fake tropical pot plants and recessed spotlights.

I glanced at the sample menu I'd been handed.

They served chicken liver parfait.

A poster informed me they held live jazz sessions on Sundays.

When she broke the news to us that the menu we were holding ran to £150 per head, we thanked her and made our escape. Outside, The BRAZZ had a small pavement café opposite TopShop. In terms of dream wedding venue stakes, it was about as far away as I could imagine.

I'd rather we tied the knot in my parents' back garden and served sausages from the barbecue. And cans of Carlsberg from Tesco. Which, I reminded Roo, was still an option… and at the rate we were going, a worryingly realistic one.

We were running out of time. The invites had to go out soon, and I was fairly certain they were supposed to include some kind of clue as to the location of the wedding…

Eventually, frustrated by events far beyond our control, we decided to sneak into the castle itself and try to see what was going on. At first it seemed quite a challenge; almost as though castles are designed to be hard to sneak into. The main gate was thoroughly boarded up, and the far side of the castle was protected by a stream running along the site of the original moat. One bridge over the stream led to a securely fenced-off loading dock, but the other gave us access to the castle grounds through a small gate with a rusty chain. A broad swathe of grass surrounded the castle, but on a level roughly equal to the bottom of the moat; the castle itself, with its imposing entrance, was high above us.

There was only one side left to explore, but I didn't hold out much hope. Assuming the air of a couple out for a casual stroll, we nipped into the manicured rose gardens of the Castle Hotel and made our way past the various outbuildings separating it from the proper castle's inner ward and its Norman keep.

We found ourselves on a barely-discernable footpath, pushing through trees at the far end of the garden. On our left, the trees gave way to a grassy bank topped by the remains of an old stone wall – a very, very old stone wall. Suddenly I realised the sounds of construction work were coming from the other side of the bank. We scrambled up it, excited – and looked down into a building site. A mini-excavator sat on a pile of sand, surrounded by wheelbarrows and bags of cement. The cobblestones of the castle's courtyard were being pulled up by the looks of things, and a posh new visitor's centre was under construction. At last we could see right into the heart of the renovation works – and from where I stood, it looked like they would take forever.

Or maybe just a decade; the blink of an eye for a monument that had survived nearly a thousand years of England's most turbulent history.

But our plans were utterly buggered.

Fascinated and dejected at the same time, we followed the line of the wall until trees screened the courtyard from view once more. We'd come to the extreme end of the footpath, if that's even what it was. I felt a bit naughty, like we'd discovered a place no-one was supposed to go. Certainly, from here it would be no trouble at all to climb down into the middle of the closed-off castle courtyard. They obviously hadn't thought fences necessary here, as though it was already inaccessible to the public. On the opposite side from the castle a dirt track led sharply upwards, through a narrow gap in the trees. Rather than go back the way we'd come we took the steep track, expecting it to come out behind one of the hotel's outbuildings.

Instead we emerged into a secluded clearing, surrounded on all sides by majestic oak trees and conifers. Between the trees, a roughly triangular patch of grass the size of a tennis court stretched back towards the hotel. The afternoon sunlight dappled the ground as we stared around us in disbelief. Somehow, we seemed to have discovered a hidden glade right in the middle of the city.

"Oh my God," breathed Roo, "I didn't know this was here!"

"Me neither. I've been through the hotel's gardens before, but I've never seen this."

"It's like a fairy glen! Where are we?"

I turned three-hundred and sixty degrees, and saw beauty in every direction. As far as I could figure, at least one side of the clearing lay directly behind the main road through town. The others were bordered by the castle's inner courtyard and the side of the hotel, but of all this the only piece visible through the trees was the ivy-clad tower of the Castle Hotel. Despite the presumed proximity of the road, all I could hear was birdsong; it was as though we'd stepped through a portal in the centre of 21st century Taunton and been transported back to the middle ages.

Magical was the only word for it.

"Do you feel that?" Roo whispered.

"I think so," I said. A ripple of excitement was spreading through me, together with a deeper, almost primal sense of oneness with my surroundings. I felt content and at peace, in spite of the rush of thoughts flooding my brain.

I felt *in love.*

"We're going to get married here," Roo said, her tone hushed with reverence. "I can feel it."

And she was right.

Tony's End?

And then, without warning, came the morning that I couldn't pee.

I'm sorry, I should probably have warned you – not everything in this book is about magic and romance.

Like this, for example; I woke up, needing the toilet – like, *really* needing it – but nothing would come out.

Understandably, I panicked.

I was in pain, and my imagination was supplying helpful images of me bursting at the seams.

So I did the only thing that came to mind.

"MUUUUUUUMMM!" I yelled.

Fortunately, my mother has lived around me quite a bit. She knows the difference between a cry for attention and genuine, pain-based desperation. And she knows that, when it comes to me, the later is true more often than not.

She barrelled upstairs to the bathroom, and burst in to see me stood there, straining at the toilet.

"Tony? What's wrong?"

"Mum… I can't wee!"

Oh, and did I mention she's a nurse? No? Well you should probably know that. It makes more sense that way.

Within minutes she was on the phone to the doctor, and I had an emergency appointment later that day. By then the pain had subsided, and I'd been able to pass a few trickles – enough to relieve the pressure on my bladder at any rate, so I wouldn't be rupturing anything important.

"Partly it's dehydration from drinking alcohol," the doctor told me, " but there is clearly something else at work here."

"It gives new meaning to the phrase 'stop cock'," I joked.

But there was no denying it – something was wrong inside me. Inside the part of me that I want nothing to be wrong with, ever.

The doctor agreed. "I'm going to refer you to a specialist," he said.

And he was as good as his word. I only waited a week for an appointment, and by the time it came around I was almost back to normal – well, normal for me.

Which, in case anyone had any doubts, is pretty far from normal.

I've always had what the medical fraternity would refer to as a 'weak stream'. Put in layman's terms, it means I stand a much better chance of pissing on my own feet than most blokes do, and I spend half my life looking for public toilets because I can't go for an hour without needing a widdle.

Of course I've wondered about this over the years, but when a Google search for these symptoms returned a result of prostate cancer, I did what most young men would do in such a situation: got drunk and stopped asking questions.

Now though, questions needed asking. My problem had been getting gradually worse, and if it carried on in this vein I'd find myself exploding in a shower of urine one fine day – which is not only a terrible way to go, it wouldn't endear me to anyone standing next to me at the time, either.

In order to test how severe the situation had become, I was sent to a special clinic where the doctors and nurses exist for the sole purpose of taking the piss out of people.

There I was plied with as much tea and coffee as I could stomach, given an ultrasound, and then pointed towards a curtained-off area in the corner of the room.

Inside I was faced with a machine which some highly intelligent person must have spent a significant portion of their life inventing; it was a measure-how-fast-you-pee-omoter. I stood there, feeling rather awkward, and emptied my bladder into a spinning metal bowl. I got another ultrasounding after that, and the doctor told me I'd only managed to empty a third of my bladder in one go. Which probably explains why I pee three times as often as anyone else.

I was given a return appointment and told to keep a diary of how often I peed, which given the frequency would amount to more homework than I did for my university degree. But still, I felt that progress was being made.

On my next visit to hospital I was given one of those fetching backless gowns, something radioactive to drink, then led into a room in which a huge scanner hung from the ceiling. It took about ten minutes for the operator to guide the scanner into position. Using a handheld remote he made the thing trundle forwards on its rails, rotate, lower, rotate some more, swing sideways, nudge forwards, extend a bit... either this was his first time, or he was just enjoying himself too much. Or both. Finally he had the scanning plate in the right position, and I obligingly stood against it.

"Crouching," he demanded, and didn't seem satisfied until I was sitting in mid-air, my bare bum-cheeks pressing into the cold metal plate and my legs trembling with the effort of keeping me there.

I've been in more compromising positions, but not many.

"Okay, like that. Just stay still..."

"I'm trying!"

"Okay, try to relax..."

"If I relax, I'll be on the floor!"

"That's okay, you're doing fine... now take this." His hand shot around the corner of the machine, holding a plastic bottle. "And pee in it."

"What? But..." I took the bottle and tried to reach underneath myself. The tip of my trunk edged inside, but nothing would come out.

"Pee now," the operator reminded me.

"I can't! I'm too tense!"

"Just relax a bit..."

I'm sure you know that if there's ever a need for a doctor to tell you to relax, it's because relaxing at that point is already impossible. In the end I gritted my teeth and squeezed with all my might, producing about an eggcup's worth of fluid in the bottom of the bottle.

And that was that.

The verdict, when it came, was both a shock and a relief.

I had a cock block.

"The technical term for it is a stricture," the doctor explained. "It's most likely a build up of old scar tissue. Have you ever had an accident with your penis?"

"No," I said, quick as a flash.

But of course, I was lying. The memory was starting to unfold for me, taking me back to one unfortunate afternoon in my youth...

I'd always loved climbing frames. My favourite trick was to run around the top of them as fast as I could, pretending I had supernatural reflexes and ninja-like agility. Come to think of it, those two attributes are still on the top of my Christmas list. I must have been a very naughty boy in a previous life to end up with two left feet and the grace of a dead hippopotamus.

Being someone who regularly walks into doors, it was hardly surprising that my climbing frame antics would end in tears. Inevitable, you might say. Anyway, one day I was chasing around the top rungs of a cube-shaped frame, when I slipped.

One foot went in front of the bar and one foot went behind it. And all the weight of an eleven-year-old boy, multiplied by the average acceleration of a small body in free-fall, went crashing down onto my testicles.

Oh man did I howl.

I screamed and moaned in such horrendous pain that all onlookers vanished instantly. I was left alone to crawl home on my hands and knees, bleating my sorrow and cradling my poor squashed spuds. The funny thing is that I'd completely blocked out the memory, like politicians do every time they buy a prostitute on their expense account. It wasn't until several years later, when I was babysitting my sister while she played on a similar climbing frame, that I overheard her telling the story to her friend. At first I'd have sworn she was making it up – but when I questioned her, she recounted the incident in such graphic detail that the memory slowly revealed itself, like a balled-up letter unfurling in my mind.

I've never forgotten it since.

And I still can't walk past a climbing frame without wincing.

"So, no history of illness or injury down there?" he pressed.

"No, no, it's all good *down there*, thanks."

"Okay then. But you definitely have a stricture."

"Right. So, is there anything you can do about it?"

"Yes, there certainly is. I'm booking you in for a procedure later on this week. How does Thursday sound?"

"Ah… Thursday's good… but, uh, what will I be having done?"

Now, in hindsight, asking this was probably a bad idea.

Because he actually told me.

In concise and clinical terms, he described a procedure which I'm sure is outlawed by the Geneva Convention.

Suffice to say it would involve opening my willy as wide as it would go – then a bit wider – and inserting an arc welder. Or what I envisioned as an arc welder at any rate.

"Not quite," the doctor said, chuckling at my imagery. "It's more like a miniature television camera. With a knife blade on the end."

I chose to picture the arc welder. It seemed safer.

I was quite subdued when I returned to Roo in the waiting room.

She was sympathetic, of course, but she couldn't really help.

Because I now had less than three days to psyche myself up…

For open cock surgery.

The rest of my family, when I told them, were equally supportive. For a bit. But it was impossible to resist making fun of me, because... well, come on, admit it – you would, wouldn't you?

Roo asked if they did requests, and suggested I get racing stripes put down the sides while I was at it. Gill weighed in (from France, I might add) with a reassurance that if something did go drastically wrong, I might at least be allowed to keep it in a jar, which would make a great decoration for Halloween.

Dad began surreptitiously leaving power drills laying around where he knew I'd find them – like in the bathroom, and the kitchen, and the bedroom... I had no idea he owned so many of the damn things. And Roo's favourite warning: "You'll be fine, so long as you don't get an erection!" had a disturbing ring of prophecy to it.

I have to say though, pride of place goes to Mum, who was frantically planning a holiday to Jordan at the time. She didn't want to go alone, so she was paying for Roo and I to go with her. It was an extraordinary act of generosity, of a kind which is often seen in my family. One particular consequence of my operation was playing on her mind, however. I don't think she even meant it as a joke – she was deadly serious when she accosted me on the way out of the door and demanded: "Make sure you ask them – how long before you can ride a camel?"

Boring

There's a certain kind of tension which is only to be found in a surgical waiting room.

Now imagine sitting in a room full of blokes, each one of which is about to have his penis operated on. Oh yes, the atmosphere in here was something different alright. Every man in there was coming face to face with his worst fear; the air was so thick with terror you could taste it. No-one spoke. Why would they? Penis health is a fairly private affair amongst men. It's very rare that I find myself in a pub-conversation about my genital hygiene, and rarer still that I'm invited to discuss any abnormalities.

Yet in private, we regularly worry if that bump is a swollen hair follicle, or if that birthmark was always that shape.

Here's an interesting test: find a man in your life, and ask him if his penis is okay.

He will say it's fine.

Then ask him if he's ever had any problems with it.

I *guarantee* he will say no.

And I *guarantee* he'll be lying.

And I *guarantee* that if you're reading this out to him in bed, he will get all defensive about it and deny lying.

You see? It's one thing we blokes are a little sensitive about. For some reason...

That waiting room was as silent as the grave.

A few of the patients had brought their significant others, to lay a supportive hand on their jittering knee. Likewise, Roo was sitting next to me, her hand clasped in mine to stop me fidgeting. But the solace those loved ones could offer was fleeting; like death, this situation was a great leveller. Every man stands alone when it comes to penis surgery.

As a nurse called my name, and led me through into a ward full of nervous men strapped to gurneys, I felt like I was taking my last walk on Death Row.

Roo accompanied me, and tried to make light of the situation by pointing out that all the beds in this ward had spread legs and stirrups.

"You've heard of the phrase 'too soon'?" I said.

The doctor, on the other hand, was unnecessarily cheerful. Trying to compensate, perhaps, for the gravity of my situation.

"All-righty-roo!" He poked his head around the curtain where I was undressing. "We're gonna have an ittle-bitty look at what's wrong with you."

At this juncture I'd like to point out that there is nothing 'ittle' or 'bitty' about the body part he was interested in. In fact my size was a bit of a concern. "Whew, if we nick *that* you could bleed to death in seconds!" he said. I think he was making a joke. One of those rare ones you can only really appreciate if you're *not* there.

"He was happy about something," Roo said.

"But what?" I countered. "Who in their right mind would want this job?

At some point he must have given up a very promising career in *other* medicine for this. I mean, I'm very grateful he did, but why? Maybe in medical school they give you a sheet with boxes to tick, and he was like 'Hm, I'll join the fight to cure cancer,' or 'I want to work with children,' or 'breast-augmentation in exceptionally beautiful women sounds like my bag'. But then, with the whole wide world of medicine to choose from, he decided to specialize in willies! In diseases and abnormalities of willies! Surely no-one – and I mean no-one – dreams of spending their day looking at scabby, spotty, fungus-infected penises. I don't care who you are or what your sexual orientation is, it would put you off cock for life."

The nurses came in next. They were doing the rounds, so I'd already heard them going in and out of the other curtained-off enclosures. I adjusted my gown in preparation, as Roo had tied it around me and had thoughtfully left my arse on display.

The nurses introduced themselves, and one of them fed me painkillers. "These won't wear off until a long time after the surgery," she explained, with a sympathy that suggested I might be needing them.

Then I had to sign some forms, which I didn't read too carefully in case they scared me. I was probably agreeing that, in the case of an accident, my manhood would be donated to the department so they could keep it in a shoe box and pull it out at parties to scare the interns.

And then the doctor was back.

"Hellooo!" he sang, "how are we doing?"

"Well, one of us is about to have his cock chopped off. I haven't decided who yet."

Okay, I didn't say that. After all this was the man who, in a few short hours, would literally have my life – and my penis – in his hands.

"I'm fine," I said instead. I was lying.

"Alrighty then, I have to ask you about anaesthetic," said the doctor. "Would you like a general? Or a local? Because if you have a local, we can either put a little tent over the site of the operation, or if you'd like, you can watch."

He said it with glee, like he was offering me tickets to a show that had been sold out for months.

Had I heard him right? *Would I like to watch?*

As far as I understood it, they were about to bore out my penis with a power drill. I don't care what kind of numbing agent they used down there, there is just no way I'd be able to sit still for that.

And if I saw it coming, and couldn't escape – well, I could bet that scenario would be featuring prominently in my nightmares for a decade or so.

"Ah, I'll have the general anaesthetic, please. And if you could blindfold me as well, in case I wake up, that would be very much appreciated."

"Aha, so funny!" said the doctor.

"No, no, I'm being deadly serious. In fact if you could cocoon my entire head in gaffer tape, that would be even better…"

"There's nothing to worry about, you're in good hands. And would you like to hear the really great news?"

"Uh… maybe?"

"You're so fit and healthy that we think your surgery will be very low risk."

"Oh. That is great news."

"Yes, quite! So we've decided to do you first. Nurse?"

And with that he swept the curtain away, allowing a pair of orderlies to grab hold of my bed and start wheeling it down the corridor.

What? NOOooooo! I'm not ready!

Even Roo was taken by surprise, and had to jog along behind me until we reached the theatre doors. "Don't worry, love," she said when she caught up with me, "I'll be right here."

Right here? I thought. *What the hell good is that?*

"I love you," I said, because that is expected at times like these.

"I love you too," she replied, "and whatever you do, don't think about getting a boner!"

And with that she was gone, left beyond the clashing doors of the OR.

A cloud of nurses enveloped me, which under normal circumstances is something I'd enjoy. Then they all started talking at once, some to me and some to each other. I felt the stab of a needle in my arm, an oxygen mask went over my mouth and nose, and questions were asked whilst they wired me up to blood pressure and heart monitors.

I suddenly remembered I hadn't said any last words. I'd planned to come up with something poignant or witty, just in case, but it was far too late.

"Count down from ten," one of the nurses said, and that was when a more pressing issue occurred to me.

"Wait!" I shouted. "I need to pee first!"

And that was the last thing I remembered.

When I woke up, I felt great. High, even. I was back in the ward, lying on my gurney with Roo sitting patiently next to me... and inexplicably, my bladder was empty.

Oh shit. That probably went some way towards explaining the look on the surgeon's face. At some point during the procedure I must have pissed all over him.

"Welcome back," he said, none too convincingly. I had a brief thought that if there ever was a guy not to urinate on, this was him. The man with the knife. Thank God it was still attached.

Speaking of which, I risked a look down.

An enormous tube snaked out of... well, out of the *end* of me. It led to a bag full of... well, you can imagine. A recovery nurse followed my gaze to where the bag hung from my gurney.

"Oh, don't worry about that. We're going to give you one of these." She flung a packet into my lap. It contained a kazoo.

"What, I whistle when my bag needs emptying?"

"Ha! No. Here..." With a deft touch she whipped off the bag, opened the packet and attached the kazoo to the end of my tube. "You use this," she explained.

Quite how was left to my imagination.

My cock was gigantic. Unbelievable. I wondered if they'd added collagen – either that, or there'd been a cock-up (no pun intended!) and they'd accidentally transplanted the knob from a giraffe.

The nurse caught me staring – at myself, for once. "It's just fluid absorption," she informed me, "don't worry, it'll be back to normal

soon."
Roo looked vaguely disappointed.

Cock Chop Post Op

I drowsed in my gurney for an hour or so, until I felt strong enough to let Roo help me get dressed. It wasn't easy – not least because I had a tube as thick as my little finger sticking out of my cock. With a whistle on the end, which I'd discovered was a tap – one I'd been assured was a temporary measure, rather than something I'd be getting used to long-term. That was a relief, I can tell you.

As we left, the nurse offered me a syringe of clear liquid. "You use this if it gets sore," she said. "You use it in… that area… you sort of… squeeze it in… put a bit in…"

I had to stop her. She was almost making me embarrassed. "Honestly, you can say it," I told her. "I've just had my penis routed out. A whole operating theatre full of people have had their fingers up there. I'd really rather you told me where I have to put that stuff."

"Okay. You squeeze it inside the end of your penis. It's anaesthetic and lubricant. It'll help."

"Thanks. I'm sure it will."

And it did.

For the next two days, even moving was agony. Going to the toilet was an experience I'm working hard to forget. I had to shuffle around the house legs akimbo, as though I'd been riding all day and had just lost my horse.

Climbing my parents' rather narrow staircase to the only bathroom was achieved mostly with my arms and teeth. By the time I'd shambled up and peed, and got back down the stairs, I invariably needed to go again… it was two very long days and sleepless nights before a nurse came to remove my kazoo.

I was in so much pain that the weirdness of the situation didn't strike me until I'd wrestled my pants down around my ankles. There I lay, naked on my bed, whilst a middle aged woman I'd never met made small talk about the weather as she poked my penis with the end of a biro. "You didn't have to take all your clothes off," she said. For some reason it hadn't occurred to me to drop trouser without first shedding my socks and t-shirt. To be honest I was just thinking about the industrial-sized cable that appeared to connect my willy to the musical instrument of choice for football fans everywhere. And about how much it would hurt when it was removed.

Down to business. The nurse was donning a rubber glove.

"That's a massive one," she observed.

And yes, she was talking about the tube.

"Well, I overheard the doctor discussing drill bit sizes before the op," I told her. "You know that thing they bored the Channel Tunnel with? I think they borrowed that in the end."

Nervous laughter followed. It was mine. Because the nurse was doing things with syringes, shooting me regular smiles in an encouraging manner. Which could only mean one thing: she was about to inflict a massive amount of pain.

"This might be a bit uncomfortable," she warned.

Why the subterfuge? I mean, I knew it was going to hurt like hell. Sure as shit she knew it. So why the pretence? At least she could treat me like a man. Even if I was about to squeal like a pig. Honestly, I don't think she was kidding anyone in the room. Had she said, "Okay, brace yourself, tense your arse cheeks and bite down on a piece of wood, 'cause this is gonna feel like I'm raping your penis with a red hot poker covered in battery acid!" – well, at least I'd have had some respect for her honesty.

It wasn't actually that bad.

It was worse.

I've never felt anything quite like it, and if I never have to again, I'll die a happy man. How to describe a sensation so unique? It was rather like ripping off a Band-Aid. One that had been stuck down with superglue. Only this Band-Aid was about two feet long – and it was *inside my penis*.

I tried not to scream, and failed miserably. Searing, blinding agony wracked me from bell-end to bowels as the tube was wrenched into the light of day. It was like the chest-burster scene in Alien, only with more gore. And nudity.

The nurse was pulling hand-over-hand, like an old sailor hauling rope, and still this thing was coming out of me.

Jesus, how much of it did they put in?

Then, with a final pop, the end of the tube emerged. My cock flopped lifelessly back to the bed with a squelch, and began drooling what I sincerely hoped was saline solution. The nurse, triumphant, brandished the cause of my discomfort as though to say, "See! I have slain the beast!"

And... Oh. My. God. It was fucking huge. I swear you'd need a general anaesthetic to get a tube that thick down my neck, let alone up my willy. Thank the Gods it was now back outside of me, where it belonged.

As for me, I bled rather substantially and passed out.

When I came to, I was treated to an interesting sight.

As a token of her respect for the courage I'd shown, the nurse had quite thoughtfully left the tube on my desk. At least, I'm assuming that's why she did it, as I can't think of any practical use she expected me to put it to. I could probably make twenty-five stout drinking straws out of it, but I don't think anyone would want to use them.

Everyone else was gone. Perhaps they'd had their fill of my cock. Or, after so long staring at my genitals, they'd decided to give me a moment of privacy.

And that, as they say, was that. I could walk again almost immediately. The pain subsided, as did (regrettably) my cock. I did consider illustrating the swelling on Facebook with 'before' and 'after' style photos, but luckily enough Roo hid the camera until I came to my senses.

At long last I had regained the ability to pee up a wall. And to write my name in the snow. In fact, with this new high-pressure nozzle I could probably have carved my name in plate steel. It changed my toilet habits dramatically. Not only could I now sit through a whole movie without having to visit the bathroom, I could pretty much go to the bathroom from where I was sitting on the couch! Not that my parents encouraged me testing this ability. But as far as improvements go, it was dramatic. Transcendent. And very nearly worth all the pain and suffering.

And yet, as I write this, I regret to report that I am back to my previous state of affairs. The doctor did warn me shortly before the procedure that in roughly fifty percent of cases, the stricture grows back, scar tissue thickening over time and closing the re-bored hole anew. Sadly this happened less than six months later, leaving me unable to sink a pint of beer without having to pee at least three times in the process.

I went back to see the doctor just recently, and explained what had happened.

He wasn't surprised. "There are two real options for you now," he told me. "The first is easy – you just repeat the same process, and we hope that this time it'll have a more permanent effect."

Now, that didn't strike me as a particularly 'easy' option. Not for me at any rate.

It did, however, give me serious concern for whatever alternative he was about to suggest. Surely if there was something easier, less painful and invasive, they'd have tried that already?

And then he said something that no man ever wants to hear.

"We can take a postage stamp-sized piece of the roof of your mouth, and sew it into a replacement tube," he said.

Which doesn't actually sound that bad, until you realize he's left out the part where they have to slice my cock open lengthwise, cut the defective bit out and stitch this replacement tube back in its place...

So, yeah. I wasn't entirely thrilled at the prospect. In fact, if you could think of a thing I'd less rather do to my penis, you're a better man than me. And I have a fairly fertile imagination. Unfortunately there are some nasty things you can shy away from in life – like work, adulthood and any kind of responsibility whatsoever – but then there are those things you can't. And it turns out that this is one of the latter.

So I'm delighted to inform you all that I'm now on the waiting list for open-cock surgery...

Watch this space!

Bargain Hunters

As I lay in bed recovering from the surgery, I milked my weakened state for all it was worth. I'd been far too busy to relax recently, so I was keen to make the most of it.

Sadly, there are two groups of people who famously know no rest: the wicked, of course – and the control freaks.

And I was guilty on both counts.

So, utterly incapable of sitting back and letting Roo and Mum organise things on their own, I took to making lists.

Many, many lists.

And then lists of lists.

There are some things that cost a ridiculous amount of money. Actually, pretty much everything for a wedding costs a ridiculous amount of money. Even versions of something otherwise quite cheap, like sandals, magically become three times the price as soon as the word 'wedding' is attached to them.

Unfortunately, we didn't have access to a ridiculous amount of money. We didn't have access to what most people spend on their wedding dress, so some serious economising was going to be in order.

I looked down the list of essential requirements I'd made, deciding which ones we could do without; none, as it happens. That's the trouble with lists of essentials – most of the things on them tend to be essential. But not to be beaten, I looked instead for things that could be borrowed, DIY'd, or bought much more cheaply in their non-wedding incarnations.

This new list included flowers, favours, invites, table centrepieces, decorations, cake, outfits and the venue.

Mum had a friend who was studying photography at the same college where she was learning massage. He needed to shoot a wedding for his portfolio, and we had a wedding that needed shooting and no money to pay him. Our two situations dovetailed nicely, so that was one major headache taken care of. We decided not to splurge on having a videographer there, mostly because I couldn't ever imagine myself wanting to sit down and watch a home movie about it. Not when there are real movies coming out all the time, most of which have much better story lines. In hindsight this is my only regret, and if I could go back and have a video made, I would do it without hesitation. True, we didn't have the budget for it, and I was relying on enough guests shooting bits of it on their phones and then letting us have the footage afterwards. In reality, this was no substitute for a well-made video capturing us both at our prettiest and happiest. Take note, people! It may seem a bit twee, but do it anyway. You can always stick it in a bottom drawer and forget about it if you want.

The cake was an easy one to sort out. Roo and her sisters have a love of cupcakes bordering on obsession, not that you'd know that by looking at them. It was a no-brainer to swap out the traditional multi-tiered monstrosity for a bevvy of miniature marvels. Originally the girls were down to make them, but Roo just happened to do a bit of research herself – by systematically finding and eating every cupcake on sale in a fifteen-mile radius.

You see – weddings are hell!

Roo chose a lady who not only made the best cupcakes she had ever tasted, but who also offered to do us a great deal on a hundred of them. With fairy wings on, naturally.

After I admitted that I could walk unaided, we drove to Taunton and negotiated with the Castle Hotel for the use of their secret garden. They were perplexed at first, having never used it for anything before, but they soon saw the potential when I outlined how I wanted the chairs setting out. They charged us £500, which included the hiring of their Grand Ballroom in case the weather turned inclement. I was one-hundred percent certain that the sun would shine on us – I just couldn't see it any other way, and I was using the power of positive thought to back that up. Still, it wouldn't hurt to have a room to store stuff in, and somewhere for me to get changed, so this was the role I relegated the Grand Ballroom to. As changing rooms go, it wasn't half bad.

While we were there, we nipped into the pub opposite to see if they had a function room. Holding the reception at the Castle Hotel meant using The Brazz, which was completely out of the question. But facing both the hotel and the castle proper was a pub called The Winchester.

We'd walked past it hundreds of times and always admired the way its stonework mirrored that of the castle. In the course of my online research I'd discovered that The Winchester actually used to be part of the castle – it had been converted from a Norman-era outbuilding, which was why it shared the narrow arched windows and crenelated roofline.

I couldn't help but think that it was far too good to be true, and at first glance it was. The manageress, a bubbly blonde lady called Kaz, showed us upstairs to a rather shabby room that they occasionally rented out for birthday parties. It was due for a complete refurbishment, she explained, which may or may not be finished before our wedding – but if not, we were free to do whatever we wanted to the place. Roo and I loved the windows, but other than that the room had little character. We considered actually renovating it ourselves, so convenient was the place, but then Kaz came out with the magic words; "If there's enough of you, I could close the pub and you could have the whole of the downstairs?"

And that was it. Sold!

Downstairs at The Winchester was a typical old-school English pub. Everything was wood, from the panelling of the walls to the polished oak bar. It had a built-in PA and music system, commercial kitchens and ample room for our guests. We could have the bar open as it normally would be, meaning guests could buy their own drinks at sensible, non-wedding-venue prices.

And then Kaz hit us with the clincher.

"I can do all the catering for you right here. And there's no charge for hiring the place, if you're all eating here."

Honestly, I could have kissed the woman!

But I didn't. Roo tends to get cranky when I do things like that.

Finding Roo's dress was always going to be a big deal. There are several different TV series dedicated solely to this one purchase – I know, because in the run up to our wedding, Roo watched every single one of them.

Which meant that I ended up watching most of them too.

Roo had been making a scrapbook of ideas for her dress, printing out pictures of gowns worn by Taylor Swift and Marie Antoinette. That was a little worrying.

I'm sure I will earn the wrath of women everywhere, and the support of men worldwide when I say this about a wedding dress – it's only worn for one day!

Yes, yes, I know.

A very special day, and all that malarkey. But still!

Luckily, against all the odds, Roo felt the same way. Her dream dress, she explained, would be one that came in two separate pieces – a corset-style top, which she could wear out clubbing with a pair of jeans, and a beautiful flowing skirt which not even she could think of another use for. Beyond handkerchiefs. But there we go, a suggestion that would see at least half her attire finding use again, so I wholeheartedly supported the search for her dream dress.

And I could hardly believe my luck when she found it on eBay, an ex-sample, for £80.

It arrived. It fit. And it was beautiful. Personally, I wished the corset had a slightly sluttier neckline, but you can't win 'em all. This one came in three pieces, the last of which was a stupendously long detachable train decorated with pastel-coloured flowers. As far as Roo was concerned, it was perfect – and as proof that it had never been worn, the original designer's price tag was still fastened into the corset.

£495, it read.

Now if that's not a bargain, I don't know what is!

Other things were also happening during this time. For Roo, the most important of these was her decision to go blonde in preparation for the wedding. She'd decided that a more 'grown up' look would be appropriate, so she let the purple fade from her locks before bleaching it so blonde it was almost white. For me, the most important decision was that I started sending out the manuscript of my first book to agents and publishers. Consequently, I began receiving my first rejections – and, as successive waves of submissions came and went, I started to realise that getting published wasn't quite as easy as I'd anticipated.

"I love your writing," one agent said, "but I can't sell a memoir written by a nobody."

As the rejections continued to pile up, it seemed this sentiment was a popular one. 'Come back to us when you're famous,' they said. Which I could appreciate, from a business perspective.

But it was a bit of a bugger.

None of this mattered though, as it was all happening in the shadow of something so much more exciting: our trip to Jordan, a country I'd wanted to visit for as long as I could remember, was almost upon us.

Mum had conceived of this holiday, and Dad was bank-rolling it. He wasn't coming because traveling to a desert halfway around the world to peer into some dusty ruins didn't appeal to him. But this was

Jordan; the Hashemite Kingdom of Jordan to be precise! An enigmatic, mysterious country, steeped in the history of ancient civilizations. The Roman cities of the Decapolis were there; Egyptian, Babylonian and Byzantine empires each claimed her in their turn, liberally sprinkling their great cities and monuments across the desert. It's the land of the Biblical Old Testament, and consequently the land of the Crusades. But above all this, there was one thing in particular that we wanted to see.

We were going to visit Petra, that 'rose red city, half as old as time' – one of the most famous temples of the ancient world, made all the more so by George Lucas, when he made it the last resting place of the holy grail in the film Indiana Jones and the Last Crusade.

I wanted to see Petra bad; it had been on my bucket list for years, as well as Mum's. And just like that, this dream was about to come true!

Courtesy of Dad's end-of-financial-year-bonus.
Did I ever tell you, Dad, how much I love you?
Well, consider this another affirmation.
Petra!
I could almost taste the sand.

Destination: Jordan

We were going to be late.

I knew this as I lay in bed, unable to sleep.

Even though the alarm had yet to go off; even though it was long before dawn, and frigid darkness held sway outside the bedroom window.

I knew we were going to be late, because there is a long-established law about being late in my family. It goes like this: Slaters are always late.

I've been a Slater my entire life, and I have never known it to be wrong.

If there was ever a morning to make an exception, it was this one; we had a bus to catch, followed by a rather expensive flight to Jordan, and airlines are notoriously unforgiving when it comes to matters of tardiness.

An hour later, everyone in the house was up, showered, breakfasted and ready to go. I'd been through all the usual stages – packing my luggage into the car, sitting waiting for everyone else, suddenly realising I've forgotten something, rushing back into the house and spending ten minutes tearing the place apart trying to find it while everyone else waited impatiently in the car, then discovering some other bugger had already packed it without telling me. Unbelievably, we were still on time.

"The boot won't shut!" Dad stage-whispered. The car was parked directly below our neighbour's bedroom window, so all our cursing had to be done at twenty decibels or less.

"What do you mean it won't shut?" hissed Mum.

"I mean… it won't shut."

"That was pretty self-explanatory," I whispered to Roo.

"Why won't it shut?" Mum demanded.

"I don't know. I think it's broken."

"What? How long has it been broken?"

"About ten seconds! This literally just happened right now."

"I can't believe this!"

We piled out of the car and stood around offering useless advice in hushed tones, as Dad tried over and over again to get the boot's latch to catch.

Ten minutes later, he was debating the use of string.

"Shit!" Mum hissed, "We're late!"

"Right. Get everything into the other car."

It was a fraught and foggy drive to Bristol bus station, but we made our bus by the skin of our teeth. We always do, somehow. Either we have the best luck in this regard, or the worst; it'd be nice, one day, to see what not being the last to board is like.

Australians often tell me how lucky I am, to live in a country where cheap flights to dozens of exciting destinations are so readily available. They never understand why England doesn't completely empty into Prague or Budapest every weekend. What they don't appreciate is that to take advantage of these cheap flights, one must generally get to London; and that getting to London, from almost anywhere else in the country, is either dramatically more expensive, or considerably less pleasant, than the flights in question. Usually both.

The three-hour bus journey felt like five. Mostly because it *was* five; predictably our coach broke down en route, and we sat in the rain in a motorway service station awaiting a replacement.

We were quite late when we got to the airport.

Luckily, the Gods that hold sway over this mysterious law kept to the rules. The plane was also late, and after we boarded it we sat on the runway for another two hours just to be on the safe side. I'd never been in a plane-jam before. It's almost exactly as frustrating as being in a run-of-the-mill traffic jam, only instead of listening to your family bicker about it, you get to listen to three hundred-odd strangers bickering.

Other than that, it was quite a nice flight.

We were met at Istanbul airport by a frantic bald man in epaulettes, who had our onward flight number scrawled on a scrap of cardboard. "Quick! Very late!" he informed us, as the group around him grew. He was wearing a jaunty captain's hat to go with his smart blue suit, but he seemed anything but confident. "Come! Follow!" he commanded.

He then escorted us at a dead run to our connecting flight. Older and less fit passengers fell away wheezing in droves, and by the time we reached the boarding gate for Amman there was only three of us left. We'd sprinted the length of the airport, leaving in our wake a sea of open mouths and confused expressions. "Who were those guys?"

people were asking, "And why were they chasing that pilot?"

Mum was gasping for air, but still with us, a fact she later put down to wearing training shoes. The businessmen in their shiny loafers and the fashionable tourists in their heels had struggled to keep up; the returning locals, aerodynamically challenged in their full traditional bedspreads, hadn't stood a chance.

Panting and sweating, we barrelled through the gate and boarded the aircraft. And then sat there for the next hour and a half while the ground crew transferred our luggage.

The Turkish Airlines plane was definitely older than I was. The food was great, but the entertainment left something to be desired; there was a single overhead TV screen at the end of each aisle, on which mustachio'd men held hands and slapped each other's faces to the wail of a badly-tuned clarinet and raucous canned laughter.

This was probably the least-strange show I ever saw on Arabic TV.

No-one was waiting for us at the next airport. Perhaps because we were the very last to arrive, having queued all the way to the passport desk before being told that visas were issued at a different desk (helpfully marked 'Visas').

We stood alone with our luggage, glancing around forlornly in search of our driver. Amman airport, at 10pm, was silent as the grave – well, until the taxi touts spotted us. Then the flood-gates opened, and I was forced to keep them at bay with our baggage trolley while Mum placed a confusing call to the hotel. They were fairly sure, they said, that we'd already been picked up. Were we absolutely sure that this was not the case?

"Yes," said Mum, "I am reasonably sure that we are not already inside a car on our way to your hotel." She said it without a trace of sarcasm, because honestly I don't think it had occurred to her that it was a strange question.

"So sorry," said the man on the other end, "it was my brother…"

Presumably his pick-up record was less than exemplary.

It turned out that someone else had seen the sign our transfer driver was holding and had pretended to be me to avoid fighting the crowd of touts for a ride of his own. But the hotel receptionist offered to negotiate on our behalf with an airport taxi driver, and Mum, Roo and I were soon on our way.

As we sped through the night, I came to the conclusion that Jordan by night is… rather dark. Streetlights were obviously not in vogue, though by the time we reached downtown Amman the headlights from the queuing traffic allowed us a glimpse into the shadowy world of market stalls and pavement vendors. Cars were bumper to bumper on all sides of us, yet still managing to travel at decent (some would say panic-inducing) speeds. Coupled with this, every driver in earshot was leaning incessantly on his horn, creating a constant cacophony; it was impossible to tell who was beeping at who for what.

The hotel, by contrast, was very welcoming. I'm a budget backpacking-type traveller, so I typically have low expectations when it comes to standards of accommodation. That said, I've renovated a fair few houses in my time so I know how simple it is to turn a hovel into a haven with a mop and a fresh coat of paint. All too often the managers of lower-end establishments don't seem to care about their upkeep, as though being cheap makes keeping the place clean and welcoming a wasted effort.

Not so the *Burj al Arab,* or Arab Tower. We were arriving at the very start of high season – hopefully good timing, as we were anticipating less crowds, milder temperatures and good deals to be had. Our room in the Tower was a great success in this regard; having booked a three-bed room for the three of us, we'd been rewarded with what appeared to be a suite. We had a living room with a sofa and chairs, a bathroom, one bedroom with two single beds and a separate en-suite master bedroom with the biggest double bed I've ever seen. Seriously – there was room for six close friends in there. It was clean, and gradually getting warm, and was costing us about £10 per person per night including a buffet breakfast. Quite simply, I loved it. The walls of the entire suite seemed to be stencilled with a leaf design in pale gold, a massive expanse of it and flawlessly done. And to remind us that we were now in the Middle East, every room featured a wall plaque indicating the direction of Mecca.

Mum's post-arrival investigation of our accommodation was thorough, and she quickly discovered the bidet jet built into the otherwise western-style flushing toilet. And being Mum, by 'discovered it' I mean: "What's that? Oh it's a… where's it turn on… oh, down here… ARGH!" The last bit was uttered as she squirted herself forcefully in the face with it. Thus ended her experimentation, proving once and for all that even age has no cure for the urge, upon finding a strange button of unknown function, to push it.

Here are a few things I learned on my trip to Amman:

1) Provided you do your research and read as many reviews as possible, budget travel really is the way forward. Keep low expectations, be pleasantly surprised, and avoid that cotton-wool wrapped 'Rich Western Tourist' experience. Unless you *want* to be insulated from the locals, which is sometimes understandable.

2) Taxi drivers can be a mine of local knowledge, especially if they like to show off their English skills. Of course, they may tell you what they think you want to hear ('Of course it's safe here at night!'), and you might have to filter out subtle declarations of poverty tucked into every comment – but you can learn a lot of key points in a short time, from a local point of view. And try out any dubious language phrases you've been practicing.

3) Jordanians love the King (wise and benevolent) and hate the government (Greedy and corrupt); NOT the other way around.

4) Don't rely on word association to remember foreign phrases, or when under the considerable stress of having to use your hard won knowledge, there's a good chance the wrong thing will come out. For example, when attempting to remember the phrase, 'Peace be upon you' (*Salaam Alaykum*), I developed a bad habit of coming out with 'Salami *alaykum*' (May the sausage be upon you)…

5) Before testing a bidet, it is wise to interpose an arse between it and one's face…*

(*Later, she tried it out again – properly this time – and emerged giggling, with two further comments; "It works… And It's VERY COLD!")

Amman by Day

We were woken by the Muslim Call to Prayer, playing on loudspeakers from the tower of the nearest mosque. It was a haunting melody with a soaring, yearning quality; at once beautiful and alien and utterly different from the harsh wail I'd heard in movies.

I lay there letting the sound wash over me, the cadence rising and falling, the words unknowable and deliciously exotic. In the apartment blocks around me, good Muslim people would be rising from their beds to praise Allah for the first time that day. All over the country, in houses, huts and palaces, over ninety percent of the Jordanian populace would be doing the same.

I stayed in bed.

After ten minutes or so, the song faded. I turned over and went back to sleep.

After all, it *was* half past four in the morning.

We were woken by the Muslim Call to Prayer, playing on loudspeakers from the tower of the nearest mosque. It was a haunting melody, and... well, it was remarkably similar to the first episode.

Only this time it was 6am.

I had several minor revelations at this point:

1) these people prayed a lot.

2) they would be praying at the same times every morning, which meant I would be awakened each time as well – so I might as well get used to it.

3) in olden days it would have been a man singing the Call to Prayer from every tower, five times a day. How gutted would you be if your local singer was crap?

The last thing I'd done before bed was post a Facebook status about how much I was enjoying my first night in Jordan, so I logged on to find a flurry of comments like:

'You've let your standards slip, mate,'

And:

'How deep into Jordan did you go?'

And:

'I hope she's better in bed than she is at writing books!'

That's the trouble with being a comedian – all your friends tend to be comedians too. I groaned, and replied that Jordan kept waking me up in the middle of the night, and that I was now seriously sleep-deprived.

"You should have mentioned how horny Jordan is," Roo added.

It was true; incessant beeping from the traffic below us had been the major cause of our insomnia. By some terrible trick of acoustics, every snort, scratch, fart and whistle from the street below came in through our window, magnified a hundredfold as though the side of the building was acting as some kind of amplifier. It was like we were sharing a room with the various tramps and late night street vendors thirteen floors below us, and it had taught us the real meaning of the phrase, 'city that never sleeps'.

As we prepared to go down for breakfast, I heard Mum calling me. Roo investigated, and came back rolling her eyes; Mum had locked herself in the loo again. Possibly this was karma in action, as she'd stolen a butter knife from the plane "in case we need it for picnics". This thought occurred to me at exactly the right time, and using the knife I was able to jimmy the lock from the outside and set her free. Mum was pleased that we didn't needed to involve the hotel management this time, and I was quite proud of myself; this was now the fourth continent on which I had successfully broken into a toilet.

We were the only people partaking of the hotel's buffet breakfast, which turned out to be all-you-can-eat cold boiled egg, and three allegedly different kinds of flatbread which looked identical to the naked eye. After watching us engage in a staring match with the bowl of boiled eggs for ten minutes, the receptionist rather sheepishly pulled out a toaster and some sachets of jam from behind his desk. Next I had my first taste of potent Turkish coffee, enjoying it until the very last mouthful. Which was when I discovered that they leave the grounds in the cup. It's little things like this that make me wish I'd done more research before a trip.

For our first adventure in Jordan, we decided to investigate Amman's most popular tourist attraction: the remains of the Roman temple to Hercules, which sat atop Citadel Hill. Our super-friendly receptionist knew a back way, which he described to us in great detail. It was the route the locals used, he explained, and so would bypass all the usual tourist kitsch. The route began right behind the hotel, and climbed through the neighbourhood which spilled down the sides of the hill. It was rough, steep going. We followed the only possible course, climbing up, around, past and sometimes through people's houses, through yards, over terraces, and up stairs in their hundreds. We climbed through a thousand years of history and chaos; past cinder-block hovels, tin sheds, ancient adobe houses, piles of rubble and the occasional gnarled eucalyptus tree. Lives flourished all around us; dogs barked as we passed, cats shot across the path in front of us. Washing lines stretched between the houses, and children scrambled back and forth, chasing balls, dogs and each other. Pausing often, we made slow but fascinating progress up the hillside, delighting in surprise views out over the city and stone steps so worn they were positively biblical.

Just below the crest of the hill we startled a family of rabbits, who were mooching about on the first patch of grass we'd seen since entering the country. We followed the grassy slope upwards, emerging beside the outermost edge of the citadel, and snuck into the ruined fortification in secret. Thus we bypassed the gate – and the entrance fee – which has made me feel guilty ever since. It's true; crime doesn't pay. Mum even suggested we try to find the ticket booth, but I felt that was going too far... at least until I saw the guards.

They were everywhere; heavily-armed police dressed more like the SAS, in black combat fatigues and boots, with rolled-up balaclavas on their heads. They were intimidating as hell, but they didn't seem to be doing much. Just standing beyond all the safety barriers, on the edges of cliffs and monuments, chatting casually to each other as if to say, 'We make the rules! Nothing is forbidden to us. Just you try it...'

"Tough gig," I remarked. "Can't see there being much trouble up here. Visitors tend to be in the 60+ bracket. Not a lot of violent crime in that demographic. I'd love to see their job description; Look menacing. Smoke cigarette. Take a phone call. Move to opposite end of site and repeat."

We strolled around the site, which covered the relatively flat top of Citadel Hill. From all sides the city of Amman could be seen stretching off into the distance, thousands upon thousands of seemingly identical buildings clinging to every inch of the surrounding hills like barnacles on a ship's hull. From this height the city was a drab, uniform brown, liberally studded with the tiny black squares of a million windows. It was an essay in population density, written in dust.

The ruins, on the other hand, were amazing. You have to hand it to these ancient civilizations – they liked their columns and they liked 'em BIG. Two in particular dominated the site, somehow still supporting a carved lintel the size and weight of a bulldozer. Chunks of carved stone were piled up around the remaining walls, some pieces so intricate they seemed machine-moulded rather than hand-carved. I always find, when looking at a site like this, that the skill level of ancient craftsmen blows my mind. I can't even begin to calculate the cost, in modern terms, of commissioning a single block of such work; yet these were pieces of decorative friezes that would have run for hundreds of feet around the building, or capitals that would have sat atop columns so massive that their details could never be seen from the ground. I'd love to cost up the materials and manpower to build a modern-day temple of Hercules in the same style, and same hilltop location, as this one. I guess the only groups who could afford such an undertaking would be the major religious organisations. Not much has changed there, then!

We poked our heads into a stone-age cave which had been discovered during recent excavations (most of the Citadel is still unexcavated). According to the guidebook, this was proof that Amman's central hill was amongst the oldest continually-populated places in the world. The cave didn't offer much proof to us though – no stone-age net curtains, or barbecued dinosaur ribs, so Roo and I left Mum trying to decide if the scuff-marks on the wall constituted cave-paintings.

We wandered back through the ruins, still marvelling at their scale.

They were crying out to be climbed.

A handful of tourists and locals were strolling casually along the low walls and fallen archways, clambering onto stone pedestals for a better view or posing atop the smaller chunks of masonry. No-one seemed to care. I couldn't resist trying a few parkour jumps across gaps in the stonework – after all, they'd survived the earthquakes that destroyed the rest of the citadel. It seemed unlikely that my training shoes would do much damage.

But then I spotted two other lads, both clearly local boys, doing a bit of the same. They'd scrambled up the massive stone walls, right to the base of the two giant columns. They seemed to be contemplating an epic jump down to a grass covered mound below. Surely, I reasoned, if they were up there then it must be allowed? It never would be back home... Perhaps these lads were kindred spirits. At any rate, if they were going to attempt something I might as well give it a go myself. Before you could say 'Bad Idea', I was leaping up the blocks towards them.

Suddenly, a harsh command in Arabic exploded behind me. The other two guys froze – then they threw a pair of worried looks over my shoulder. I crapped myself, jogged along the wall in the direction I was facing, and jumped off the far end to safety. Roo was waiting for me in the shadows. A quick glance back the way I'd come showed the would-be athletes surrendering themselves to a whole pack of armed guards. Neither group seemed particularly cheerful.

We moved as quickly as we could in the opposite direction, putting a sizeable chunk of temple between me and the soldier-police. I even took my bright red jacket off in case it made me more recognisable – though the fact that I was being very obviously arm-steered by the only blonde woman we'd seen since we entered the country probably didn't help.

'Go in springtime, the guidebook said, there'll be no crowds…'

As my almost-partners-in-possible-crime were frog-marched away by the police, Roo and I peeked out from behind a two-thousand-year-old corner. "See how they're carrying those machine guns?" Roo gestured at the departing escort. "There is a time and a place for climbing old buildings and jumping off them," she said. "This is NOT that time."

She had a point.

Minutes later, shunning the more impressive ruins in favour of the rocky fringes, we came across Mum. She was also looking a bit nervous, to the point where I had to ask her if she was okay. I was half afraid she'd been accosted by an overly aggressive souvenir salesman, but I needn't have worried.

"I'm alright," she said, taking a calming breath. "I just got shouted at by the police for climbing on the ruins…"

Roo looked back and forth between the pair of us, and shook her head in despair. "We are *so* going to get shot on this holiday," she muttered.

Dinner

Climbing back down through the flotsam and jetsam of Citadel Hill, we descended through a way of life largely unchanged since the ruins above were last inhabited. There was electricity in some of the places, and the sound of petrol-powered traffic filtered up from below, but the women still rubbed their washing against corrugated boards whilst chatting with their neighbours, and judging by the smell of the place at least a few people still threw buckets of shit out of their bedroom windows. Stepping around dogs and children and piles of rubble, twisting and turning through steep alleyways, we made our way down stairs made alternately of thousand-year-old stonework and shoddy concrete blocks.

By the time we reached 'street' level, the three of us were exhausted.

We'd missed lunchtime, as denoted by the midday Call to Prayer. It was worrying how well our stomachs had begun to synchronise with the wailing of the Calls, because there were five of them in every day.

The other impressive site in Amman was a huge Roman amphitheatre, right in the centre of downtown. From the top of the citadel it looked close enough to walk to, and it was – at least, it would be, if walking were possible. However, the pavements in Amman had a far grander purpose than mere surfaces for walking on. They were the place of business for a horde of trinket sellers, fruit sellers, clothes sellers, the occasional washing machine seller... You name it, if you wanted it in downtown Amman, you could probably find it spread all over the pavement within fifty yards of your front door. Which would be great, if you wanted stuff. Walking, however, required space to put your feet in, which was far less common. It also required concentration, dexterity, and the ability to politely decline the thirtieth offer of 'genuine antiques, very cheap' whilst dodging traffic, dogs and the last twenty-nine antiques vendors who weren't prepared to take no for an answer. It was chaos, though a friendly-natured chaos – but to someone like me, who struggles to eat and breathe at the same time without killing myself, it was an accident waiting to happen.

Or ten of them.

We took refuge from the heat and the endless array of stalls in a first-floor café. From there, we gazed down on our route to the amphitheatre, which was just across the road. The traffic was ceaseless, somehow moving at substantial speed despite the lack of visible gaps between the cars. Traffic lights and crossings were scattered around the nearby junction, but none of them seemed to mean anything to the drivers – they changed colour prettily, like the lights on a Christmas tree, and were given about the same amount of attention. Which is to say, none whatsoever.

We ordered falafel sandwiches, as they seemed relatively safe whilst still dipping a toe in the waters of 'foreign cuisine'. Then we spent a peaceful hour watching the traffic, waiting for the food. No-one seemed in much of a hurry here, which was quite refreshing – except that, by this point *we* were in a hurry. It was 4pm when the sandwiches arrived, and it took us less time to eat them than it did to cross the road.

We reached the amphitheatre to find it would be closing in ten minutes, but spurred on by a reinvigorated sense of wonder we covered every inch of the structure in that time. It was vast, and remarkably well-preserved. Steps ran up between the rows of seats, much like in a modern stadium. Unlike a modern stadium they were tiny, narrow, crazily steep and crumbling, but we raced up and down them to check out the view from every angle. It seemed so solid, so complex and durable, it was hard not to think of it as a modern building. Studying Roman Britain in school in England, I'd been treated to endless pictures and videos of small stone walls, apparently delineating some of the most impressive structures ever built. The school year had culminated in a visit to several archaeological sites, where we were treated to a first-hand encounter with the small stone walls – surrounded, as always, with rather ambitious illustrations of what the walls could have looked like. Towering bath-houses and magnificent villas – it all seemed like a bit of a stretch, when most of the evidence consisted of a handful of pottery shards and a ditch filled with rubble.

But this was the real deal; the Roman Empire, in quite a lot of its former glory. Even the humblest of these stones had a massive quality, an indestructibility, and they fit together flawlessly. And this was just one, and certainly not the greatest, of Jordan's ancient structures.

Beneath and behind the terraced seating, tunnels disappeared deep inside the amphitheatre, hinting at passageways and rooms within. We searched in vain for an entrance that wasn't closed off with a steel grill, but given the lack of health and safety measures encountered so far we had to assume the inside of the amphitheatre was truly dangerous. Or else they were trying to keep people from setting up stalls in it. In hindsight, this seems the more likely situation; I think if you found room anywhere in downtown Amman to spread a picnic blanket, by the time you turned around there would be a stall on it.

Maybe three.

Running the gauntlet of souvenir and antique stalls leading back up to the hotel,

I realised that there was no flat land in this city. Every building clung to one hillside or another, and every alleyway we passed led to a steep flight of crumbling steps; anyone living here would gain thighs like tree trunks and lungs like Zeppelins.

Well, except the women. They didn't seem to go out much. I had the unusual experience of seeing more pre-Christian archaeological sites (3), more city-dwelling wild rabbits (7) and more kilt-wearing Jordanian-Scottish bag-pipers (2) than I saw women on my first day in Amman (0).

That evening, while recovering from our exertions in the hotel, we were treated to a glimpse of just how strange this country was to us. It also proved that Mum's capacity for understatement is truly impressive.

She was sitting in an armchair watching TV. She'd been flicking through the Arabic channels in search of an English one when she stopped, suddenly entranced. I didn't notice at first, busily writing in my journal while Roo used the laptop to check her emails, but Mum continued to watch, enthralled, for several minutes.

"That's an unusual sport," she said, finally.

I looked up.

On the telly, on Dubai Sports 2, commentators chatted and important statistics flashed across the screen as several bearded men dressed in full traditional bedspreads were attempting to throw enormous fish. Each was holding what looked like a narwhal by the tail, then spinning, spinning and releasing it at high velocity. It was like the Olympic hammer toss only, y'know, with fish.

It was one of the few moments in my life when I was genuinely lost for words.

So we sat there, all three of us, and stared at the TV while another three competitors sent their choice of sea mammal soaring skywards.

CAN I KISS HER YET?

"You're right, Mum," I said at last, "that *is* an unusual sport."
Roo nodded. "Especially for the fish," she said.

For dinner that night we were faced with a choice; to venture out into the city again, braving the endless string of stalls and vendors in the dark whilst searching for a genuine cultural experience – or to hide in the hotel and eat burgers. I chose to bridge the two. I conceded that the hotel lobby was closer than anything not in the hotel lobby, but when we settled ourselves at one of the two tiny tables I asked the receptionist-cum-waiter (and quite possibly cum-head chef) if I could try a traditional Jordanian dish.

He very enthusiastically explained that I could indeed, and that he'd be delighted to serve me with Jordan's most popular delicacy: *mansaf*.

As we waited for our food, I preached to the others on the importance of embracing every facet of Jordanian culture. We would be here for less than two weeks, after all, and this was the first country any of us had visited in the Middle East; therefore, it behoved us to take a few risks.

Thus ended the lecture, as our receptionist was back with a tray of food fresh from a nearby restaurant. He assembled it on the check-in counter, and then brought our meals over to us one by one.

When he placed the *mansaf* in front of me, I had to admit it looked utterly revolting. I caught a slight snigger from Roo, who had just been served her pancakes. But I knew my iron stomach would prevail, and before long I'd be one cultural notch up on her and ready to boast about it.

So I tucked in.

The lamb (or possibly goat), was still on the bone. It was stringy and gelatinous; it had the consistency of those bits you cut off and throw away, the ones you can't even bring yourself to feed to the dog because the very thought of them being eaten turns your stomach. It was a like a large knuckle joint, all sinew and cartilage and tendons… I had a feeling I'd been given a leg. Which if you've seen a sheep lately, doesn't do much to whet the appetite. But no matter; someone must have thought this was edible, so I couldn't let it defeat me. I ate as much of the oozing meat as I could ferret off the bone, then started in on the sauce.

Which was made of rancid yoghurt.

Now, I'm not being mean here; the description of the dish is 'Rancid Yoghurt Sauce', although I'm sure it translates into something less off-putting in Arabic. I didn't want to think about how they made it, or about how impossible that would be whilst adhering to any sort of health-and-safety principles. I just ate the stuff – or at least, as much of it as I could get down. Quickly realising I couldn't stomach spoonfuls of the stuff, I poured it over my rice. Each splash releasing a waft of delicate fragrance which my nose identified as feet dipped in mouldy cheese.

"You look like you're enjoying that," Mum remarked, as I shovelled the foul stuff down my gullet at high speed.

"Mmm," I mumbled, not trusting myself to comment further.

"Perhaps we should all eat *mansaf* tomorrow night?" She didn't sound convinced, and a sideways glanced revealed a look of disgust on her face.

"I'll pass," said Roo. "It smells like unwashed armpits and looks like it's been eaten once already."

There was nothing to say to that, because it was true. So I closed my eyes – and, as far as possible, my nose – and continued shovelling. Because this was *cultural*, God-damn it! I was doing it for the greater good. For the team. And I wasn't going to let us down.

That night, Roo consoled me through the bathroom door as I knelt on the tiles in front of the toilet. I'd been throwing up for hours; there couldn't possibly be anything left inside me. My guts, however, weren't taking the risk. Whatever *mansaf* was, my body clearly thought I'd been poisoned. I'd left the hotel lobby at a run, barely making it back to our room before the first heave overtook me – and I'd been crouched in the bathroom ever since.

In terms of cultural appreciation, it was not my finest hour.

"You can order a cheeseburger next time," Roo called through the door. "I won't tell anyone, I promise!"

Floaters

We'd been very lucky with our choice of hotel. Toxic *mansaf* aside, the Burj Al Arab was a brilliant find; very cheap, comparatively luxurious and well-positioned for anyone disinclined to pay entrance fees. But far and away the hotel's biggest advantage was the staff – specifically the receptionist, who was the only member of staff we'd actually seen since our arrival. I think he was living on the sofa behind his desk.

He'd welcomed us, provided all the information we could need about Amman and her monuments, and organised us a series of day trips to visit the more far-flung sites in the area. For our driver he supplied his cousin, Ahmed, who looked identical – and turned out to be every bit as helpful as the original.

Ahmed was waiting for us in the hotel lobby, even though we were up especially early to leave time for breakfast. We gobbled down some toast (made with rare 'sliced' bread, presumably kept expressly for difficult tourists like ourselves – and judging by the texture, kept since the last such tourists departed), and piled into a rather impressive Mercedes S-class for the trip to Mount Nebo.

"Nice car," I said to Ahmed.

"Yes," came his nonchalant reply.

And then he powered out into the traffic, the engine growling like a beast restrained. We went all of twenty feet before we stopped, thoroughly ensconced in gridlock. The road, which we'd struggled to cross the previous day, was three lanes wide in each direction. Officially. However, six lanes of cars were now crammed onto each side of the carriageway, making a mockery of anything so arbitrary as road rules. The honking surrounded us, a ceaseless cacophony to obliterate all sense of reason. We edged forward, Ahmed somehow finding a gap between the two cars in front. I'd hesitate to ride my bicycle down that gap, but Ahmed's Mercedes surged forwards, coming to rest within inches of shearing the wing mirrors from both vehicles. In this fashion we continued for the better part of an hour, violently shoving our way through the melee at every opportunity. All the other drivers were doing the same – darting in and out at crazy angles, often sitting broadside across the stream of traffic just to have a chance at an emerging gap three lanes over. It was the fastest, most high-octane traffic jam I've ever been in.

How Ahmed's car remained unscathed, I'll never know. I've seen people take risks in developing countries, with shitty cars most students wouldn't be seen dead in, but this Mercedes looked brand new.

Being a tour guide must be big business, I thought. *Ahmed must make more than I do. Wait a minute, what am I on about – I don't make anything!*

After a near miss that actually made me pee a little, I decided to tackle Ahmed about it. I tried to keep the tone light, jokey, as I usually do when I'm fearing for my life.

"Woah, don't people need to pass a driving test here?" I asked.

"Yes."

"Well what is it? Drive through downtown for forty-five minutes, and if you're still alive you've passed?"

"Yes," he said again.

Ah… that explained it.

'Yes' was the only English word Ahmed knew.

This being Jordan, most of the major sites had some kind of biblical significance. Our first stop was not on the regular tourist trail, however. An hour out of Amman, Ahmed managed to convey that he was taking us on a special detour, and set off at breakneck pace down a narrow track suitable only for four-wheel drives. We descended a long, switch-backed trail, plumes of dust rising from the unsealed road, and skidded to a stop at the bottom of a gorge. Ahmed led us over rocks, past a ruined shack, and into a cave through which a small stream bubbled. At the source of the stream, he proudly tapped the rock with a stick he'd picked up.

"Moses!" he proclaimed, jabbing the stick down again.

It was Mum that put it together; "Oh! It's where Moses struck the rock, and a spring came out!"

"Yes!" said Ahmed.

Mum was excited. "Let's drink from it!"

I glanced around the cave, which may or may not have been the scene of a miracle. Mostly, it was full of rubbish; food wrappers, cigarette packets, and the occasional used condom.

"Um… let's not. Just this once." I turned to Ahmed. "Very nice," I said. "Shall we go now?"

"Yes!"

There was no doubt about it, though – this was Moses country. Regardless of whether or not he sprung that spring, our next stop was Mount Nebo, which a whole fistful of popes had certified to be the real deal. It was supposedly the place where the great man had stood, looking out over the lands of far-off Israel, and been told by God that his descendants would rule over them forever.

"Forever?" exclaimed Moses, "Wow God, that's a pretty sweet deal."

"Oops! Did I say forever?" God sort of scratched the back of his neck and looked at his sandals for a bit. "Um, well, you *might* have to fight for it. Four, maybe five thousand years of ceaseless violence and bloodshed. But you'll get to keep *most* of it. *Eventually.*"

To which one must assume Moses gave a dramatic Jewish "Oyyy!"

The drop-off from Mount Nebo was epic, plunging eight-hundred metres down towards the river Jordan, offering a view that took in thousands of miles of what appeared to be mountainous, scrubby desert. It must have looked like the promised land to Moses, but in fairness he'd been through some fairly tough times up until then. My parent's back garden would have looked like the promised land after forty years wandering the wilderness. Unfortunately, the poor bloke popped his clogs right there, too, so he never got to experience the promised land first hand. If he had, he might have realised how soundly he'd been ripped off, and he'd have shown up in the next life with a few choice words for God.

We marvelled at an intricate mosaic floor, the last remnant of a church built in the 4th century, that was currently protected by a large hessian tent. We were rather less impressed by a great sculpture to Moses, which appeared to be made out of construction waste left over from the building of the visitor's centre.

Next, we visited the place where John the Baptist did whatever it was he was famous for. Bee-keeping, wasn't it? Anyway, we paid a suspiciously cheap admission fee – I think they forgot to charge for Mum, perhaps because only her forehead was visible above the counter – and then we were led along a winding trail lined with gnarly tamarisk trees. At John's 'high tide' baptism spot, both Mum and I took the chance to taste the water, finding it surprisingly salty. Then we made our way down to one of the most significant archaeological discoveries of the 20th Century. Whilst clearing mines after the 1994 peace treaty was signed between Jordan and Israel, the remains of an ancient church was found. Further investigation led to the discovery of five separate churches, each predating the other, all built on exactly the same spot. The oldest featured stone steps leading down into what, two thousand years ago, would have been the edge of the River Jordan. This was the site of John the Baptist's ministry. The river has shifted course over the centuries; these days the steps lead down into a stagnant puddle of disturbingly yellow water, which I had absolutely no intention of tasting. Still, it was oddly awe-inspiring, to stand in a spot where, on a certain day two millennia ago I'd have been able to see Jesus himself having that water poured over his head.

Ugh! I hope he brought a change of clothes.

Our guide took us to the current bank of the Jordan, where a concrete platform allowed tourists to dip their feet in the legendary river.

"Can we swim in it?" I asked.

Mum clutched my arm, as though to restrain me in case I didn't like the answer.

"No," said our guide.

"Oh. Why not?"

"See those men?" He pointed across the river, where steel mesh and barbed wire fenced off what looked like an exclusive holiday resort. I spotted the guards, lounging around in their camo-suits, cradling their weapons.

"Yes?"

"This river is the border between Jordan and Israel. If those men think you are trying to swim across, they will shoot you."

"Oh. Fair enough then."

Inexplicably, Mum's grip on my arm had tightened.

"It's okay," I told her, "I'm not going to try and swim across just to prove a point."

"I know," she replied. Without letting go of my arm.

"So…"

"Shall we dip our heads in?" she said, sounding excited.

So we did.

And then, one by one, so did everybody else in the group. Presumably because they didn't want to miss out on any extra enlightenment we were getting.

Our last stop, and the highlight of the day, was the Dead Sea. I've never been able to float; when I did a life-saving course, I was the least-popular victim, to the point where most of my fellow students refused to rescue me. I couldn't figure out how I'd pissed them off, until one lad told me: "You're a sinker, man. It's like your whole body is made of lead!" The poor girl who was picked to tow me on the exam nearly drowned. She passed anyway, because (as the instructor said), "Slater doesn't count as a real person."

So I was keen to put the famous buoyancy of the salt-heavy waters to the test.

The Dead Sea can be accessed all along its coastline, but if you want to do it in comfort you have to pay to enter a resort. The cheapest ticket buys you access to the public beach, but it's still a hefty fee (£15) considering all it entitles you to is the use of an outdoor shower.

The narrow strip of beach was buzzing with tourists from all over the world.

We scrabbled over slippery rocks and into the sea, and were at once amazed; it was impossible to keep our limbs under water, even for me. Laying back, staring up at the sky, I was treated to a mouthful of brine, courtesy of a large German fellow in shorts that last fit him in 1978. It really was a fantastic experience though, and we lounged around pulling silly poses for Roo, who was in charge of our brand-new, indestructible waterproof camera. She didn't trust me with it, as I've broken every camera I've touched, including hers. In theory, this super-tough Panasonic model was meant to be the solution; the only problem was, it cost so much that we daren't put it to the test. Consequently, I wasn't allowed near the thing.

Halfway up the beach there was a table bearing three terracotta urns. For a measly three Jordanian pounds, the old woman guarding the vessels allowed us to delve inside them, coming out with handfuls of thick black mud, which we smeared on ourselves until we were coated head to toe. I say we – Roo declined this particular experience, on account of the smell.

I'm reminded of this experience every time an immaculately-manicured young woman accosts me in a shopping centre and tries to sell me beauty products that, despite bearing the name, have never been anywhere near the Dead Sea. I always chuckle, but I'm not laughing at her idea of a 'good price' – I'm laughing at the memory of Roo's reaction that day, when I decided to give her a spontaneous hug.

She seemed most bothered by the gigantic black hand-prints I left on her ass.

Lunch was provided at a huge, empty restaurant set back from the beach. It was an all-you-can-eat buffet of entirely cold, largely unrecognisable dishes, and it cost as much per head as our entry fees – a whopping £15, which we politely declined. This severely limited our options, as the only other food source available was an ice cream kiosk. They did stock chocolate, however, so a lunch of ice creams and Mars Bars rounded out our Dead Sea experience.

It was a long, subdued ride home; quite honestly, we were knackered! It was hard to believe how much we'd seen in one day, and how much ground we'd covered. Covering it again, all the way back to the hotel, I couldn't help but notice that in between the towns and cities most of Jordan's countryside looked barren. The smaller settlements appeared ramshackle and run-down, a far cry from the affluence of central Amman. Coming from a land as green and verdant as England, this semi-desert seemed harsh and inhospitable. *Nice place to visit*, I thought, *but I couldn't imagine living here.*

We were all starving by the time we got back to the hotel.

"What do you want for dinner?" Mum asked. "Something… cultural?"

"Hm." I weighed my options carefully. "Isn't there a fried chicken place next-door?"

"I think so."

"Right! Bollocks to the culture."

Roo was doubly pleased, because we were sharing a bathroom, and as she was keen to tell me, "*mansaf* smells as bad on the way out as it does on the way in."

So we went with the chicken.

And it was good.

Road to Ruin

We were sad to leave the Burj Al Arab. It had been a great base for our explorations, and I'd developed a fairly intimate relationship with their toilet.

There was more to discover in Jordan, however, and we didn't want to be like the bus-tourists we'd heard loudly declaring that, "Jordan can easily be done in a day".

We ate the last sliced bread we were to see in the country, and collected Ahmed on the way to his Mercedes. There were two places we wanted to visit today, which were a couple of hours apart by car, after which Ahmed would be taking us to Madaba, the City of Mosaics, and leaving us there. All we had to decide was which site to visit first – Ajloun Castle, or the Roman city of Jerash; we figured Ahmed would be the best person to ask, seeing as how he was doing the driving.

I didn't want to insult his intelligence, but it was important we get this right, so I held up two hands.

"Go to Jerash?" I asked, nodding at my left hand, "then castle?" I shook my right. "Or castle... then Jerash?"

Ahmed seemed to ponder this for a moment, and was about to respond when Mum chimed in. It had never really occurred to me before that speaking pidgin English was a skill, and that it was one I'd unconsciously honed over my travels. Mum, on the other hand, did not have this advantage. So she said to Ahmed; "It depends if Jerash is open later, 'cause if it is we could nip to the castle first and get it over with, then we'd have longer to traipse round Jerash. What you reckon?"

Ahmed, veins popping out of his head, replied, "Uhhhrrr...?"

Mum could see that some clarification was in order, and she was happy to give it to him; "What I mean is, does one of them stay open later than the other? I know Ajloun is closer to Madaba, but we don't want to miss out on it because we take too long in Jerash. If we do the castle first we'll have to double back on ourselves, and we don't want to be rushed when we get to Jerash. You see what I mean?"

Ahmed looked at her, then back at me, with panic in his eyes. He licked his lips several times before he responded; "Uh… you go Jerash?"

Poor bloke!

We went to Jerash.

But we went to the castle first.

There are stacks of castles in Jordan. Most of them were built by the Crusaders, but Ajloun is the exception; an anti-Crusader castle, it was built by Saladin's nephew – with a bit of help from his friends, I'd imagine. It always staggers me when I visit these places, just how insanely difficult they must have been to construct. Ajloun Castle was perched on the pinnacle of a seriously steep hill; an exceptionally strong defensive position of course, but simultaneously an absolute bastard to build in. Stones the size of a fridge-freezer had somehow been hauled up there in the hundreds of thousands. I was out of breath just walking up to the entrance, and all I was carrying was a bottle of water. Mum had to stop and rest twice. "This had… better be… worth it!" she gasped.

It was. Ajloun was a thing of beauty. Those massive blocks of pale sandstone fitted together almost seamlessly. The cream-coloured walls, metres thick, were dressed inside with masonry that would do a modern master proud.

Tourists were thin on the ground, so I climbed through a hole in the roof to explore some bits that were probably out of bounds. Unfortunately, they don't tend to light such places, so I couldn't see a lot.

I heard Mum chattering away to someone below me, and then she called: "Tony, there's some local people here who'd like to meet you!"

So I leapt straight back through the hole, landing in a crouch on the floor below – right at the feet of two astonished young Arab girls. "*Salaam Alaykum,*" (Peace be upon you) I said as I stood up. The girls stared open-mouthed for a few seconds before fleeing down the corridor, giggling and pushing one another.

"I think you frightened them," Mum said.

"Yeah. I do seem to have that effect on women."

We arrived in the ruined Roman city of Jerash just in time for the circus.

Now, before you coulrophobic types start sweating, let me explain that 'circus' is the Roman word for the Greek 'hippodrome'.

And if that doesn't make things any clearer, let's just call it an amphitheatre on steroids. The Roman circus at Jerash was a truly massive structure, built to hold chariot races; a 15,000 seat stadium, not too different from a modern one. As long as two football pitches, it encompassed a 245 metre track; sixteen rows of tiered benches would have wrapped around the action on the sandy arena floor, though the 500-seat section we were in was all that remained. Luckily, only ten people turned up for the show so we weren't too crowded.

The spectacle we had paid to see was a reconstruction of gladiatorial combat. We'd read about it on the internet while researching Jerash, and we couldn't resist taking a look.

"Don't pay any bribes," warned the bloke who sold us our tickets.

He needn't have mentioned it, as 'Do Not Bribe The Gladiators' was printed across the bottom of the programme we were given. And on the tickets.

It was a bit like seeing a 'Don't Feed The Animals' sign at the zoo – I wanted to know if they'd suddenly become more dangerous once money was involved.

The show itself was interesting, if fairly tame. One (very lucky) company of the Jordanian Army got to dress up as Roman soldiers and perform battlefield manoeuvres, like the infamous 'turtle', while trumpet fanfares and commentary blasted from an old-school PA system. A quick costume change saw them re-emerge as gladiators, and they spent the next ten minutes flinging nets at each other and duelling with swords.

It must have been a cushy job, compared with patrolling the Israeli border, but I doubt it earned them much respect. 'Join the army, they said... you get to wear a skirt and fight with a trident...'

The charioteers came next, whipping their horses to breakneck pace as they raced up and down the central *spina*, or fence.

After the show, we were called down to take photos with the gladiators.

"But don't pay them any bribes," the ticket seller reminded us.

Which was easier said than done. The biggest of the gladiators, a massive body-building-type, offered me a go with his sword – an activity which was strictly forbidden according to the pamphlet. Not something I was likely to refuse though! Next he took a stand behind Roo, his sword poised to cut her throat, as she knelt in the sand in what I nicknamed the 'mother-in-law position'.

Then he asked me for five *dinars*, and I paid the bribe because, to be honest, I was scared of what would happen if I didn't. From the size of him, I'd say that cash went on meat and steroids. Most of the other tourists had wandered off by this point, and the rest of the gladiators, scenting bribes, closed in around us.

Roo and I were rescued by a charioteer, who whisked us aboard his spindly transport and took us on a hair-raising lap of the arena. Now *that* was five *dinars* well spent!

Unfortunately this action, whilst timely for us, left Mum alone with the pack – and she was forced to bribe herself all the way out of the circus.

Unbelievably, Jerash was almost completely devoid of tourists. Perhaps because it was the low season? Or possibly because the place was so damn big, you could lose a thousand tourists in there and it would still seem empty. There was not one but *two* open-air theatres, one so complete that we could walk through the passages running inside the walls – though not without a moment of trepidation for the hundreds of tonnes of stone seating which carried on right above our heads.

There were more incredible ruins than I could ever describe, giant gateways the size of an office block, temples, roads, and columns as far as the eye could see. One immense concourse, a paved circular plaza fringed with columns, was big enough for a 747 to turn around in. Everywhere we went, the stonework stretched on – buildings upon buildings, some nothing more than rubble, some so well-preserved they could almost be lived in. As a lover of ancient history, I had never seen anything to compare with it – and I still haven't. Jerash was, in a word, spectacular. It was also a great place to climb, and I frequently found myself looking down on my fellow tourists from the top of a crumbling temple wall or a gravity-defying archway. At one point I glanced down to see what was crunching underfoot, only to discover I was walking on a mosaic – forgotten, unprotected, uncared for, it had been ruined and scattered in all directions. Nor was it alone – whole avenues of smashed mosaics lay beneath the layers of dust and sand, victims of a site so enormous that there was no realistic way to preserve it all. I bent down and snuck a couple of the mosaic tiles into my pocket, while pretending to tie my shoelaces. An English woman saw me do it, and shrugged. "Might as well," she said, "it's just being destroyed here." And she bent down to do the same.

Foreign Food

The excitement of our stay in Jordan had only been marred by one reoccurring problem: food.

Whilst living in Thailand I often ate only one meal a day unless I was diving, and Mum has been "on a diet" pretty much consistently since 1978. Roo, however, has the metabolism of a racehorse. If she doesn't eat every few hours she will literally pass out. Because we were traveling such long distances each day, and because most of that distance seemed to be completely devoid of human habitation, we had started taking meals into our own hands; for us, this meant stealing flatbread and cream cheese triangles from the breakfast buffet and using them to make sandwiches in the back of the taxi. On the morning we checked out, however, there hadn't been any cheese left, and it seemed a little too blatant to ask for them to be replenished and then rob the lot.

We'd snacked on ice cream in Jerash, but it was a long drive to Madaba and we were seriously in need of something more substantial. I mentioned this to Ahmed – though not in those exact words – and he pulled over in the next town we passed through. Motioning in no uncertain terms that we stay put, he left the car and disappeared into an alleyway. A few nervous minutes passed until he emerged, arms laden with paper bags. He flashed a huge grin at me as he handed them into the car. "For me, very cheap! For you, very expensive!"

The bags contained falafel sandwiches, a staple snack food in Jordan; they were fresh, still hot from… well, whatever it is you cook falafel in; and they were delicious. Ahmed ducked back out and bought us a can of Coke each to wash it all down with. Not only had he used his local discount on us, he refused to let us pay him at all.

A free lunch tastes great whatever country you eat it in!

The upside of arriving in Madaba outside of tourist season was that our hotel generously upgraded us to a huge corner room. The downside was that, to conserve power throughout the nearly empty hotel, the management had decided to turn the heating off. This wouldn't have mattered much in the day, but like all cities in the desert, Madaba was bloody freezing at night. We toughed it out, wrapped in every spare blanket we could find, before I gave up and begged the manager to turn the heating on. He was confused at first – apparently Jordanian tourists were usually tucked up in bed fast asleep by 9pm – but he grudgingly agreed to run the heat for half an hour. I could tell he was thinking, *Crazy Westerners, sitting up all night in their rooms!*

We had stuff to do, though.

Diaries to write, blogs to update, trips and hotels to book. We were doing this on the fly, much to Mum's dismay, but so far it was working for us; we were finding plenty of discounted rooms at short notice, much like the one we were now staying in. It was obviously a hotel for Jordanian businessmen rather than scruffy English tourists, but so long as it offered us a roof over our heads, we were happy.

Well, a room-temperature above zero would have been nice, but you can't have everything.

Mum was using the miniscule laptop we'd brought with us, sitting on her bed and frowning at the screen, when she complained, "I can't read my writing!"

Roo and I exchanged a glance. "Um, Mum," I said, "you do know you're typing, right?"

"You know what I mean," she said. "I'm trying to tell Dad what we've been doing, but I can't read my journal." She showed me the book. It did look like she'd been killing blue insects with the clean pages rather than writing in it. I guess as a nurse, it's to be expected that she shares the doctor's curse of utterly illegible handwriting.

Roo was laying on her bed, cradling the guidebook, trying to make notes on what we'd be seeing tomorrow. Sighing, she dropped the notepad and rolled over onto her back. "The trouble is, this book is going in one ear and out the other," she said.

"That sounds painful," I told her. "Just don't get any blood on the pillows."

I was on a roll that night.

But what I wouldn't have given for a roll the next morning.

Instead, we had our first taste of the typical Jordanian hotel breakfast, which we were to enjoy – if enjoy is the right word – in similar form, every morning for the rest of our trip.

It's our own fault, of course. We were expecting the Western standard – sausage, bacon, eggs, the odd croissant perhaps, with a bit of ethnic Jordanian food mixed in for variety.

No.

There was a long table running down one side of the dining room, festooned with bowls of mysterious liquids and sauces, dishes filled with strange-coloured powders... I felt like I'd stumbled into a high school chemistry class. Nevertheless, we picked our seats and sat there staring at each other, all wondering what to do next. There were no waiters; this was a buffet breakfast, which we'd been excited about because it gave us the chance to steal a bit of food for lunch. Only, before we could do that, we'd have to figure out which bits actually were food, and which were just the table decorations. The candles I could recognise, but they still looked more edible than anything else on offer.

Once, on holiday in Egypt, I sampled a bright blue powder which was piled up enticingly next to the cumin and crushed garlic on every spice stall in the Bazaar. A stall holder pantomimed that I wet the tip of my finger and dip it in for a taste... then laughed like a drain when my face screwed up in disgust. It was laundry detergent. You've got to get your kicks from something, I guess – I think if I worked on a spice stall in that market, I'd be doing the same thing. But I developed a certain distrust of foreign powders that day, which seemed to rule out roughly half of my breakfast options at a stroke.

I tried to stay positive, though. "When in Rome," I reminded Roo, as we approached the buffet table – ignoring the fact that, had I been in Rome, I'd blatantly be having pizza for breakfast.

"What's that one?" Roo asked, pointing at a wide dish full of brown goo.

"Not a clue," I said, "sorry."

Her fingers hovered over the serving spoon for a second, before she decided not to risk it. "What's that one?" she asked, pointing towards the next dish in line.

"Sorry love... no idea."

"Oh. Right. What's *that* one?"

We approached a tureen, labelled in Arabic, and I lifted the lid for a look.

"Is it soup?" Roo asked, hopefully.

"Erm... I'm not quite sure. You wanna try some?"

She stirred the pot with a ladle, causing various floating things to surface momentarily. "Ugh, no," she said, "it's cold. And it's got *bits* in it."

By the time we reached the end of the buffet table all three of our plates were still empty, apart from the pieces of flatbread we'd picked up at the start.

Mum glanced around, clearly embarrassed. "I think I'll go back and get one of those cold boiled eggs," she murmured.

Ten minutes later, after retracing our steps up and down several times, we'd amassed a selection of unidentifiable food items that we were willing to try.

I'd taken some small, hard nuts, a pile of brown powder that could have been absolutely anything, and one of those triangular foil packets of cream cheese.

Roo had found a pastry that oozed clear liquid, a spoonful of seeds which may or may not have been sunflower, and an unidentified piece of fruit that looked like it had been sat on.

Mum, who doesn't eat bread on account of it making her feel "a bit bloated", had gone for the only thing she could recognise – a double serving of bread, with a cold boiled egg on top. Which turned out to be pickled.

"Cream cheese?" I offered her.

"Oh God, it's Laughing Cow! The picture is the same, even though the writing is in Arabic. Quick, go and grab some more for later."

By later, she did of course mean lunch – so, our uninspiring breakfast looked set to be followed by an equally uninspiring picnic.

"There must be something here to eat though," I said. "Why don't we sit and watch what everyone else does?"

Both Mum and Roo were far too polite to adopt this strategy, so I cast a few surreptitious glances around the dining room. As far as I could tell, the other diners were slavering their flatbread in oil from a bottle in the middle of the table, liberally sprinkling it with an assortment of herbs and powders, and then tucking in to it with great relish.

So I tried it. It wasn't what you'd call a complete success. The net result was that instead of having stale bread, I now had oily stale bread with bits in it. And a trail of olive oil that led across the table to my plate, down into my lap, and right back up my shirt to where it was dripping off my chin.

"I think I'll try one of those boiled eggs," Roo said.

"They're pickled!" Mum warned.

"Oh." Roo was half out of her seat, but she quickly sat down again. And we were back to staring at each other. "How's the bread?" she asked me.

"Oily."

"I can see that. How does it taste?"

"Oily."

"What did you put on it?"

"I haven't a fucking clue. But it's starting to burn the inside of my mouth…"

"Well then," Mum chipped in. "Are we done with breakfast?"

All It's Cracked Up To Be

As we left the hotel, the receptionist furnished us with a poor quality photocopy of a hand-drawn map. This would, in theory, lead us to the amazing mosaic floors for which Madaba was famous. Most were in churches, but there were so many of them that some were in private houses. There was also a Mosaic Museum marked, and a School of Mosaics, and… well, that was about it. If you're not into mosaics, Madaba probably isn't the best place for a holiday.

Following the map carefully, we set off for the nearest of the sites – a mosaic map of the known world, dating from around the 5th Century AD.

As we wandered along, Roo and I were holding hands which meant that Mum, quite naturally, walked on the opposite side of me. Now, Roo is super observant but quietly spoken, whereas Mum, like me, walks around in the perpetual state of fugue that is our genetic legacy. Only, she is also going deaf. So our exploration of Madaba was punctuated with exchanges like this:

Roo: "Hey look, a fried chicken shop!"
Me: "Mmmm, chicken…"
Walking, walking,
Mum: "I think that place sells chicken."
Me: Yup, Chicken. Mmm."
Then, a few paces later,
Roo: "Wow, nice mosque!"
Me: "Oh yeah! Awesome!"
(thirty seconds' delay)
Mum: "Is that a mosque over there."
Me: "Yup. Mosque."

By the time we'd been walking for an hour, I was killing myself laughing.

I was also starting to question the accuracy of the map.

You see, Madaba is a fairly small place, and the church we were looking for should have been less than ten minutes' walk from the hotel.

I was beginning to suspect we were lost, but then we rounded a corner and found it – not, as expected, the Church of the Map, but instead the Church of the Apostles – which, according to our map, was the furthest point away from where we'd started. Somehow we'd circumvented the entire town! Ah well.

We went in anyway, and were treated to a glimpse of a woman emerging from the sea (mosaic style), which was in fantastic condition considering it was over fifteen-hundred years old. A raised walkway ran around the inside of the church to keep the floor safe from tourists, and we duly walked around it before pulling out our cameras.

At this point a uniformed guard hurried over to tell us that no photographs were allowed... well, unless we paid him 5 *dinars*. This we did, and his demeanour changed completely. Pulling aside the railings he led us down to the floor, onto the surface of the mosaic itself, and let us take our photos at point-blank range. This was a phenomenon that was to repeat itself throughout the day in Madaba – photos were banned everywhere, but the guards always asked us for a bribe to look the other way. We couldn't take them all up on it, or it would have been a seriously expensive day – and we'd have ended up with dozens of photographs of mosaics, which I doubt would have changed our lives for the better.

Instead we marvelled at the perfectly preserved paving of a Roman Road which had been discovered beneath the town, and shopped for scarves in the endless procession of kiosk-like shops which lined every street, spilling out onto the pavements with brightly-coloured woven goods, beads, trinkets and postcards.

Most of the souvenirs were way out of our price range. The value of money seemed to have slipped a few notches over here, or else they were used to tourists who were considerably richer than we were.

It was like something out of Back To The Future.

Every so often a beggar would shuffle up to me, piteously dressed in non-designer labels and last year's Nikes, and say, "Please, give me ten dollars to buy a coffee?"

Having spent all morning on our feet, we were forced to supplement our lunch of stolen cream cheese and flatbread with a falafel sandwich from one of the omnipresent vendors, before setting out to find the same thing we'd been searching for all morning – the Byzantine Mosaic World Map.

And I have to say, against all the odds, it actually was worth it. Featuring trees, rivers, castles and cities laid out street by street – all labelled in delicate tile-work – it was the 5th Century equivalent of

Google Maps. The accuracy of the map (unlike the one we'd been following to get there) had allowed archaeologists to pinpoint a host of significant sites dating back to the biblical era, such as the Baptism site we'd visited earlier.

We'd now seen every possible kind of mosaic, including some laid directly on top of each other in what must have been the Roman version of redecorating. For our last stop, we somehow managed to navigate our way to the Mosaic Museum.

We never did determine if the museum was closed for renovations, or just crap, but either way no-one challenged us as we strolled inside and poked around amongst the exhibits. One room held a series of glass cases, some empty, some full of costumed mannequins, and Roo couldn't resist climbing into one of the open displays to pose alongside the traditional Bedouin dress of centuries past. We left the way we'd come, past a deserted office, through an unmarked door and back into the street. By this point we'd had enough of Madaba's dusty streets – even enough, dare I say it, of her mosaics – so we found a barbecue restaurant and ordered chicken 'taouk', which turned out to be delicious shish-kebabs.

When we got back to the hotel it was, unsurprisingly, like an icebox. Being the only man I was again nominated to go down and ask reception if they could turn on the heating. The manager rather amused me with his surprised response of "Again?"

I left him shaking his head at the peculiarity of foreigners, who want their room warm every night, rather than just on special occasions.

The next entire day was spent in a taxi, crossing hundreds of miles of empty desert at the heart of Jordan. Awed by the alien-ness of the landscape, we sat in stunned silence as fields of orange sand strewn with rocks rolled by. The desolation stretched to the horizon in every direction and its scale was breath-taking. Every now and then we'd pass a handful of bare concrete houses surrounded by market stalls made of sticks. The contrast with Amman's affluent, modern cityscape was hard to believe – clearly not everyone in Jordan drove a brand new Mercedes. Even the presence of vegetables for sale in the tiny settlements seemed incongruous; where on earth were they growing it? The only produce we saw being farmed seemed to be cacti, which again begged the question – why the hell would anyone want to farm a cactus? Can you milk them?

"Maybe that's where prickly pears come from," Roo mused.

Still, the vegetation brought a bit of colour to the journey and some welcome interest to the eye. At one point, Mum hadn't said anything in over an hour when she sat bolt upright, stared straight out of the window and said, "That's a very big cauliflower."

We were understandable impressed by her contribution. It certainly gave us something to discuss for the next hundred kilometres…

We stopped at Kerak to explore an epic Crusader castle. The concept fascinated me. Picture it: you're deep in enemy territory, fighting a series of the most brutal campaigns in ancient history. What do you do? Why, you start carving monumental blocks of stone from the surrounding countryside of course, and spend the next ten years building castles! How did they even know where to begin? Some of the knights must have had a degree in architecture. At any rate, they'd excelled themselves by going completely arch-mad. There were three-way arches, four-way arches, big arches on top of little arches, and one gigantic barrel-vaulted great room the size of an aircraft hanger. It was hard to believe this was all built by hand, out of the heaviest and most difficult to manoeuver materiel possible – on one of the most inaccessible pinnacles in the whole damn country. And they clearly hadn't given in to the urge to build a little castle. You know how, when you get halfway through a big job you start thinking of ways you could cut corners to finish it quicker… not these boys! These knights must have been a damn sight better with a chisel than with a sword by the time they were done. No wonder they lost control of the Holy Land – the whole army must have been suffering from chronic backache. Their castle, however, was amazing, and well worth a visit.

We stopped again an hour later to marvel at the immensity of Wadi Mujib – a vast canyon, its far side just visible through the heat haze, swallowing the road until it looked like an ink-scribble on the valley floor five-hundred metres below us.

Night fell, and still we drove.

And then we caught sight of twinkling lights in the distance.

Collectively, we caught our breath, because this was *it*.

This is what we'd been waiting for – in Mum's case, for most of her adult life.

We had finally arrived at Petra.

Or more accurately, we had arrived at *Cleo*Petra – a cringe-worthy name for an otherwise cheerful hostel in the nearby town of Wadi Musa.

Roo showered and then collapsed onto the bed, conquered by that peculiar fatigue that comes with mileage rather than physical exertion. It had been a long day, and I was equally eager to remove the sweat and grime that accumulates when exploring ruined cities. The shower, however, presented a unique conundrum, and Roo dragged herself out of bed to see why I was having an hysterical laughing fit in the middle of it.

"What's wrong?" she asked. Presumably she thought I was drowning.

"It's got a step in it," I giggled, pointing to the bath.

This was true; the bath, which had the shower over it, was only half-size. The back part of it was raised, for no good reason I could think of.

"Yes…?" Roo sounded confused.

"Well, I can't stand on the upper step. I can't get my head under the shower." I demonstrated this. "And if I stand on the lower step… well, look what happens!"

The bottom bit was fairly small, obliging me to stand right against the wall. At a certain height, a tap protruded from that wall to facilitate the filling of the bath.

And as I stood there, taking my shower, my balls rested lightly on the tap.

Roo started to snigger.

"It's even worse if I turn around," I explained. "Look what happens when I try to soap my legs!"

I shuffled around and bent over – presenting my arse to the tap, which nestled itself uncomfortably between my buttocks. "Why would you put a tap at exactly that height?"

Roo was lost for words.

"I mean, I'm just trying to have a shower here, and I'm being forcibly violated by the plumbing!"

Roo shook her head in disbelief. "I can't believe I'm marrying you," she said. "I managed to shower in there without getting a tap stuck up my ass."

"It's not my fault!"

"It could only happen to you."

"Are you saying my bum's too big?"

"I'm saying nothing. Just… make sure you wipe that tap when you're finished with it."

Petrafied

Wonder of the classical world; capital of the ancient Nabataean civilization; the rose-red city, half as old as time; a lot has been written about Petra over the last few hundred years.

I hadn't read any of it, of course.

I *had* seen the film Indiana Jones and the Last Crusade, and that had left a permanent impression on me – from that moment on, Indiana Jones is who I wanted to be when I grew up.

Still is, to be honest.

But it has to be said, considering this was meant to be the highlight of our trip, that my research and preparation was a little on the shoddy side.

Here's what we did know: Petra is famous the world over for its massive, temple-like facades carved from the sheer rock walls of the canyon. It is a city of the dead, in that it's a complex of tombs rather than of residences, though plenty of Jordan's native Bedouin have lived in them. Apart from this, we knew that it was beautiful; that it is utterly unique; and that it features on every 'things to see before you die' list ever created.

And for anyone planning a visit to Petra themselves, here are a few things we did not know.

Fact No.1 We Did Not Know About Petra: You can do it in a day. Apparently. So said Mr and Mrs Modra, a fit looking couple in their early forties. Mind you, they were Aussies, so it's possible there was a bit of bravado in their statement. They did have that slightly feverish, gung-ho look about them – the 'up at 6am, took a shit in the bush and wiped my arse with a cactus' type breed. Depressingly enthusiastic outdoorsy-type folk. Anyway, they were clearly nuts as they were actually *driving*. Our guidebook had a whole chapter about driving in Jordan. It was one word long and said: 'Don't.'

Fact No.2 We Did Not Know About Petra: It is the biggest rip-off in the world.

No, really! For two reasons. First, it is literally the biggest – over 500 individual tombs, so many you'd be dead of boredom and needing one yourself long before you saw them all. Luckily, they're scattered across thirty-five square kilometres of rocky desert, most of which is only accessible by goat.

Second; because it costs *fifty pounds each* to get in! For one day. Yes, that's right – US$80 per person! Which is why Jordan isn't on the backpacker trail. You can buy a cocaine plantation in some South American countries for that.

But was it worth it? Well, that's a tough question for me to answer, really.

Because I didn't pay it.

You see, I've always been a big believer in Fate, and this is why:

Following my rather intimate encounter with the shower at CleoPetra, we all headed into the tiny town centre of Wadi Musa (which the unkind might point out is really just a roundabout) to get the quickest, easiest food possible before we passed out eating it. We chose a kebab shop at random (there were three of them, and nothing else); and there, on the mezzanine dining level, we met Mr and Mrs Modra.

We were the only other western tourists in the restaurant, sitting at a table festooned with brochures and enjoying a bird's eye view of our food being cooked, when they pounced.

"G'day!" said Mr Modra. "Y'all sound like you're from England!"

We spent quite a while chatting with the Modras.

They were in the middle of a major trip, exploring every country they could get visas for, and – to cut a long story short – they'd both bought two-day passes to Petra, hiked the crap out of the place in one, and wanted to move on. They offered us their passes – for free – on the off chance we could make use of the second day.

Which we most certainly could. Especially when we noticed how much they'd cost. We scurried back to the hotel and checked with the receptionist. "Yes," she confirmed, "Fifty *dinars* for one day. For two days, only fifty-five."

One Jordanian *dinar* is pretty much equal to one UK pound.

Collectively, we suffered heart failure. Our guidebook listed the entry fee as *twenty dinars* – circa 2009. Who could imagine the price would almost triple in just over a year? Faced with becoming so broke we'd be eating cream cheese for the rest of the holiday, we quickly formulated a plan. Roo and I would go in posing as the Aussie couple.

Mum would buy a full price ticket for herself – for two days, since it was only five quid more, and it would give her the option to pace herself.

And that was that.

As the morning of the scam approached, Roo and I got progressively more nervous. I like to pretend that I live on the edge, but I'm not really a law-breaker – at least, not often enough to become blasé about it. My brain swam with all the things that could go wrong. I imagined all the questions the guards could possibly ask, and tried to come up with a plausible answer for all of them. We couldn't prove our surname was Modra, as printed on the tickets, because we'd left our passports in the hotel safe. We'd brought no other ID for fear of pickpockets. I didn't sound like an Aussie because I'd only just moved there from England. Our first names were... Shit! Why couldn't I remember our names? And what if they'd taken photos...?

But no.

In the event, the guard's ticket scanner didn't even work. He gave it a couple of ineffectual wafts, frowned at the screen, then banged it repeatedly against a nearby rock. This didn't seem to do it much good, so he passed the scanner back into his booth and waved us through. Grand Larceny had been committed, and it was only 9:30 in the morning!

Fact No.3 We Did Not Know About Petra: The horse ride to the entrance is free.

This is a country where, despite the cost of living being similar to the US or UK, people still seem to think of tourists as purveyors of great wealth. God knows why – they must get their customer relations training in Bali. Everyone we met had their hands out for cash, from the kids in the street (wearing trainers I couldn't afford) to the taxi guides earning £70 for four hours' work. So when a bunch of guys hanging around the ticket office started to follow us and demand we get on their horses, we ignored them and walked on. They shouted that it was free – but this was a tactic we'd seen before. Whilst *entirely* free to get on, getting off at the other end requires the application of a tip; probably around five *dinars*. Which is pretty steep for a five minute ride.

And yet it turned out to be true! Mum had been given a leaflet with her ticket, which we were all too nervous to stop and read whilst the guards could still see us. We read it later that night in the hotel. Apparently a horse-ride to the canyon *was* included in our ticket price – they mentioned it almost by way of apologising for the exorbitant entrance fee. A shame, really, as the walk in was much longer than expected, and took at least half an hour off our tomb-raiding schedule. But the leaflet also explained that it was customary to tip the guide afterwards – and sure enough, they suggested five *dinars*.

Fact No.4 We Did Not Know About Petra: It was not discovered by *Indiana Jones*. There is no immortal knight inside, no spinning blades or bottomless chasms. Behind the gigantic facade carved into the wall of the canyon, there is only an empty square chamber the size of a tennis court. And it was closed.

Which was a bit of a bummer.

Quite a lot of the tombs were closed, actually. No explanation was given – just steel or plastic barriers stretched across the entrance of all the most popular sites mentioned in our guidebook. 'With a funeral chamber in the upper story, it's a must-see…' the book gushed.

Nope. A mustn't see.

A soldier with an AK47 was lounging against the entrance to Tomb #67.

"I want to go inside," I complained.

"No. Is closed." And he patted his gun.

Had I paid to get in I'd have wanted to swear at him, and point out that I'd just paid his wages for two days of sitting there, stroking his weapon, telling people what they couldn't do.

But I hadn't, so I didn't.

It made me wonder, though, just where all that entrance money ended up. The tombs at Petra were carved out of solid rock over 2,000 years ago. The place has hardly changed since then. It's been attacked and conquered, sacked and relieved, stolen, lost and rediscovered by every civilisation this part of the world has known. How much 'conservation' were they really doing? Aside from sweeping up the cigarette butts? Despite it being low season, the car park was rammed out with tour buses, at least fifty by my reckoning. If only a thousand of us were there that day, the authorities had made fifty grand. What the hell kind of conservation they were undertaking on that budget? Building a life-size replica out of Lego?

So, my best piece of advice about Petra is, DO go there. It's phenomenal. And it's ridiculous to go all the way to Jordan and then miss it. But DON'T pay full price. Plan to spend a couple of days in town, and try to hook up with another group matching your description. Get them to buy two-day tickets and go in on day one, and then buy their second day off them for half price. Everyone's a winner baby! Smile sweetly at the guard as you go in, and imagine just how many beers you can buy for the cash you've screwed his employers out of. (Approximately five in Jordan – or closer to twenty if you wait till you get back home to buy 'em).

Oh, and take your free damn horse ride. Hell, take mine too for that matter...

Stalling Tactics

The entrance to Petra is through a narrow gorge called the Siq. Now, when I say narrow, I mean it – as the Siq twists and turns like a jagged knife-cut through the solid rock, there are places where it's just three metres wide. The sun, visible only in the slot above the sheer walls of the Siq, casts slender beams like search-lights into the depths of the canyon. More than any place I've ever been, it just *felt* mysterious – like the entrance to some fabled lost city. Which is exactly what it is. The difference in temperature between the pools of shadow and shafts of light was about ten degrees, so stepping from one to the other caused a ripple of heat (or cold) to run over me. We had plenty of chance to appreciate this effect, as the Siq turned out to be almost a mile long. We'd rather cleverly managed to sneak into the gap between two large tour groups, meaning so long as we kept our pace right we could achieve that holy grail of tourism: a photograph without half-a-dozen people in flip-flops and Hawaiian shirts in the background.

All of a sudden we rounded the last bend and were rewarded with the sight we'd all been waiting for; a sliver of Petra's most famous structure, the immense Treasury. That vertical slice was all we could see for the last part of our journey through the Siq, enticing us onwards into the sunlight. Then the canyon opened out to into a wide valley, and the Treasury was revealed in all its glory. It really was magnificent. A columned façade over forty metres high towered above us, sculpted straight from the cliff face. The masons had worked top-down, carving away the side of the mountain while they were still standing on it. It looked like the entrance to some vast underground palace; I could hardly believe it housed nothing more impressive than an unadorned square chamber and a couple of side-niches.

Our plan for 'doing Petra' (no pun intended) was to thrust in as deep as possible (okay, I intended that bit). The part that most tourists failed to reach was also the most impressive, and we aimed to get there as fast as we could, bypassing the crowds around the closer tombs and visiting them on the way back. But no plan survives contact with the enemy; in this case, that enemy was an army of Bedouin merchants, all of whom had set up shop here, and all of whom were determined to sell us something.

I struggled to comprehend the depth of the scam. We'd *paid* to get in here; well, Mum had. But instead of being free to explore, we were besieged by vendors, pulling at our clothes, shoving fistfuls of beaded necklaces into our faces. We'd bought tickets into an enclosed version of the tourist-scamming hell we'd been trying to escape since we set foot in the country! On top of which, the Bedouin traders were presumably coughing up a chunk of their profits for some form of license to harass. Somebody, somewhere high up in a Jordanian government building, was laughing into their quail omelettes.

Hundreds of stalls lined our trek through the canyon, all selling the same silk scarves, 'authentic' antiques, buckets of fake silver jewellery and resin-cast 'fossils'. It would have been interesting, if every historical site we'd visited so far hadn't been lined with identical stalls selling identical 'handmade Bedouin products'. I was starting to think that these mysterious Bedouin were bloody productive, given that there were only a handful of them scattered around the remotest parts of the country. And, as closer inspection of the trinkets revealed, at least some of these Bedouin lived in China.

Dodging past rows of tombs cut into the canyon walls, past the ruins of Roman temples, past fallen columns and mysterious caves, we found our way to the furthest end of Petra, where the canyon met the mountain. Here were the steps we'd been reading about – eight-hundred of them, which roughly translates into a fifty-four floor building. It was going to be an epic climb, and Mum had been wrestling with the decision to attempt it all night. Now, faced with the challenge, she came to the conclusion that nothing the steps would bring could be worse than sitting alone at the bottom – and thereby becoming the sole target for every passing salesman in the area.

Up we went.

The crumbling stone steps, hewn from the rock thousands of years ago, were anything but boring. Narrow and twisting, wide and shallow, suddenly steep and precipitous, they wound their way back and forth across the mountain. On one side, then the other – occasionally both – vertical drops for hundreds of feet led to a nasty finish on a carpet of fallen boulders. A knee-high wall provided the only safety barrier, and the really exposed sections didn't even have room for that. Mum, bless her heart, toiled up the lot of it – sweating, panting, stopping for breaks – but she, like me, loved every minute of it.

Well, apart from the stalls which lined the entire route.

The vendors' persistence was truly impressive. After fighting my way past a dozen tatty stalls, shouting "No, NO!" in five languages – one of which was even their own – what in all the hells made the stall holder at pitch #13, watching my progress from his ragged awning, think, "Eh up! This bloke looks keen…"

By stall thirty I'd started swearing at them. By stall ninety I'd run out of swear words and my throat was full of sand. Luckily enough, stall ninety-five or so seemed to be selling cans of cheap cola – no doubt for the price of a Stella in a swanky Soho nightclub. But between me and the outrageously priced beverages lay at least four more stalls. I could see the owners rubbing their hands in glee. "This one's lost the will to fight already," they were saying to themselves, "he hasn't cursed anyone for ten stalls! Surely he will buy my shit just to shut me up. Quick! Rasheed! We must be extra persuasive…"

The view from the top was spectacular. After ascending a load more stairs which no-one had told us about, we were rewarded with a vista to rival the best I have even seen. The mountain fell away below my perch; thousands of feet straight down, to a valley floor that was impossible to see. On one side stretched the whole of Palestine; the great wide swathe of mountains which separated Israel from Jordan. On the other side stood Mum, shrieking, "Get down from there, you'll fall to your death!"

She does get overworked about such things, but she did have a point – as a family, we're known mostly for our clumsiness.

Roo was holding my hand and edging me gently back from the precipice.

"I'll get a better photo from there," I said.

"Yes my love, but if you die horribly in Jordan it'll put a big hole in the wedding plans."

"Well. Fair enough then."

Next we paid a visit to the real reason for climbing all this way; the largest building in Petra, the Monastery, was carved from a sheer rock face, high up on this distant plateau. Stylistically it was very similar to the Treasury, only much bigger – fifty metres square, a truly gigantic sculpture giving clear evidence that, even in ancient Nabataean culture, one-upmanship was alive and kicking.

The closer I got to the wind-blasted façade, the less I could see – it was simply too big to take it all in. At the base of the cliff a small crowd of tourists milled around, tripping over each other with their necks craned back. The interior of the tomb was empty of people though, and it wasn't until I got right up to it that I figured out why; the square opening was over eight feet up. No-one was even trying to get in, so I couldn't resist practicing a bit of Parkour. I leapt onto the wall and swung myself up into the entrance, really grateful for the grip on my Merrells. I helped Roo up, and together we explored the interior – which was, predictably, an empty square chamber. Back at the entrance we were attracting a lot of attention – of the good kind, for a change. Several people asked if I could help them up, and I happily obliged. Then, our expedition completed, Roo and I hopped gracefully from the ledge, landing as we'd practiced in a shock-absorbing roll.

Ten minutes later, returning from a different viewpoint, we noticed the same group of people standing forlornly on the edge of the Monastery entrance. It hadn't occurred to them – or to us – but none of them could get down again.

We were happy to let them figure it out, though.

After pausing for a Coke in a Bedouin-run tent café, Mum bravely suggested we start back down the steps. It was more punishing in this direction, the solidity of the steps and their unevenness taking a toll on our knees and ankles. A young Arab clucked to his donkey as he passed us, leaning back in his saddle against the incline. Sure-footed, the donkey plodded down step after step, picking a path so precarious it had me clutching at the rock wall for support. Of course, there were no handrails.

"Hire a Porsche?" the man asked as he came level with us. "Air conditioned, see!" he waved his hand above the donkey's ears.

I had to smile. "Sir, your Porsche is trying to eat my hat."

With a chuckle he was off, slapping his ass (by which I mean, his donkey). The beast paid him no heed, taking its own sweet time to choose the footing.

"I think I'd be more scared, doing this on a donkey," Mum said.

"I think the donkey would be, too," I quipped. And ran.

Luckily, she was too out of breath to chase me.

Getting The Hump

The next day would have been our second exploring Petra.

I think it's safe to say, we were all glad it wasn't.

On our way out we'd visited every tomb we could find – bloody hundreds of the buggers – and one other thing we could all agree on was that we were totally tombed-out. We'd seen chambers cut so that the marbled patina of the rock provided all the decoration a tomb could ever need. We'd seen tiny hovels and giant arched structures supporting bridges and more arches and finally a tomb perched on the top. Tombs up the side of cliffs, impossible to visit without Spiderman to give you a leg-up, and tombs stacked three-deep that could be climbed like a ladder. Steps that led up to tombs, steps that led nowhere, and, at the final whistle, a sprint back up the Siq to get out before we missed the bus back into town.

We'd narrowly avoided adding that walk to our tally.

And so, with sore feet, aching knees, and dreams invaded by gap-toothed Bedouin merchants selling maps to the exit, I was more than happy to spend most of the morning in bed.

We passed a casual day, eating sticky Jordanian sweets from the bakery and mooching about town – both of which took less than ten minutes. Mum found a grateful recipient for the second day of her Petra ticket, a German girl who had just arrived at the hostel. Then we devoted the afternoon to repacking our bags in preparation for the next leg of this adventure; a trip into the desert, a 4x4 experience, an overnight stay in a (doubtless authentic) Bedouin camp, and to cap it all off – a camel ride!

Mum was to be seen eyeing my crotch, which is unusual even in my family.

"I'll be fine," I told her, "there's nothing a camel will do to me that I don't do to myself."

Honestly, I think it sounded better in my head.

The four-wheel-drive experience was fantastic fun, in a devil-may-care kind of way.

We'd been warned in advance that all Bedouin vehicles were in poor repair, and none would be considered safe enough to drive on the roads. The one we got into rattled along in fine form, though the driver was always careful to park it on a downwards-facing slope. The reason for this was obvious enough – it couldn't start by itself, didn't even have an ignition, in fact – and so every time we set off again, after playing in the dunes or climbing odd rock formations, we were treated to a frantic Bedouin-style bump-start. On the one occasion this method failed, we were treated to a Tony-style push-start, which, it must be said, would have been considerably easier on tarmac. I fell flat on my face in the sand as the Jeep roared into life, but it hardly mattered; I'd spent half the morning rolling down sand dunes anyway, so it wasn't like I was trying to keep my hair clean.

Our dinner that night was outstanding – cooked at our authentic Bedouin camp by a Bedouin man in a Bedouin-style hole in the ground.

(In case you're wondering, yes, I *am* trying to get you to say the word 'Bedouin' so often that it starts to sound strange and loses all meaning. Email me and let me know if I succeeded.)

We'd seen plenty of genuine Bedouin encampments as we crisscrossed the country by taxi; each consisted of a single long, white tent, the pitched roof covered with old tires to weigh the canvas down. Everyone slept in this communal tent, as well as eating and drinking in it, whereas our tent was surrounded by rows of miniature square tents, like little sentry boxes, each with a selection of mattresses on the floor. It was far more comfortable to sleep that way, but was obviously designed for tourists, and was more reminiscent of a Roman encampment than a Bedouin one. Still, our meals were taken in the central tent, all prepared by our host Walid, who was a permanent resident. He was obviously a bit lonely, and spent most of the evening trying to entertain his guests – a German couple, two Czech ladies, and us. He started by trying to convince us to dance with him – I gave it a go, and spent an awkward few minutes slow-dancing with the over-enthusiastic Arab to what appeared to be Jordanian hip-hop. I've no idea what traditional Bedouin dance is like, but Walid's moves seemed to involve holding me a little too closely for comfort. After the hilarity of that spectacle, none of the other tourists were keen to give it a go.

I can't imagine why.

Next Walid deployed his instruments – by which I mean, he got out some bongo drums and maracas and tried to turn us into a percussion group. After a half-hearted attempt, we excused ourselves to go and look at the night sky. The moon had risen, bathing the desert in light. It washed out most of the stars, which was a shame, but the amount of light it gave off was incredible. We went for a walk without any fear of getting lost, but Walid insisted on accompanying us, trying to make polite conversation in broken English. That was becoming a chore, so we fled the scene again – despite it only being 9pm – and went to bed in our box tent, leaving the door open to the pleasantly cool night air.

After breakfast we were bounced off to the nearest village in the back of a pick-up truck. The village was a permanent settlement for Bedouin who had got sick of the nomadic lifestyle; built (poorly) from concrete blocks and corrugated iron, the whole place resembled a disused farmyard. Here we stored our bags in a shack while we awaited the arrival of our steeds. When they came, they matched the village perfectly; ragged, flea-bitten, with great bald patches on their fur and flies circling them in clouds. It looked doubtful whether they would last the day. Their master was a middle-aged Bedouin man wrapped head to toe in his traditional white robe – complete with the tea-towel wrapped around his head. I'm sorry, I know that isn't politically correct, but I can't help it – we have exactly the same tea-towel in our kitchen drawer at home.

Mounting the camels was surprisingly easy, as with a few harsh words and some mild physical abuse, the guide got them to lie flat on their bellies. Mum's ridiculously short gnomic legs still couldn't reach the saddle, but with a bit of help she was up – shrieking when the camel rose from its knees, tipping her so far forward she nearly belly-flopped onto its face.

And then, we were off! Our trusty guide strolled casually along in front of us, leading Mum's camel, with mine and Roo's tied on in single-file. That pretty much governed our pace, so there wasn't going to be any galloping on this excursion. We started off on a sandy track into the desert, with the striated splendour of the gorge walls rolling sedately past to either side. The swaying motion of my camel was easy enough to get used to, but the saddle – which was wooden, with a woolly blanket thrown over it – was not. It was Roo who discovered the only comfortable position; sitting with our legs up, thighs hugging the beast's back, ankles dangling around its shoulders. As adventures go, it was rather anticlimactic; the guide led us straight along the same track, then after half an hour he turned around and led us back. He managed to spend roughly 80% of the time on his mobile phone, laughing and cursing in equal measure, which did little to enhance the mystery of the experience. We took plenty of photos of the surrounding rock formations, and even a few of each other.

"Careful! Use the wrist-strap!" Roo warned, as she reluctantly handed me the camera. Well-trained by this point, I put the cord around my wrist before pointing the camera back at her.

"I thought the whole point of buying an indestructible camera was that I'd be allowed to use it," I complained.

"You can use it, just be careful! It's only meant to survive a fall of two metres, and we're quite high up."

"But it's sand underneath us. Not concrete."

"Yes, but if you drop it now, we can't get off to pick it up! How long will it take to persuade this guy to stop the camels? We'll never find it."

"Point taken."

"Shall I take it back then?"

I sighed. "Yes, I suppose so."

I leant out of the saddle and passed back the camera, nearly being pulled off my camel when she took it because I'd forgotten to undo the wrist-strap.

A few minutes later, I was gazing off into the distance when Roo's camel decided to take a big bite out of mine.

"Shit!" Roo said, as her camel moaned, "I think my one wants to shag your one!"

"How romantic!"

Roo's camel, clearly not impressed with that observation, then turned its attention to her. She deflected a few snaps, then the camel lunged.

I was looking the other way – chuckling at her predicament, to be honest – when I heard her shout: "Fuck *off!*" And there was a *crack!*

"Did you just punch that camel in the face?" I asked her.

"Yeah."

"Oh."

"The little shit keeps trying to bite me."

"Fair enough. Sounded like a hell of a clout!"

"Yeah, I hit him with this," she held up the indestructible camera. "It was in my hand. And look! Not a scratch. £300 well spent, eh!"

Our transfer driver was waiting in the Bedouin village by the time we got back, and he set off for the port city of Aqaba at top speed. He was a very different kind of driver to the ones we'd had before –

uninterested in us, with no desire to communicate as he put the pedal to the metal. Within minutes of setting off he was cranking the tunes – and the three of us, squashed in the back, had to bite our tongues to keep from laughing out loud. He was playing a song which, to him, must have sounded full-on gangsta, but he obviously didn't have a clue what the lyrics were saying. I later discovered it was a 'tune' by Eminem. The style was fast and rappy, but the words slightly undermined the image he was trying to present:

"The way you shake it… I can't believe it… I ain't never seen an… Ass Like That!

The way you move it, you make my pee-pee go: De Doing Doing Doing!"

The driver mumbled along to the chorus, glaring at the road and nodding his head with attitude. Then he skipped the CD back to the start and played it again. And again. And again.

For two hours.

My best guess is, he was trying to learn English that way – in which case, someone, someday, is going to be on the receiving end of a truly strange conversation from him.

Thankfully, the next two hours were spent listening to his other CD – a peculiar medley of song-snippets, where half a verse of Brian Adams' *Everything I Do (I Do It For You)* would play, fading out randomly to be replaced by thirty seconds of *My Heart Will Go On* from *Titanic*. There was only about five songs in total, but they'd been chopped up like confetti and mixed around in bowl to produce this CD. It was a truly surreal accompaniment to the timeless expanse of mountains as we passed back through *Wadi Rum*.

Exodus

For the last two nights of our holiday, Mum had treated us to a posh hotel in the seaside resort of Aqaba. It had a pool, it had a gym – it even had an open-air terrace on the first floor, festooned with cushions, where Shisha pipes could be smoked. As always I was keen to try a new experience, and ordered one filled with apple-flavoured tobacco. Mum was horrified, but I rather enjoyed it for the first ten minutes or so. That was when I realised I was only halfway through, as most people tend to smoke shisha in groups, sharing a single pipe. By the time my smoke ran out I felt thoroughly sick, and I wasn't getting any sympathy from Mum. I felt like I'd been caught stealing cigarettes, and had been forced to smoke a whole pack as punishment – something which my parents never had to do to me, I hasten to add, but which I'd been clever enough to inflict on myself aged 33.

I believe the technical term for this is 'fail'.

I quickly redeemed myself, however, by discovering an unsecured wireless network that could be accessed by sitting in the corner of the terrace. It probably came from the hotel next door, but it was fast and reliable enough for us to spend the rest of the evening online, thus avoiding the astronomical charge our hotel made for internet access.

I'm going to call that one a 'win'.

We then had the rare privilege of going to bed knowing that we could lie in for as long as we wanted in the morning – no bags to pack, no taxis to scramble into, no frisky camels to fend off – just the bliss of a clean bed in a pleasant hotel room, and a day where the most strenuous thing we had planned was a spot of sunbathing.

Ahhh!

One major benefit of splurging on a decent hotel was that they were used to catering for Westerners – the breakfast, consequently, was all we could have dreamed of. I must have spent an hour in there, going back for second, third and fourth helpings – cereal, toast, fresh fruit, croissants, cake (Roo was most excited by this one)... even eggs, cooked individually to our liking right there on the buffet table.

We'd found paradise at last, at least as far as I was concerned.

And then, by way of exploring Aqaba, we went shopping.

I know! The irony is not lost on me. But there's a huge difference between wanting to shop, and being forced. Although a short while later I was heard to say (whilst searching desperately for a toilet), that the next time someone asked me to go into their shop, I'd go in there and piss all over the floor, since they all claimed to have exactly what I was looking for.

We bought some antiques; it was borderline impossible not to, and Mum's bartering skills were a wonder to behold.

"How much you wanna pay?" she was asked.

"Oh, I haven't got enough money."

"No, really, how much you wanna pay?"

"Really, I haven't got any money at all."

She carried on like this for a good ten minutes, with the guy getting more and more frustrated. Finally, having started out demanding 20 *dinars*, he dropped his price one last time – to 1 *dinar*.

"Oh well, I think I can afford that," Mum relented, fishing a note out of her purse. "Here – have you got change for a fifty?"

Later that evening Roo and I went out for a stroll, hoping to investigate the maze of streets without being hassled. Although most of the sellers had cleared their wares from the footpath, there were still a few die-hards left in the alleyways, burning the midnight oil in hope of a sale.

We were wandering along the seafront, my arm decorously around her waist, when a group of lads on the other side of the road noticed us. Cat-calls and shouts in English and Arabic sailed across the street, followed by the lads themselves once there was a gap in the traffic. There was at least half a dozen of them; ages were difficult to guess, though I'd say most of them were between sixteen and eighteen. Their taunts, at least the ones we understood, were fairly inoffensive, probably due to a limited English vocabulary. Lots of "Sexy lady!" and "Hey, English!" floated along behind us. Already used to being shouted at, we ignored them and carried on walking.

Then a stone was thrown, bouncing off the back of Roo's head. She cried out, more in surprise than in pain – but that was enough. I spun around to face the gang and stomped towards them with balled fists, spitting out threats and curses. My rage took me right into the middle of the group, and almost before they'd had time to react I was at point-bank range, eyeballing them one at a time and demanding to know who had thrown the stone.

And that was where the rebellious youths of our two countries differed. If I'd tried this in England, I'd probably have woken up in hospital. But these lads were instantly terrified, begging my forgiveness and pushing the young perpetrator to the back of the group. As I advanced, still cursing, they backed away, raining apologies and the blessings of Allah upon me. Then they turned and ran, leaving me glaring and fuming at fresh air. I got the impression they wouldn't be going tourist-baiting for quite some time.

Even so, we cut short our walk, heading straight back to the hotel.

We really had no idea what kind of people prowled the streets of night-time Aquaba; we'd either been lucky or unlucky so far and without knowing which, it made sense not to push it.

I've found that controlled aggression can be quite handy in sorting out these kinds of situations. Nine times out of ten, harassing locals have no desire to fight and will retreat rather than face me if I look set to explode. I guess they're fed a steady diet of Vin Diesel and Bruce Willis movies, so they readily associate westerners with violence. It's bound to backfire sooner or later though, and I'd rather Roo wasn't with me when it does.

The next morning, after another delicious buffet breakfast, we waited for the bus that would take us back to the capital, Amman. Following that we'd be heading back to the airport for our flight back to England.

"It'll be nice to get home and see your Dad," Mum said, "but I'm sad to be leaving Jordan. It's so mysterious, so full of wonders."

"Yeah," I agreed, "but I am looking forward to going a whole day without someone demanding I look in their shop."

Roo was almost as excited to be leaving as she had been when we got here. "I can't wait to see my hamsters again," she explained.

Amazingly, we scored the best seats on the whole bus – right at the front, on the top deck. With nothing restricting our views of the surrounding countryside, we settled in for a real treat of a journey.

It was not to be. The bus driver had other priorities, and wasn't in the mood to provide a relaxed and serene passage. Instead we were treated to four hours of Arabic electronic pop music, played at deafening volume for the entire length of the country. It's true what they say: in a sealed tourist bus, no-one can hear you scream... And if they did, they'd probably think it was part of the music.

Now, I often get asked for advice about traveling to the various countries I've visited, so I've dug around in my brain to come up with a couple of tips for anyone planning a trip to Jordan.

Do Take: One of those sunglasses-on-a-cord type thingumies. Going from dark castle dungeon to sunlit courtyard and back several dozen times in one day necessitates repeated donning and removal of eye-protection. At one or more points in such a day you WILL a) drop them directly in front of a giant tourist with size 14 feet and have them stood on; b) return them to a 'more convenient' pocket, only to realize far too late that said pocket is crushed against the rough rock face when climbing a gorge wall, and; c) put your replacement pair somewhere so safe that you'll assume you've lost them and go buy some more. (If you're my mum, you will also drop them down the toilet. But that's another story).

I now own four pairs of sunglasses: two crushed, one miraculously rediscovered and one shitty, overpriced pair that I needn't have bought at all.

Don't take: That awesome pair of special trekking trousers you got (in the sales) just for this holiday. Partially because they scream 'tourist'; partially because you'll wear them last, or not at all. But mostly because for no advertised reason, they will chafe you in parts you didn't think could be chafed. Then you will hike in them, and sweat, and unsightly patches will appear in locations you didn't realize you could sweat from. Then you will try and ride a camel in them. The wet patches and the sweat will combine with the rhythmic swaying motion of your arse on the saddle to speed up and magnify the chafing process dramatically. By the time you get off even the *thought* of standing with your legs together will make you wince.

Do Take: Super grippy shoes! Great for hopping from rock to rock, even better for climbing. They bestow the ability to look cool and impress people by swiftly shinning up large boulders whilst everyone else is still cursing the lack of good hand-holds. I do love my Merrells. Technically they are 'water shoes', and are mostly made of mesh for quick drying. This means they fill with sand in one step and refuse to ever let it all go. Thus, every time I entered the marble-tiled foyer of a posh hotel I left a small trail of sand in my wake. Which leads me on to my next point: Do take a spare pair of shoes. They're great for when your best shoes are inexplicably still full of sand. But don't put the first pair away in your backpack (I learnt this one the hard way). They are, after all, still full of sand. No matter how hard you shake them first, for the rest of the week you will rediscover the desert every time you put on a clean pair of underwear.

Mum was right; I *was* sad to leave Jordan. It's an incredible place, with history literally lying around on the floor for you to pick up, take home and give as presents to horrified (yet secretly pleased) archaeologists you may know.

Above all the amazing sights and sounds, the interesting smells and the tastes that left me bolting for the toilet, the two things I remember most are 1) how amazing the ancient sites would have been if they weren't crammed with assholes trying to sell me shit, and 2) the millions of assholes trying to sell me shit. Oh, and 3) all the unnecessary shit I bought.

Seriously though, it's a beautiful and fascinating country, and the ancient sites simply cannot be beaten. I could have spent a week in Jerash alone, and I know that Mum is already dreaming of a return visit for exactly this reason. I have my fingers crossed that I'll be invited – after all she's bound to need some company.

It's no place for a gnome.

But there was one other crucial detail, almost overlooked in the madness and excitement of that holiday – one that was to have significantly longer-lasting repercussions.

When Roo left the UK, she'd been on a tourist visa, and close to the end of it too.

Now she was returning triumphantly, the holder of a shiny new Working Holiday Visa. The rules surrounding it were far less strict, allowing her to stay in the country for up to two years, allowing her to work during that time if she felt the urge – but pivotally, there was one other difference to her previous visa; on this one she was allowed to get married.

It had been quite a feat to attain it, of course. There was paperwork to be submitted, ID documents to be certified, interviews to be undertaken, *et cetera*. The rules also stated that she couldn't apply for this visa from inside the UK, and that once outside the UK, she could only apply for it in her home country.

Major bummer, eh?

Sometimes I wonder how people manage without having an identical twin sister living in Australia.

Paperwork

We arrived back in the UK, legal at last; finally we would be able to get married without the pesky intervention of the government. But there were still a few legal hoops we had to jump through. Most notably, we had to give our 'banns'. This is a weird English custom dating back to the twelfth century, where couples have to give official notice of their intention to marry several weeks in advance – presumably giving time for anyone to come forward if they know the bride and groom are secretly related. It's usually a formality, handled (for a small fee) by the church or registry office where the wedding is taking place. Only England and Wales had this requirement, which is why Gretna Green, the first village over the border in Scotland, became such a popular wedding destination for couples whose parents didn't approve of their match. Or for couples who were brother and sister.

With time sprinting ever more rapidly onwards, I took it upon myself to deal with these bits of bureaucratic bollocks. And that's where I hit a snag.

Had we come from the same town (or church parish), it would have been as simple as rocking up at the registry office, showing our IDs, and filling out a couple of forms. But when we got there, Roo's Australian passport gave the staff some sort of allergic reaction. We were told that we needed to give our notice at a 'designated office' – the nearest of which was fifty miles away in Exeter – and that only there could they tell us the correct procedure.

I couldn't fathom what kind of 'correct procedure' could be required, beyond making an appointment, but I gave them a call to find out.

It wasn't the happiest phone call I made that day.

"You want the bad news?" I asked Roo.

"Can I have the good news first?"

"Okay then... erm... I love you."

"Oh-oh."

"The bad news is, we can't get married until we give notice. And they won't let us give notice until we've got a thing called a Certificate of Approval."

"Oh! Right. So how do we get that then?"

"It can only be issued by the Home Office. We have to write to the Home Secretary and ask for his permission."

"Oh. Can't we just go and see him?"

"Well... I think he's a fairly busy bloke."

We consoled ourselves with a visit to the giant Hobbycraft store in Bristol.

Deciding to make our own invitations was a no-brainer. I'm a big fan of the personal touch, and I knew our guests would appreciate the value of something homemade over expensive customized stationary. With no definite plan for what we wanted, we did our usual trick – looked at everything and bought nothing. Then, to make ourselves feel better about wasting four hours wandering around a craft shop with only four sheets of paper in a bag to show for it, we nipped next door to TK Maxx and bought some shoes. Well, that made Roo feel better anyway. New shoes seem like a miracle cure for anything that's ailing a woman. I just consoled myself with the fact that I'd spent all morning in a shop the size of a national stadium and still only spent £20.

That afternoon we began a process of creation that would take days.

I artfully ripped up the sheets of parchment-paper, onto which we printed the text of our invites in a medieval-looking font.

We spent another morning cutting out small letter D's (for 'Dear...'), a task which is impossible to accomplish without a vast quantity of puns. There's a chance that most of this was my fault; I am known for having a D-based sense of humour.

"D-sist!" Roo demanded, after a particularly bad joke.

"Oh dear," I said, when we'd finished, "we've got all D's bits left over..."

A tube of gold powder, which was our only other purchase besides paper and shoes, proved to be worth it's weight in... well, in gold. For the price we paid I think it actually was gold. But it adhered well to the glue we applied with the rubber stamp, giving us sparkly raised knot-work in the corners of our invites. Less joyful was the way it also adhered to everything else – the table, the carpet, our fingers, and anything we happened to touch while it was still on our fingers.

As a result, golden glitter worked it's way into the most private crevices on my body. Places where the sun never shines were now self-illuminating via the magic of sparkly powder. Roo was finding the stuff in our bed for weeks.

"Are you sure you're not having an affair with a unicorn?" she asked.

My paperwork didn't end with the invites, however. I was expanding the net with my book submissions, sending out sample chapters to more niche publishers. For a while it looked like I'd have a chance with Summersdale, a publisher specialising in travel books. Unfortunately, the things that other publishers had liked about my book made it a poor fit for the rather poetic and highbrow world of travel literature. "Ecuador isn't a popular destination for budget travel," I was told, by way of explaining their rejection. But that was obviously just an excuse.

What they really wanted to say, but were too polite to, is "This book is coarse, crass and full of swearing. For starters you write far too much about your willy."

All of which is true, in case you haven't noticed.

Based on this complete lack of interest from the publishing industry, I very nearly decided to abandon my efforts. I'd never dreamed of being a writer after all, I just had some crazy-assed experiences that I wanted to share with the world. For some reason I felt sure that people would want to read about my exploits in Ecuador, but apparently I was in the minority.

And then I discovered self-publishing. I spent two days at a conference in York, and came back with a new fire lit beneath me. There were people out there that were making money by publishing their books online with Amazon. It was fast, it had potential, and literally anyone could do it. After a conversation in a bar with a drunken Irishman, I had decided to take my book down the DIY route. I doubted it would lead to fame and fortune, but at least it would get the damn thing out of my hands. And then I could stop mucking about with books and get back to that other thing I had going on.

You know, that whole wedding malarkey.

Jeez, those things take a lot of work.

My next wedding-based purchase was a pair of rings from the 'Tree of Life' collection by Clogeau, the Welsh company who supplied the gold for Kate and Will's royal wedding. Roo had seen the rings, and fallen in love with them, before we'd even started planning the wedding. Now we bought them – not from the tiny jewellers where we'd been visiting them every week, but online, direct from Clogeau. I hated myself for doing this, contributing to the demise of the traditional High Street, but we saved almost 50% on the price. The rings arrived in beautifully finished wooden boxes; sessile oak leaves in gold and white gold for Roo, and silver with gold vine accents for me (because let's face it, it'd be broken or lost within a year).

I very publicly bragged about booking a harpist, which made Gill shit bricks as she realised she hadn't booked any musicians yet. She was still working in France at the time, which I felt was cutting it rather fine; she was getting married in less than six weeks.

Then I very quietly booked a limo to take Roo and her sisters to the wedding, choosing to keep it as a last-minute surprise for her. The money wasn't really in the budget, but I'd been driving some hard bargains recently, and I had a feeling we were a little bit ahead. Plus, there are some things that are just more important than money; Roo's happiness, especially on her wedding day, was one on those things. She'd been sacrificing as hard as anyone, buying bargain items whenever she could. Her latest acquisition was a pair of diamante-encrusted, transparent plastic flip-flops (or thongs, as those crazy Aussies call 'em). She planned on wearing them to the wedding, regardless of the fact they'd only cost £10. "No-one will see my feet when my dress has a two-metre train," she pointed out, "and I love them – they're just so *sparkly!*"

I was also kind of grateful she hadn't decided to wear high heels – not because we were getting married on grass, but because they'd have made her taller than me.

Our next shopping trip found us in an 'alternative fashion' shop. Roo has always been kind of alternative, and she can't walk past one of these places without going in for a look. But it was me that found something this time, spying a pair of black trousers that had an embroidered, almost medieval look.

I tried them on, but they were extremely tight, in a way that is popular with punks and emos.

"I can't wear these," I said to Roo, as she hovered outside the changing cubicle, "they're borderline indecent."

"Oh, let me have a look," she said. So I swished aside the curtain of concealment.

"Oh, Tony! They're *amazing!* You have to get those!"

"Ah..."

"No. It's decided. You're getting them."

And she marched over to the cash register and paid for the trousers while I was still struggling to liberate my arse from them.

"But they're so tight," I complained, as she ushered me out of the Blue Banana.

"They're perfect," she replied, "and anyway, men in medieval times wore tights. You've seen Robin Hood, haven't you?"

"Yeah, but I'm not sure that's what I want to style my wedding outfit around. There'll be people there, you know, relatives and stuff. They don't want to see me in tights. No-one wants to see me in tights."

"I think you'd look great in tights," she said.

"Yes, well you're bias. And these things are ridiculous."

"Try them on at home, with your shirt and boots, before you decide."

"What, when I've bought my shirt and boots you mean?"

"Exactly."

Of course, my boots arrived a week before the wedding. I'd spent weeks browsing eBay for them; Roo knew what a picky bugger I could be, and I'm sure she was counting on it. The third and final incarnation of my shirt was sewn for me by Mum, a task which she completed one day before we got married. So by the time I got to see my entire outfit all assembled, it was far too late to change any of it.

I regretted buying those trousers from the moment I tried them on at home, until the moment I took them off after the wedding, and I've never dared to wear them since. Roo wonders why, as she loved them; I had to point out to her that not everyone enjoys seeing my package highlighted so dramatically.

She said she couldn't quite put her finger on the problem. I responded that, if she had, it would have completely changed the tone of the wedding.

We might even have been arrested for public indecency.

Which is also fun...

Always A Bridesmaid...

A month after our triumphant return from Jordan, Gill arrived back from France with her husband-to-be – a tiny little blonde bloke called Chris. Theirs had been the ultimate whirlwind romance; they'd got engaged only a few weeks into their relationship, whilst sharing a hot-tub in sub-zero temperatures on the side of a mountain in New Zealand. Some drink had been involved, I have to say; it had been my leaving party, after all. But they'd stuck to the promises made that night, and had been together ever since, working ski-season after ski-season, following winter around the world.

They were both rather pale.

Chris had been a dream find for Gill; always into short blokes, she'd finally found one who was short, athletic, handsome (although don't tell him I said that) and an excellent skier. Actually, don't tell him I said that, either. Gill was head-over-heels in love, and when Roo and I had decided to tie the knot this summer in England, it made perfect sense for Gill and Chris to do the same.

Only, they were getting married before us, because neither of them wanted to wait that long.

Kids, eh?

Well, they looked like kids.

Especially when they were standing next to Roo and me.

Gill's wedding, despite being organised entirely by remote control from France, was remarkably successful. Chris had actually had a life *before* deciding to be a ski-bum – during which, he'd been a geneticist. Consequently his bank balance was more than sufficient to fill the gaps in hers, and they'd managed to find a perfect wedding venue in a cliff-top castle on the south coast.

It was a gorgeous place, a two-hundred year old stone fortress surrounded by beautifully manicured gardens leading down to a private beach.

It was also one hundred and twenty miles, and nearly three

hours' drive away.

Packing the car for the trip was fairly stressful, as we were well aware that if we forgot anything vital, we wouldn't be coming back for it.

Granddad would be traveling with us, much to his mock horror.

When I told him Roo would be behind the wheel, as I'd still not passed my test and so wasn't allowed to drive on the motorway, he rolled his eyes and said, "Oh no, that's all we need – women drivers!"

The journey passed reasonably quickly, though I didn't envy the relatives coming down from Manchester. We unpacked the car and the camper van, which my parents had brought on account of it being stuffed to the gills with wedding paraphernalia. Preparing the old fort for the arrival of a hundred-odd guests was the next priority, and took most of the evening. Roo and I had a nice little chamber on the lowest level of the fort, right at the tip where the front and back walls came together. That night we snuggled up together, and talked long into the night about Gill's wedding, how it was going to go, and everything we still had to do for ours.

It was quite a list.

The wedding day dawned beautifully clear and sunny. This was ideal as Gill's plan, like ours, involved an outdoor ceremony. Staff from the castle were on hand to move dozens of wooden chairs down from the fort to the gardens, while Roo and I started to get organised for the day.

Our biggest task reared its head with the arrival of the first guests. They'd had a long drive, and they were hungry – only, there wasn't any food for them. The main meal was part of the reception in the evening, and a local catering firm had been hired to provide a full-on medieval banquet. Until then, however, nothing was planned... and as more and more guests piled up in the castle, we realised something had to be done about it. A quick trip to town sorted most of it, and a further trip to town sorted more. The next couple of trips to town, for niggling items we'd never even thought we would need, like tin foil, lemons and vegetarian cheese, were a bit more frustrating. There was only one shop in 'town', and it took us twenty minutes to get there; we could be reasonably sure that by the time we got back, someone would have discovered something else we needed. In between trips we greeted guests, served food, poured drinks, led tours of the fort, cleaned up and washed dishes, cooked soup and pizzas and pastries, made sandwiches and platters of cheese, bought matches and tobacco and favourite tipples for guests that hadn't brought their own. In between this, we did what we could to help prepare for the wedding ceremony itself. Roo had hair and make-up appointments, leaving me to run the kitchens and organise the arriving caterers, musicians, celebrant and guests.

Granddad needed help getting dressed, and most of my family converged at the same time to lend a hand. At first he didn't understand why he was being asked to change his shirt. "What's wrong with what I'm wearing?" he asked.

"We're just getting you into your posh clothes, Gramp."

"Oh, alright. Why is that?"

"For the wedding, Gramp."

"Oh! Who's getting married?"

We looked at each other and burst out laughing.

I went outside to help with the final preparations, only to find that the wedding party was ready, but there were no guests. So it was back up to the fort to explain to everyone in it that they were in danger of missing the wedding they'd driven all this way for. Slowly they trickled down into the garden, until finally they were all milling around in the right general area. I wheeled Gramp down in his chair, and had to leave him, rather confused, in the midst of all those people; it had just occurred to me that I'd better get changed into my own wedding outfit. I'd barely had time to pee, let alone get myself ready, and I didn't want to be the only person there in jeans and a t-shirt.

I was the last man in place, and the music began before my bum even touched my seat. Suddenly there was Gill, looking like she'd stepped from the pages of a bridal magazine. Her hair, piled artfully, cascaded down her back in curls and ringlets. I felt a lump in my throat. I hadn't seen Gill in a dress since… well, ever. I think part of me secretly believed she'd end up getting married in scuffed trainers and a baggy jumper. I'd never really noticed before, but my baby sister was *beautiful*. Stunning, even.

Unless she's reading this. In which case, Hey Gill! You looked alright.

Chris stood at the altar in a blue shirt, looking smarter than I'd ever seen him. He didn't look old enough to be getting married; between the small heels on her shoes, and her tiara, there was a good chance Gill would be taller than him.

Roo walked down the aisle behind Gill, her elaborate hair-do gleaming platinum-blonde in the sunlight. She didn't look bad, either.

As she passed where I was standing Roo shot me an alarmed glance, to which I could do nothing but shrug. Whatever was going on, it was beyond my power to understand, let alone do anything about. "It's my dress," she explained, once we were free to talk. "You didn't lace it up tight enough at the back! I could feel it slipping down with every step. I though I was going to arrive at the altar with it round my ankles!"

Luckily, this did not happen. The ceremony itself was brief, eloquent, and I don't remember much about it because I spent the whole time trying to stop my eyes leaking. I didn't succeed, but I wasn't the only one. Must have been something in the air.

A round of champagne came next, followed by photographs taken in strategic locations around the castle grounds. Roo and I barely had time to feature, as we were suddenly busy again; the ceremony itself had been like the eye of the storm, and beyond it the whirlwind raged anew. Guests needed direction, drinks needed serving, toilets needed pointing out, caterers needed informing, tables needed moving, crockery needed discovering, and Granddad needed convincing not to try finding his own way home. "Where are we again?" he asked me.

"We're in Cornwall, Gramp. At Gill's wedding! She's just got married."

"Oh!" he said. "I thought there was something going on."

But the chaos backstage was like the turbulent current beneath the surface of an otherwise placid lake; as far as the guests knew, everything was running smoothly, perfectly even, and we were at great pains to keep it looking that way.

The spit-roasted pig was a big hit. I'd toyed with the idea of incorporating one into my wedding, but the cost was prohibitive. It was great to experience it as a guest though, even if I was a bit too busy to eat more than a sandwich.

Dad had waited his entire life for what was about to come next, and he was on fine form. As he stood up to make his Father-of-the-Bride speech, he kept one hand in his pocket.

"I'd like to raise a toast," he began.

And then he pulled his hand out of his pocket, and slowly raised it.

He was holding a piece of toast.

The collective groan nearly shook the building.

Once the speeches were done we cleared the tables, moved them back out of the way, set up the music and got the disco rolling. For this part we got to do what we do best; dance like idiots, in the hope of encouraging other guests to start strutting their own funky stuff. We then spent a large portion of the evening in the kitchen, washing dishes, pouring drinks, serving up left-overs for anyone still hungry and directing guests to their rooms, the bathrooms, the roof and the beach.

It was great fun, as we were joined by several of the guests at different times, and tried to get a sneaky drink in here and there.

It was also utterly exhausting!

The day had been an emotional rollercoaster for a variety of reasons, but as it drew to a close Gill and Chris started saying their goodbyes. They'd opted for a more traditional end to their wedding, where the bride and groom leave to start their honeymoon while the guests carry on partying. It was a pity, as the average level of drunkenness in the huge dining room had finally crossed a certain threshold, and people were starting to dance and prance and generally make fools of themselves. Still, the newly-weds had their priorities straight; this was, after all, their wedding night.

So with much fussing, many hugs, kisses, cheers and a few tears, Gill eventually extricated herself and her new husband, and escaped to where a limo was waiting. Their destination: the honeymoon suite of a boutique hotel. Chris's mum had organised all this as part of her wedding present to the couple, so while we changed out of our posh clothes and began the clear up, Chris and Gill were whisked away for a night of luxury.

Gill later told me that the hotel was incredible. A private staircase led to a bedroom converted from the attic, the sloping eaves and great wooden beams creating a cosy and intimate feel. Champagne was waiting for them on ice, and the bed was littered with rose petals. She'd been overwhelmed with happiness and a little tipsy, and she'd spent the rest of the night enthusiastically celebrating the start of life as a married woman.

The next morning she'd dragged Chris out of bed and down to breakfast, as they had a honeymoon cruise booked and an airport to get to. She was surprised to see her mother-in-law already sitting at the breakfast table with her partner, both tucking into eggs and bacon.

"Oh!" said Gill. "Sorry, are we late? I didn't think you were coming to pick us up for another hour."

"No, in the end we decided this place was so nice that we decided to stay here as well." She offered Gill a conspiratorial smile. "We had the room below yours."

Gill opened her mouth to ask how she'd known that, and then stopped herself just in time.

It occurred to her that there are some conversations you don't want to get into with your mother-in-law; at least, not in the middle of the hotel dining room.

"So," she said instead, "I'm starving. What's for breakfast?"

Mere Formalities

With Gill and Chris's wedding over and the happy couple enjoying their honeymoon cruise, it was time for me to turn my attention back to my own wedding.

There were still a few niggling things to sort out – the kind of trivial items that always end up getting left until the last minute.

Finding someone to marry us, for example.

I don't know exactly what constitutes short notice in the wedding celebrant industry, but this was probably it: I had exactly one month until M-day.

If I couldn't find someone quick, I'd be asking Gill to get herself ordained in the Church of the Flying Spaghetti Monster so that she could marry us. I had no problem having my ceremony conducted by a Pastafarian, but it would be tough on Gill being both the best man *and* the minister...

I found InterfaithFoundation.net, a searchable database of exactly what I was looking for, and sent off a slew of emails. All the ministers I contacted got back to me straight away, all were polite, and all were available.

And all were way out of budget.

The median price for a homemade ceremony such as ours was apparently £300 – not including travel costs, preliminary meetings or rehearsals. I'd budgeted half that, figuring £150 for an hours' work was more than sufficient, but I hadn't taken into account how much effort these people would have to put in behind the scenes. All of them suggested we arrange a chat to discuss what we wanted from the ceremony, with a view to creating it from scratch. I'd already planned on doing that myself, and had spent days scouring the internet for Celtic prayers and Wiccan hand-fasting rituals. It hadn't occurred to me that whoever we chose to do the ceremony, they would also want to put their own stamp on it.

The I spotted an advert posted by a lady called Angela, who lived in Bristol. She did blessings and namings, but weddings weren't listed as part of her repertoire. *Might as well try*, I thought. So far we'd managed to save a lot of needless expense by looking for the non-wedding equivalent of things. Our outfits were a perfect example; Roo had recently added a stunning full-length white cloak to her ensemble, for less than £50. She'd bought it from a website that supplied costumes to role-players; if she'd gone shopping for such an item in a wedding shop she'd have been lucky to get change from £200.

And the magic worked again!

Angela got back to me straight away, and as soon as I read her email I knew she was the one. Her tone was polite and friendly, but excitable – just like us. She'd been considering the move into weddings, and felt it was fate that we'd asked. This would be her first, and the timing couldn't have been better. I hadn't even noticed, but the date on my email was 21st June – the summer solstice. She'd taken this as a sign, and offered to help us develop and write our ceremony as well as performing it, all within the budget I'd asked for.

We went to meet her a few days later.

Angela lived in a gorgeous Victorian town house in a leafy Bristol suburb. She was blonde, middle-aged, with a kind face that was used to smiling. She sat us down, made us fruit tea, and started to talk about what we wanted. I'd emailed her what I'd found so far, and over the course of the next few days we hammered out our perfect ceremony in a flood of emails. I wanted just enough Wiccan elements to lend a sense of ritual to the service, whilst still keeping the more traditional elements of a western wedding. I chose readings as a way to involve more people in the ceremony, and we finished with the hand-fasting, where our hands would be tied together briefly as a symbol of our union. This is the origin of the phrase 'tying the knot', and for the first time I felt a sudden confidence surge within me. We had almost all the elements in place, against all the odds.

This was actually going to happen!

I think this was the first time it hit me.

I'll admit, I cried a little.

With that taken care of, there was the small matter of our last legal hurdles to surmount. Our Certificate of Approval from the Home Office had been issued without any questions, almost as though they knew it was a waste of time and paper as much as we did. Oh, for a world without bureaucracy! The COA had arrived at a time when we were busy helping to organise Gill's wedding, so it had vanished into the growing 'To Do' pile. Now, at long last, we found the time to drive to Exeter, to do that whole 'Giving of Banns' malarkey that seemed at once utterly pointless, and bizarrely pivotal.

I'd phoned ahead for an appointment, and we were shown straight into the registrar's office.

I handed him the precious piece of paper bearing the Official Seal of Approval from the Home Office – noting as I did that I could have made a more convincing certificate on Photoshop in about five minutes.

"Ah yes, that all seems to be in order," he said.

"Great! So what do we do next?" I asked.

"First I have to ask you if you intend to give notice of your upcoming marriage."

"We do," said Roo and I together, sharing a smirk of triumph.

"And do either of you know of any reason why you can't be married?"

"We don't."

"Very well," said the registrar, "I hereby announce that— oh, wait a moment!"

He scrunched up his face and studied the document before him, bringing the piece of paper up close to his reading glasses. "I'm terribly sorry," he said at last, "but this certificate is no good."

"What?" I gasped.

"I'm afraid it expired. Last Thursday."

The drive home was not a happy one. Nor was the fruitless evening I spent once we got home, scouring the internet for guidance. I couldn't find anything; all mentions of the Certificate of Approval seemed to have been removed from the websites I'd been using. Eventually I discovered why; the CoA scheme was undergoing a transitional phase, and was soon to be replaced with a new set of rules designed to make the approval process more streamlined. And while we were waiting for that to happen…

There was nothing.

"I'll have to call them," I told Roo. "As soon as they open on Monday morning."

We spent a miserable weekend shopping half-heartedly for wedding favours, before coming to the conclusion that pretty much anything would blow our remaining budget when multiplied by eighty.

On Monday I was up early, navigating my way through the fearsome array of automated menus that surround the Home Office telephone system like the walls around the building. I swear they're designed to keep you out.

I was thin on patience by the time I managed to get a real live human being on the other end of the phone. I poured out my woes to her, and vented a bit of my frustration at how little information was available online.

"Yes, the Certificate of Approval has entered a transitional phase," she explained. I had a feeling she was reading it off the same web page I was looking at.

"But can you tell me what that means, please?"

"The old rule has been abolished, and the new law won't take effect until... well, until it's been invented."

"So what is the rule right now?"

"Right now there is no rule."

"So what does that mean for me?"

"I'm not sure about that. Hold the line, please..."

I spent two hours on the phone to the Home Office, talking to officials of escalating importance. Not one of them knew what was going on. And not one of them could give me a definite answer to the burning question: *are we allowed to get married?*

Call me a worry wart if you will, but I felt a powerful urge to get that detail ironed out. It would put a real crimp in our wedding plans if they suddenly became illegal.

On my second day of trying, I managed to get through to someone high enough up the ladder to have some kind of clue. After outlining our situation for what felt like the hundredth time, I finally felt like I might be getting somewhere. This lady was very precise and officious, but she seemed to have access to information other than the public website.

"Okay, I think I've found out what's replacing the COA scheme," she said.

"Great. What is it?"

"Nothing."

"Eh?"

"The COA is being replaced with nothing, meaning it will no longer be needed. They're removing that requirement completely."

"So I don't need a COA anymore?"

"Well, that depends on when the new rule comes into force. Technically at the moment you would still need the COA because it hasn't been replaced yet."

"Even though it's going to be replaced with nothing?"

"That's correct."

"So, my COA has expired. I need a new one. How can I get that?"

"Oh, I'm afraid they're not issuing them anymore. Because

they've been abolished."

"Okay, I get that. But what does that mean for me?"

"I'm not quite sure... please hold the line..."

Several days of confusion passed, filled with panicked phone calls and emails, before Roo and I found ourselves in Exeter once again.

"So," I said to the registrar, "as far as I can tell, we don't have to do anything special. We just have to announce our intentions as normal. Does that sound okay?"

"Yes, I can see how that might be the case."

"So, does that mean we can get married now?"

"I would say that's quite possible."

"And will it be, you know, legal?"

"Ah... I would think so."

"Riiiight."

We left his office not substantially more confident than when we'd entered it. We'd officially given our 'banns' to the good people of this Earth – specifically the bit surrounding Exeter. Why any of them would care was beyond me. Perhaps a few centuries ago these announcements were carefully studied by anyone who could read them, on the off-chance that someone they knew was marrying their own cousin unawares. Still, as a third-generation only-son marrying a girl from Australia, it didn't seem terribly likely that we were related. And if we were, I sincerely doubt anyone in Exeter would have known about it.

A Beginning And An End

Two other things happened between Gill's wedding and mine; I finally released my first book, 'That Bear Ate My Pants!' – and I lost my beloved Uncle Paul to Motor Neurone Disease.

Paul been fighting the illness for a couple of years, but he had a rare version that started inside and worked its way out. Amongst the first things to go had been his ability to talk, leaving him communicating with grunts and gestures, and eventually special software on an iPad. His slide downhill had been rapid and tragic, all the more so because he'd been such a competent, active man. Paul had survived the trip down to my sister's wedding, but he took ill just before the ceremony and was rushed to hospital in Cornwall. We'd carried on regardless, as he would most assuredly have wanted us to, and Gill's wedding had been a triumph marred only by his absence.

After a few days in hospital, Paul had been transferred by ambulance back to Manchester, and eventually they allowed his family to take him home.

There was nothing more they could do for him at this point, and it was better for him to spend his last weeks surrounded by his family rather than stuck in a hospital bed.

Meanwhile, I'd been planning a truly epic day of promotion for the launch of *That Bear*. Creating the eBook had been relatively easy, but both the blessing and curse of self publishing is that you have to do everything yourself. I'd hardly slept in a week, sitting up till 6am planning strategy and creating lists of people, online forums and websites to target. I didn't mind doing it all myself because I'm a control freak and perfectionist of the highest order. Unfortunately I'm also crap at most things, which leads to a rather ridiculous situation where I do something quite badly, over and over again, desperate to improve it yet not actually getting any better.

By way of an example, see my books.

But my family would never let me do something like this without their support.

Roo was determined to help, and she came up with an idea to rent a bear costume and run around the town centre, handing out flyers. She took a break from organising our wedding – now in less than three weeks – to phone around every fancy dress shop in the west country, looking for an adult-sized bear suit. Gill returned from her honeymoon just in time to suggest we incorporate a gigantic pair of underpants, with her inside, into our strategy! It sounded like an unbeatable combination. If you wouldn't take a flyer from a chick in a bear suit, how can you refuse one when it's handed to you by a giant pair of y-fronts?!

Gill spent an entire day carefully crafting her underpants from cardboard, and we were ready to go.

Then we got the call that no-one wants to get. Uncle Paul was starting to lose his battle. We'd all known it was coming, but the timing (for me) couldn't have been worse; it was fairly inconvenient for him too, as I'm sure he'd rather have lived past sixty-five. I threw a load of socks and t-shirts in a bag, grabbed my laptop and drove three-hundred miles to Manchester to hold his hand as he lay dying.

Launch day was a surreal experience. I'd stayed up all the previous night writing emails. At midnight and one minute, I fired out the first batch of messages, crossing my fingers that somewhere, someone out there actually gave a shit.

It's hard to say exactly what I was doing from then on. I sat down in front of the computer, started typing and BAM! 20 hours had disappeared. Time was just absorbed wholesale by the process of conducting a hundred micro conversations simultaneously over Facebook message, Group threads, Email, and Twitter.

And it was punctuated every couple of hours by a pause while I sat by my uncle's bedside, stroking his hand and watching the machines force air into his lungs. "I did it, I launched my book!" I told him. "I'm gonna be famous, uncle!" I got a brief glint of his eyes and his hand trembled for a moment as he fought past the weakness to give me a shaky thumbs-up.

Back at my temporary command centre, the messages had started to pile up. Some folks had bought my book and wanted to be sure I knew it. Some had read the beginning and wanted to tell me what they thought of it. Occasionally, someone I'd never heard of entered into a dialogue after seeing on Facebook or Twitter that I'd surpassed Bill

Bryson in the Kindle Travel charts.

It was true. Once people started coming home from work around 5:30pm, things had started to hot up. I'd sneaked a peak at my sales after watching my Amazon sales rank leap from 16,000 to 4,500 – only to discover that I'd sold 4 books. I took a walk out into the sunshine and told myself it didn't matter; then I looked in on my uncle, and told myself there were other things that did matter.

But suddenly, like a monsoon, messages pelted into my inbox from friends who had bought the book. Everyone seemed to want to tell me about it, which thrilled me, and I spent the next few hours writing back to them all, whilst continuing my Facebook campaigning and keeping a weather-eye on Twitter. Soon the messages were arriving faster than I could respond to them, as congratulations on my ranking (which I hadn't had time to check) started coming through. I'd broken into the top thousand! Impressive, considering half a day earlier I'd been off the board.

I could go on, but I won't. It was more of the same from here on; the thrill of rising rankings, the desperate fear of slipping back again, and mountains and mountains of words. I must have typed enough to fill my next three books, just keeping up with all the messages, comments and Tweet mentions. When the dust settled I was utterly exhausted. I'd made it as high as no.450 in the overall charts on Amazon.co.uk, and had hit no.7 on the Travel Books Bestseller list – two ahead of ole' Bill himself. It was a monumental success as far as I was concerned, although the numbers were less than astounding. To my knowledge, my efforts on Twitter (and the re-tweets and mentions by others) netted me exactly zero sales. I had a Facebook Event set up and personally invited 250 people. 66 joined, thereby committing to buy a copy on the day. And on the day I sold 53 copies in total. But you know, things could always have been worse. I had only to look in the front room for proof of that.

We came home a few days later. Paul was still hanging on, so Mum stayed there to be with him. The rest of us said our goodbyes, knowing that this time, it really was goodbye. Paul had only days left to live. The next time we saw him, it would be at his funeral. "You're the strongest man I've ever known," I whispered to him as I hugged him for the last time. His eyes flicked up, the only part of him he still had some control over, and he winked at me.

Two days later, Paul passed away, on July 5th, at 11pm.

We all miss him terribly.

But even though my heart wasn't really in it, I had to get on with other things.

Which for now meant selling my book.

Gill and Roo were still planning their promo stunt, and one unfortunate side-effect of the delay was that I would be available to help them. On launch day I'd hardly dared leave my computer to pee, and the girls had originally planned to do the bear-and-pants-show without me. Now, a week later, I had no excuse at all. And neither did Mum, so I roped her in too.

We stayed up all night printing flyers and reinforcing the gigantic pair of cardboard underpants – a fairly typical evening in my house. In truth, I spent a large part of the night screaming "BASTARD!" at the printer, which had chosen exactly that moment to start misbehaving. I spent an hour tinkering with it, and when I finished screwing the top back on I discovered a handful of plastic components that I swear had never been in there in the first place. After that, it wouldn't print at all. There was a strong possibility I'd left my other screwdriver in there somewhere.

"You'd make a terrible surgeon," Gill said.

Next I made a 'press release'. Then I looked up 'press release' and destroyed mine, as what I'd made didn't even remotely resemble a press release. Well, it had a button that you press to release, and that's all I'll say about that.

I emailed every radio station and newspaper for miles around, telling them to expect a 'promo team'. I may have oversold us slightly; I suspected they'd be a little disappointed if they showed up in the pouring rain to find Mum waggling her ass in a bear suit, while Gill handed out limp leaflets. The Red Bull Display Team we were not. But I needn't have worried; none of them turned up anyway.

So on a beautifully clear Somerset morning, we descended on the town of Taunton.

The poor buggers never knew what hit them!

Bear-Faced Cheek

Mum chose to wear the bear first.

At a gnomic five-foot nothing and a quarter, she looked less like a bear and more like an Ewok, but I was just happy I didn't have to be in there. Faced with the prospect of torrential rain, we were over the moon when the day dawned clear and sunny. No-one wants to hug a cold, wet bear. Sure as shit no-one wants to wear one. Gill had even more to lose; rain and cardboard are natural enemies, and she had no desire to spend an entire day wearing the world's biggest pair of soggy underpants.

My first victim was an older woman, slender with long grey hair. She was unlikely to buy my book, I thought, but an ideal test subject; my sales pitch had yet to be practiced. Hell, it had yet to be invented. I approached her and muttered something about having written an eBook.

She turned on me, eyes blazing with righteous fury. "I don't approve of THAT at all!" she declared.

Oh bugger.

She then proceeded to tell me in emphatic detail, how technology was the work of the devil. How our society is being destroyed by it, even as we speak. How we are sinking further and faster, and the only way to free ourselves is to wipe it all out forever!

"I've just paid this young man in cash," she indicated the green-grocer's stall behind her. "Credit cards ruin people's lives – credit cards and COMPUTERS! If I could, I would burn the lot of them."

There really wasn't much to say to that. I hadn't been cursed so thoroughly since... well, ever.

"Would you like a flyer?" I offered.

She glared at me as though I had stood on one of her doubtless many cats, and I retreated slowly.

The rest of the morning passed without incident. Not without interest though. Once the crazy woman made her departure, I offered a rather more subdued sales pitch to the green-grocer she'd so kindly paid with pure, innocent cash. He was more receptive.

"Sounds great," he enthused, and whipped out an iPad from under his stall. He concentrated for a few moments, tapping the evil device on various corners with a grubby finger. "There!"

He proudly showed me the display, featuring the front cover of 'That Bear Ate My Pants'. "Got it! I'll read it tonight."

I was stunned. For a techno-whoring minion of the antichrist, he was a jolly nice chap.

There was a bloke collecting for Guide Dogs for the Blind, sitting outside the car park on a stool with his bright blue plastic bucket. We'd all donated after parking, and had threatened to come back in costume. Now seemed like the perfect time for it. Gill handed him a flyer and he glanced down in surprise.

"We're advertising my new book, all about my crazy adventures in Ecuador!" I explained.

His brow wrinkled. "But I can't read. I'm blind."

"Oh. Um. Sorry!" It honestly hadn't occurred to me.

He was still clutching the flyer the next time we walked past.

Gill was wearing the pants. Her new husband, much amused, was trailing us and taking photos. Every so often she would stop and ask him to help her adjust the string shoulder straps. Every time she would mug an unhappy face at the nearest passer-by and tell them, "My pants are falling down!"

Roo was a great advocate, loudly proclaiming the merits of the book to everyone in earshot. "Buy it, it's hilarious!" she told a passing businessman.

"Fuck off," he replied.

After that she decided to take a turn in the bear.

We de-beared and de-pants'ed outside Debenhams, so we could swap jobs and take turns to use the loo. Roo suited up and immediately started dancing to the music in her head. Within minutes she had been offered a job by the café next-door; they needed a human statue for the upcoming flower festival. Apart from us getting married that week (and going to Uncle Paul's funeral in Manchester), we really didn't have much else on, so she took the job.

We moved to our local seaside town of Burnham-on-Sea for the afternoon shift, and the lifeguards were fascinated. When the Giant Underpants shoved their way into the hut there were gales of laughter on all sides.

"Hot pants," one of the lifeguards quipped, eyeing up my sister.

"People have been trying to get into her pants all day," I warned.

"Well, I'm the one in authority here," said the oldest bloke; "Quick – knick-her!"

I groaned all the way down the beach.

Roo had been swamped with children all day, and she was in her element, hugging them and posing for photos. I took full advantage of the distraction to chat to their parents about my book, and it was working a treat. Until, just as we were leaving the beach, I was accosted by a tiny blonde girl of about six. "*Excuse me*, what are you doing?"

I favoured her with a grin and launched into my spiel. "I'm telling everyone about my new book, 'That Bear Ate My Pants!' It's very funny, and there are bears in it doing very funny things!"

It wasn't my standard spiel, but I'd become a pretty good ad-libber. I handed her a flyer to seal the deal and strolled off.

A few steps later I turned to check on the bear, only to discover that the blonde girl was walking along behind me. "*Excuse me*," she said again, "can I have one of those for my friend? He wants one too."

"Here you go," I told her, handing her another flyer. She skipped away merrily.

"We'd better move on asap," I said to my team.

"Eh? Why?"

They followed me quickly back up the boat ramp and onto the crowded street at top speed. "Where are we going?" Gill asked when she caught up with me.

"Away!"

"Why?"

"Well, those flyers I gave to the little girl?"

"Yeah?"

"The tag-line on them reads, 'Jesus Christ! I'm about to be eaten by a bear!'"

"Oh...! Right. Yeah, we'd best get moving then..."

The flyers did their trick though. I was delighted to see some people had kept hold of them, and were brandishing them at me the same way you'd show a crucifix to a vampire. 'Keep away,' their eyes said, 'you've got me already...'

Of the teenagers we met, some were clearly too cool for school.

These types, terrified of anything that could endanger their street cred, fixed their ludicrously outsized sunglasses on the horizon and strode past as quickly as possible. But one group of lads showed an interest. They dared each other to hug the bear (something that kids as young as 18 months had been managing to do all day without being dared). "Is it a boy or a girl in there?" one lad asked.

"Girl," I replied.

Suddenly they all wanted a hug. One even tried a little dry-humping. His mate noticed and dragged him away with a stern warning. "Matt, bestiality is NOT the answer!"

Then Gill offered a flyer to a confused looking man. "But I am here on holiday," he said, in heavily accented English. "I don't know what to do?"

"Where are you from?" Gill asked.

"Cherr-many," Came the response.

Gill brightened, and gave the bloke a wide smile. "Welcome to England!"

This marks the first time in the history of our two great nations, that a citizen of one has been welcomed to the other by a gigantic pair of cardboard underpants. At least as far as I know.

As the day drew to a close, and our dancing bear had hugged her way into heat-stroke, Gill (still in the pants) tried to flyer a flyer-giver – only to find that the man was advertising The Path To Heaven. In fact he had a large placard with a flow chart, neatly depicting which sins pointed you towards Purgatory and Hell (and in which order), and which acts of redemption allowed you to ascend to the clouds. It looked very well researched.

But he didn't even offer us a flyer. I could tell from his expression that he had already decided our fate; there was no place in his heaven for people like us.

It had been a fun and fairly successful day, and I learned a few things which I thought I might share with you all:

1) NO-ONE can resist ANYTHING when it's handed to them by a walking pair of underpants.

2) Children love bears. Especially smiling ones. This worked well, but it did make a lot of people think I'd written a children's book. Perhaps I should consider writing a children's book. Or renting something scarier next time, like a werewolf.

3) Life behind a keyboard isn't nearly as fun as getting out there

in the real world. Especially if you're a complete lunatic. I can't imagine we made many sales from our activities, but we sent some photos and an article to the local paper. They were bound to print something – literally nothing else happened in Somerset that week.

4) Hot day plus hot bear costume equals one sweaty fiancé. The Giant Underpants were far better ventilated. That is not a sentence I get to use very often.

5) My family love me very, very much. And I use this love to make them look foolish, and then write about it. But you know, I'm okay with that.

I just have to hope that they are…

Understanding

Now, If you're not a wedding-y type person, then you might want to skip the next few chapters. Although having said that, if you're not a wedding-y type person I'm afraid you might have picked up the wrong book...

Sorry about that!

With the launch of 'That Bear Ate My Pants!' over, there really wasn't anything else I could do on that score. And anyway, as Roo kept reminding me, I had a wedding to finish organising.

Women, eh? So demanding.

I decided to refrain from telling her, "It's only a wedding."

I didn't think that would end too well.

We visited Angela in Bristol and had another close read-through of the ceremony in its latest, hopefully final, incarnation. It was a good job we did; due to my inimitable typing skills we had come frighteningly close to promising, in front of the entire congregation, that we would 'grow string together'. Hm. "Perhaps from my nose?" I suggested.

Then Angela took Roo off into a separate room to go over the vows she had written. I'd been dreading this part. Sure, I can churn out a few words here and there, but I've never been particularly good at expressing sentiment. I can tell jokes about marauding animals and bodily fluids until the cows come home, but the kind of serious, honest, poetic writing skill required for this was beyond me.

Consequently, the vows Angela was about to inspect, didn't exist.

Well, unless I finished writing them by the time she was done reading Roo's...

No chance.

I followed Angela into her study, and straight away she told me not to worry. "It's not an exam," she said, "and there is no way of failing at this. You're probably stressing too much, and over-thinking it."

"I am struggling a bit," I admitted, which could be considered a slight understatement.

Angela turned a caring look on me, her eyes welling up with empathy.

"It's easy," she said, "ask yourself; what does Roo really mean to you?"

I stared back at her, eyes wide, mouth more than likely hanging the same way, and nodded my approval.

And that was that.

Ten minutes later, with tears streaming down my face, the vows were finished.

They were absolutely perfect.

Not eloquent perhaps; as anyone who has read my books can attest, eloquence is not exactly my strongest attribute. But based on advice from my reviewers I'd managed to avoid swearing *and* mentioning my testicles, which I felt was a step in the right direction. I'd poured out my heart and soul onto that tiny piece of paper, and suddenly I felt a great burden lift from me. It was as though the act of writing those few small truths had brought them into sharper focus for me; it had distilled the whirlwind of thoughts in my mind, and in the process had calmed the chaos. I now knew precisely how I felt – about Roo, about myself, and about our life together – and with that realisation came understanding, and a healthy measure of peace. I *was* doing the right thing here. No matter what doubts would assail me (and it went without saying they would continue to do so) – I knew now, in my heart of hearts, that I was right for Roo, and that she was right for me. Without ever mentioning it, I'd been secretly worrying that I didn't have much to offer her. But I'd been looking at it from the wrong perspective. Now I saw that there was a simple, beautiful truth that ran counter to this fear; I was offering her everything.

Every part of me, body and soul; every secret unmasked, every thought, every effort would be dedicated to her; she would be mine, a prospect I was already looking forward to – and I would be completely and utterly hers.

It was the only thing I had to give, and in that moment the scales fell from my eyes and I realised that, for Roo, it was enough.

She wanted me every bit as much as I wanted her.

Fair trade.

I was still thinking about this a few days later, as I sat alone in the back seat of Dad's car on the way up north to Uncle Pauls' funeral. We'd had to leave Roo behind to look after Gramp, who wasn't in the best of health himself, but she'd taken on the task without question. Now more than ever I felt the need to have her at my side, but we both had to be strong in these difficult circumstances. I would only be away from Roo for twenty-four hours, but I was missing her after twenty-four minutes.

I helped to carry Paul's coffin, with tears streaming down my face; I would miss him, too, and for a whole lot longer. But all my sympathy was focused on Margaret, Pauls wife, who had been at his side the whole way through his illness. Now she was facing the rest of her life without him. It made me realize just how precious it was, this thing that Roo and I had. How valuable our time together was. And that, no matter what else happened, so long as we still had each other, we'd be okay.

On the way back we stopped off to visit another relative on a different side of the family. I couldn't help but notice that her garden was covered in blossom, blown from two trees at the front of her property. The petals were light, almost translucent, and dry rather than moist.

"They're sycamore," she said, "there's only two trees in the area like them, and we've got both of them!"

A mad idea had taken hold of me, and I spent an hour in the back garden filling two huge bin liners with blossoms. "We're not allowed to use paper confetti near the castle," I explained, "but this will do perfectly!"

The next coup was over wedding favours. We'd been worrying about this for a while, as giving our guests something to remember the day by was high on our list of priorities. The sycamore blossom gave me the answer: seeds! Both Roo and I are tree-lovers, and given the chance we'd have planted one on that special day to symbolise our marriage. Alas, we were technically homeless and planning to emigrate to Australia. But most of our guests were firmly established in their homes. If we couldn't grow trees for us, then some of them could! I shopped around online for acorns, and ended up going one better when I found a company selling Giant Sequoia Redwood seeds! "What about wildflowers?" Roo asked.

"If that's what you want," I said.

"Of course that's what I want!"

So she bought ten thousand of them.

Tiny glass bottles was our next discovery, and we bought enough of those to give every wedding guest one filled with the wildflower seeds. Another company sold us tiny chocolate squares with our photo on the wrappers. A silver leaf charm per person, and sparkly organza bags to put them in, finished it off. We had our nature-themed, practical favour bags, and they hadn't cost the earth.

To anyone who planted those seeds without realising that some of them were for gigantic Californian redwood trees, you have my apologies; there were a few inevitable mix-ups at the bottling stage. But don't worry, they stop growing after a thousand years or so.

We'd taken Gill's idea of having big books on a table for people to write nice things in, and adapted it slightly by including scraps of parchment, left over from the invites, in the favour bags. We hoped this would encourage our guests to write us messages, which we intended to collect at the end of the night.

Assuming we survived.

And then I struck gold; there was a florist selling a box of offcuts from her fake flower arranging business, mostly leaves and assorted foliage. I bid twenty quid for it, paid seven, and must have been the most grateful customer she ever had. All I was buying was her rubbish, but when it arrived – a suitcase-sized box crammed full of exquisitely modelled plastic and fabric leaves, stems and vines – I was so excited I did a victory lap around the house. A dozen cheap pillar candles from TK Maxx and a half-kilo bag of scatter gems from eBay completed the picture – and our perfect, nature-themed table centrepieces were complete. They were also damn easy to transport and set up. A few days before the ceremony I simply rocked up at the Winchester and handed over a big cardboard box. A handful of greenery made a nest for a single candle, and handful of gems strewn artfully around that completed the arrangement. I demonstrated one for Kaz, and she agreed to do the others on the day. She did a beautiful job; I think it took her less than a minute per table. The effect was magical, elegant, and looked like we'd spent considerably more than £30 all-in.

With the first guests scheduled to arrive in a couple of days, there seemed a very real danger that a wedding was about to take place. I still hadn't quite got my head around it, mostly because I'd been too busy finding places for people to stay. I'd negotiated a deal with The Days Inn, a nice motel not far from Taunton. Everyone would be staying there after the reception, including Roo and I; we'd never stayed in posh hotels, and there was no reason to start just because it was our wedding night. And there was no choice because, with minibuses booked to shuttle everyone to and from the Days Inn, every penny of the budget was finally spent.

Leaving me with nothing to do but pray for rain.
Or not, ideally.

Full House

Timing is everything, or so they say.

By way of an example, Cassie, our twelve-year-old border collie, choose this precise moment to have a stroke. It happened overnight, and we didn't even know about it until morning.

The sight that greeted us as we came down the stairs was unbelievable.

Cassie had survived, poor thing, but she had temporarily lost the ability to a) walk and b) control her arsehole. So she'd started to take a shit, and finding herself unable to stand had proceeded to drag herself up, down and around the entire ground floor of my house, still crapping like fury and carting most of it along with her. She was now a black, white and brown dog. As for the house... well, there's nothing like a living room striped end to end in diarrhoea to take your mind off of an upcoming wedding.

We were still scrubbing the carpets when the first guests began to arrive.

With Gill's wedding and mine so close together, most of our family had only been able to travel to one or the other. Roo didn't have as much extended family as me, so she'd gone ahead and invited the lot. From a cautious beginning, when we'd tried to keep the numbers to an intimate (and budget-friendly) thirty, the total of people invited had grown closer to eighty. Of those, we had fifty-six confirmed guests attending, most of whom would be coming down on the day. We'd specifically planned our ceremony in the afternoon to give them plenty of travel time. But not everyone was driving from the north of England. Roo's family were flying in, from Emmen and Ijmuiden in the Netherlands, and from Perth in Australia. They couldn't risk arriving late. So they were arriving now.

Roo's sisters flew in first. All three were going to be bridesmaids, and I'd sent them money to buy their dresses in Australia. It made sense, as they could shop together and try their outfits on, but getting them to agree on one dress – or more specifically, getting them to agree *with me* on one dress... that had been the hard part. Like Roo, they are all tall, slim and beautiful, so I knew they'd look fantastic in the simple green gowns I'd chosen. Whether they'd ever forgive me for choosing them was another matter entirely.

The girls were fascinated by the hamsters, and immediately began discussing plans to include them in the wedding as miniature bridesmaids. There was talk of walking them down the aisle in tiny harnesses made of white ribbons; it was about this point that I bowed out of the conversation, having more mundane chores to accomplish. It was good news that the girls were getting on well with the hamsters, as they'd be sharing a bedroom; it was going to be quite a squeeze too, as by then the available floor space was split roughly 80-20 in the hamster's favour.

A day later, Roo's dad Gerrit arrived, to a tumultuous applause from the Dutch contingent. They hadn't seen each other in years despite being closely related, having lived most of their lives on opposite sides of the planet.

Next to need a pick-up from the airport was Linda, my best friend from my year in Thailand. With her she'd brought our guest-of-honour and flower-girl – her two-year old daughter Saoirse. Don't worry – I can't pronounce it either! Linda had named me Godfather at Saoirse's christening, although so far I'd been as rubbish at that as I am at most things.

Roo was delighted to discover that Linda would be wearing wings on the morrow – and that Saoirse would be dressed as a fairy!

I'd had to put Linda up in a B&B in the village; as a result of this sudden influx of wedding guests, accommodation in Holly Cottage was at a premium. My parents have always collected vehicles, and not for the first time they'd been pressed into service. One extended family from Manchester had filled the caravan and another occupied the camper van. Power cables snaked out through the front door to provide these guests with a few creature comforts, but the only bathroom was still the one on the top floor of the cottage. It was taking a pounding. With over twenty sweaty bodies needing cleaning daily, the shower was in near-constant use. There was only one problem with that: Holly Cottage wasn't in the best of shape. In fact it was in need of complete renovation, but all my parent's time and money had been spent trying to maintain their collection of rental houses in South Wales. That shower had been in the cottage when they bought it almost fifteen years ago, and it was starting to show its age. To say it leaked would be a gross understatement. To say that ninety percent of the water going through it came out of a hole in the ceiling below would be way more accurate.

It was a full-time job just emptying the pots and pans we'd placed to collect the leaks. One day soon that whole chunk of ceiling was going to collapse – I just had to keep my fingers crossed that it would hold out until everyone had gone home.

In the meantime, every room was buzzing with people, creating a kind of carnival atmosphere. Dad had pulled out all the 'emergency chairs' (everyone has them!) – and then he'd outdone himself by finding an 'emergency sofa' in the shed.

Gill's bedroom was full; my bedroom was full. The spare bedroom was full.

Roo and I were sleeping in a bright pink tent in the front garden.

The tent was a beaut, though. Two bedroom pods and a joining porch area, I'd won it on eBay a week before the wedding, when it had first occurred to me that accommodation was going to be an issue. As the cottage filled up, Roo and I had pitched the thing on the Land of Dubious Ownership – a patch of ground in front of the house, which my parents have been trying to claim for the last ten years by putting a white plastic fence around it.

This is where we would be spending the night before our wedding. I thought it was quite appropriate, considering we'd first got together in a tent.

Only this time my sister wouldn't be sleeping on the other side of me.

With all the guests collected and accommodated, clothing packed and drink starting to flow, we were in the final furlong. Only a few key tasks remained; Mum had to finish sewing my wedding shirt, which was kind of important, I had to transfer the music for the reception onto my iPod, and apparently we needed flowers.

Speaking as a bloke, I find the whole trade in flowers to be faintly ridiculous. Sure, they're pretty to look at, but they're dying from the moment they're picked. Nothing says true love like murdering a bunch of innocent flowers so your better half can watch them decompose. Well, unless you count paying hundreds of dollars for the privilege. Ask any florist what your wedding flowers budget should be and they'll spread their arms in a shrug, whilst gazing up to heaven. This roughly translates as 'as much as you've got, I can spend it twice.'

Thankfully, we were never put in that position. From the start we'd planned on getting married outdoors, as close to nature as possible. Although my dream of a forest wedding hadn't quite been pulled off, we had an excellent, some would say vastly superior alternative. We would still be surrounded by nature, screened away from the rest of the city by majestic conifers and ancient stone ramparts. There were flowers all over the place, along with birds, bees and butterflies – and yet we had a bar and a posh hotel bathroom within a hundred metres.

But the real bargain came when Mum nipped round to the supermarket on the last morning before the wedding and bought every flower in the place. Daffodils, tulips and all kinds of wildflowers; they were half price for some reason, and for less than fifty quid she cleaned them out.

That evening, Roo's sister Sonja marshalled her troops. Every woman in the place (and there were quite a few of them by then) gathered in the conservatory, armed with scissors and ribbon. Over a couple of hours they dissected the cheap bunches of flowers and transformed them into bouquets fit for a princess. Or several princesses in fact, since we needed rather a lot of them.

There was one last flower-related mission that Roo and I had to accomplish. This we chose to do under cover of darkness, for no reason other than it seemed appropriate. We met outside, both dressed in black. There's only one streetlamp near my parent's house, and we naturally gravitated towards it before realising that kind of defeated the purpose. Then we scurried off into the night, Roo cutting a considerably more stealthy silhouette than me, and together we approached the house of our immediate neighbours. Ivy webbed the stonework of their cottage, completely dominating the two-storey end wall. It spilled over into their yard, climbing across the low wall that ran around the front of the property – and it was from here that we collected it, prising long strands away from the gate it was slowly engulfing. I teased it out and Roo snipped it, and in minutes we had all we needed. We could have just asked for it of course, but this way was much more fun. And it also saved us having to explain to our neighbours that the wedding they'd be attending the following day was an affair so slapdash and cheapskate that we were actually collecting our decorations from the side of the road.

So. Once back inside, Roo wasted no time in creating a masterpiece. She took a scrap of material she'd found in the sewing shop's bargain bin and roughly stitched the strands of ivy onto it lengthwise. Checking it for flexibility, she practiced draping it across our wrists – where tomorrow, the celebrant would be tying it. As with everything else we prepared in those final rushed hours, it was perfect; either we were being very lucky, or we were incredibly bias.

There was a slight danger that, if the latter were true, our guests would be treated to one of the crappest, most half-assed spectacles the world of weddings has ever known.

To look at it through someone else's eyes, we were getting married in an inner-city hotel's front garden, in homemade and second hand clothes, having the reception in the local pub and doling out tree leaves and birdseed as though they were suitable presents. Compared to the fairy-tale weddings some of them would have attended, there was a good chance ours would seem a bit naff.

But you know what? We've never set unnecessarily high expectations for ourselves and then struggled to achieve them. We have dreams of course, but we try to be happy with our lot. Life is much less stressful that way, and we get to enjoy every minute of it. I honestly wouldn't care if we were getting married in a field. It would be perfect for us no matter what happened.

Nocturnal Activities

I was up late that night, going over the timing with Gill. I'd made detailed crib sheets for everyone that was helping out. Each one was different, highlighting the points appropriate for that person. My cousin Dale, for example, was charged with getting all the guests from the Days Inn to the ceremony; his sheet had a list of passengers for each minibus, with notes in the margin about which of them spoke no English, along with a timeline of the day and all the phone numbers of the key players. I'd organised everything down to the last detail, and I wanted to be doubly sure this wasn't a wasted effort.

It was boring stuff to listen to though, so Roo decided to get as much sleep as she could. "Don't stay up all night," she warned me, "we're getting married tomorrow."

"Thanks, I'd forgotten," I said. "I won't be long, I promise. I'll try not to wake you when I come in."

So she went to bed alone, feeling her way across the road and into the tent in total darkness.

Two hours later I did the same thing, tripping on guy ropes and wincing at the noise of the door zipper. I managed to get undressed without standing on her, but there was definitely something strange going on beneath my feet.

I took a step towards the bed, my legs slid from under me, and with a colossal cry of "SHIT!" I crashed down on top of Roo.

So much for stealth. A flying elbow to the ribs has to be one of the world's rudest awakenings.

"OW!" she yelled, "What the hell? Did you mix up 'not waking me' with 'practise wrestling moves on me'?"

"I'm so sorry," I said, as I climbed off her. "The floor of the tent is weirdly slippy!"

"Just be careful," she said. "And please don't give me a black eye before tomorrow."

"I won't." I leaned over to kiss her, but she jerked upright again.

"There's something on my face!"

"What? A spider?"

"I don't know! Get it off, get it off!"

I swiped in her general direction and nearly delivered that black eye. Even in complete darkness I could tell she was still wriggling, brushing frantically at the covers. "What's wrong, love?"

"Ugh! I think there's insects in here! They're all over the bed!"

My skin crawled. There was something cold and moist stuck to the bottom of my foot. If Roo thought we were having an infestation, there would be no chance of her sleeping tonight. *Deny everything*, I decided. "It's just your imagination," I told her. "I cleaned the whole tent this afternoon, and it's been zipped up ever since. And I'm coming to bed now, so I can protect you."

She didn't sound too impressed by this, but she snuggled up against me and pulled the duvet over her head. "Next time, I want to stay in the house," she mumbled.

"Next time we get married, you mean?"

She chose not to respond to that. Soon her breathing smoothed out and her body relaxed.

I thought I'd be too stressed to sleep, but once away from the noise and confinement of the house I found the cool darkness was just what I needed. Even the threat of creepy crawlies couldn't keep my eyes open for long.

It wasn't until the next morning that we discovered Sonja had covered our bed in fresh rose petals – and we only noticed then because I woke up with a mouthful of them. Our midnight bug hunt had left petals stuck all over us in the most unexpected locations – finding and removing them was a fascinating, if somewhat unusual first activity for the morning of our wedding. Sonja had been very sneaky to pull this off without us knowing. It was very thoughtful of her, even though it nearly resulted in us getting married in A&E.

The morning passed in a blur of activity. I was up at seven, showered and shaved, contributing to the deluge of water pouring from the kitchen ceiling. I cleared up the mess I'd made and took a look at the 'order of the day' document I'd been writing until 3am. My first major task was to collect Linda and Saoirse from their bed and breakfast, while Dad fetched Linda's sister Irene from the bus station. All the girls were getting their hair and make-up done together, only a few steps from our front door. One of our neighbours, a lovely lady called Faye, was a professional hairdresser; she'd offered to do them all as a wedding present. Only Gill was going to miss out; as best man, she no longer counted as one of the girls. And anyway, I needed her.

I made a flurry of phone calls, checking in with various guests and those I'd recruited to help me run the day. I checked my lists, made lists of my lists, and started packing the car. Gill would be driving me into Taunton in Granddad's tiny Nissan Micra, setting off a few hours before everyone else so that we could take care of the last few jobs when we got there.

Speaking of transport, Roo came to me with a sight concern.

"Are you sure there's enough space in the cars for us?" She bit her lip nervously as she counted passengers on her fingers. "If Gill and Chris are going together with you, that just leaves your parents' cars. Four spaces with each of them... Sonja and the girls is three, plus Dad, Linda and Irene and Sushi... are we taking your Granddad in the same trip? Maybe I should drive one of the other cars. I guess I could put my dress on when I got there..."

It was time to unburden myself. The limo was the last secret I had, and part of me wanted to keep quiet until it rolled down the street. But there was a fine line to tread here; no matter how delighted she might be by the surprise, it wasn't worth ruining her morning by letting her worry about a non-existent problem.

"It's all good, love," I said. "I've taken care of it."

"Oh? Are you coming back?"

"Nope – I've arranged for a car to come and get you."

"Oh, right? Coming to get who, exactly?"

"Coming to get all of you."

"But we won't all fit!"

"You will in this car."

That's when it dawned on her. "No..."

"Oh yes! But you'd better get over to Faye's. She's got a lot of work to do."

I gave her a kiss – the last we'd share before I left for the wedding – and I strolled away, feeling like the king of the world.

However, nothing makes you feel you feel small and insignificant like the power of nature – specifically the enormous chunk of nature I had to load into the Micra's boot. Over a metre in diameter, the slice of tree-trunk had been sitting in my parents' garden waiting to be made into a table-top for at least a year. It was an epic addition to our cargo. It was also quite rough, as I'd never found a spare eight hours to sand it smooth. Gill helped me manhandle it into the boot. The suspension gave a moan of distress and the car settled about six-inches lower than it had been.

"Shit, I hope we make it there," she said.

After all, there was going to be three of us in the Micra; I think between us and the contents, we outweighed the car quite substantially.

I nipped over to Faye's house to give Sonja money to pay the limo driver. He was doing us a cash-in-hand deal, which presumably meant he was squeezing us in on his lunch break and pocketing an easy £100. I had no problem with this at all; like all the best solutions, it made everyone happy. The girls weren't pleased to see me though, and refused to let me in until Roo had been hidden away upstairs.

"It's unlucky to see the bride before the wedding," Sonja reminded me.

"I woke up with her in my tent this morning," I reminded her, "although she was so plastered with red rose petals I thought she'd bled to death in the night."

There was evidence that the girls were enjoying their make-overs – empty champagne bottles and glasses littered the tables amidst bottles of nail varnish and hair care products that were beyond my comprehension. Anti-colour-lock-frizz-ease-shine-nourishing-serums and formulas dominated the kitchen countertop. I decided discretion was the better part of valour at that point, and bid a hasty retreat before my ignorance was exposed.

And just like that, it was time to go.

Gill was driving with Chris in the passenger seat, as I had work to do. I'd brought a few spare sheets of paper and a biro, and I now had almost half an hour of uninterrupted thinking time – to write the speech I'd be giving at the reception that afternoon.

Other than this minor detail, I felt I'd pretty much covered all the bases.

I had clothes, I had vows, I had rings.

And for the sake of completion, I should mention that sharing the backseat with me on that journey was half a wrought-iron birdbath, several bin-liners full of sycamore blossoms, a small piece of carpet and a large stone frog.

Pretty typical for a Thursday morning.

Last Minute Preparations

When we arrived in Taunton, the first thing I did was haul the giant chunk of tree trunk out of the car. It took all three of us to carry it up the stairs into the secret garden. Jokes were made about the size of my wood, which helped to ease the pain of the splinters in our arms. When set on the legs from the iron birdbath, against the backdrop of conifer trees, it made a perfect altar. I added a few items to the top of it – an exquisite piece of black granite from Mum's rock collection, symbolising earth, a candle for fire, a small bowl of water, and some incense, which is generally used to signify air. With the elements represented, the altar was done for now – draped with a few flowers and bits of ivy, hopefully it wouldn't trigger any accusations of Satanism from our more religious guests.

The chairs had been set out exactly as I'd requested, which was a relief. Beyond that there was nothing to detract from the area's natural, timeless state. I set up one of the empty chairs in honour of Roo's mum Frieda, with flowers and a framed picture of her on it, and the frog ornament in the grass underneath (as she'd had a lifelong love of frogs). Making this little tribute had been an easy decision for us – we wanted to feel like Frieda was with us at the ceremony, and it was a happy choice to include her. Likewise, we invited the spirit of Roo's cousin Petra to attend – a talented artist, she'd been killed recently in a car crash, otherwise she'd have been here with the rest of the Dutch delegation. As Petra's obsession was with butterflies, we'd bought some decorative ones online, and we hung them from trees here and there around the garden.

Standing in front of the altar, surveying the scene, I felt a ripple of anticipation run through me like an electric current. This was it – in a couple of hours I'd be stood here for real, exchanging the vows I'd printed onto two small parchment scrolls. I hadn't read Roo's, of course – she'd taken over the computer to print hers – so that particular piece of magic would only be revealed when the time was right.

It was all coming together, and so perfectly I could have cried – if I'd had time. But I had more pressing concerns. The last pile of stuff in the car was for the Winchester, and it was vital it be delivered – a laptop containing the music for the entire evening, which still had to be tested with their speaker system, plus party favours, candles, guest books and last minute instructions for Kaz.

As I turned to leave the garden, I noticed something really special; a brilliantly-coloured butterfly was doing a dance right above the altar.

I had to smile. Thinking about it, there were three distinct possibilities:

1) It was just a butterfly. This was, after all, a garden.

2) It was fate; a tiny portion of Petra's spirit had come to watch us get married… or

3) It was sexually attracted to the numerous plastic butterflies we had scattered liberally around the place. In which case it was in for a long and frustrating day.

All was well at the Winchester. Kaz had made a clean sweep of the place and it looked gorgeous – gleaming wood, glowing brass, pristine white tablecloths on the heavy oak tables. Both my laptop and the back-up iPod I'd brought connected easily into the pub's stereo system, so the music was a go.

"Oh, but my chef's called in sick," Kaz said, "so I might need you to give me a hand later in the kitchen."

"Wha…? I… But… What?"

"S'alright, I'm only messing with you! Relax – it's your wedding day!"

"I can't relax *because* it's my wedding day. I've got too much to do."

"Sounds like someone needs a double whisky."

"Bloody hell! Good idea."

With that taken care of, some of my other concerns seemed to melt away. I'd already accomplished almost everything on my list, and I still had some time to spare. I called the limo company to check they were on schedule, and the minibus company to check they were, too. All was green.

Thunderbirds are go.

So I dispatched Gill and Chris to intercept any early arrivals, gathered my outfit from the back seat of the car and headed into the Castle Hotel's ballroom to put it on. A million things were running through my mind; would my cousin at the Days Inn be able to get all the guests on the minibus? Would they be too late and delay the ceremony, or too early and be bored? I got a last-minute text message from one of my best friends, saying she wouldn't be able to make it – her car had exploded on the motorway, and she was now sitting in a field waiting for the RAC. She attached a picture of her and her boyfriend; both were dressed in full-on Robin Hood costumes that they'd made specially. She was understandably gutted, as was I – the party wouldn't be the same without her.

Was that it? All the day's bad luck falling on one unlucky pair? Or was some unnamed disaster still lurking in the wings? A catastrophic change in the weather? An accident, a timing error, or something I'd completely forgotten to buy or plan or organise? I was starting to go a little bit crazy, so I nipped back to the Winchester for another dose of medicine.

After that, the inside of my head seemed much calmer.

Everything was ready; everything was in motion.

It was too late now to worry about what might have been missed, as there was nothing I could do to fix it. Time to kick back and go with the flow...

All I had to do was wait for the photographer, who would be taking pictures of me getting dressed for the ceremony. I wasn't sure why, but apparently that was considered appropriate. While I waited, I had a look round. If the weather had gone against us, this would have been the room we got married in. It would have swallowed our crowd easily enough, and it certainly looked the part – an elegant room, albeit fading here and there in its grandeur. There were easily a hundred chairs in there, with space for a hundred more – those would be the ones that now lined the secret garden outside. It must have taken ages to carry them all out. A bank of double-height windows ran down one wall, lined with voluminous velvet curtains. I hastily pulled them all closed; it was slightly unnerving, wandering around such a massive and elaborate room in my underwear.

From the huge entry doors I heard the softest, tiniest, barest minimum of a knock.

That knock could only come from one person; Sally, my best friend from my student days. With her would be Chris, and they would both be wearing head-to-toe black, just like I did back then. The three of us had been so tight throughout university that it bordered on the incestuous.

As I got to the door, sure enough I heard Chris' singsong Welsh accent on the other side, asking, "Are you sure this is the right place?"

I flung open the door to greet my friends, bellowing, "HEELLLOOO!"

The pair of them stood there, looking shocked. Sally cast a critical eye up and down me, which is when it occurred to me that I was still wearing nothing but my underpants.

"Yup, this is the right place," she said.

The photographer wasn't far behind, which saved me having to explain my indecency. Actually, I didn't even try – both Chris and Sally had seen me in far worse, and far more compromising situations. To be honest, I think they were more surprised that I'd shaved than they were at my semi-nudity.

The photographer explained that, whilst shots of the bride in her 'boudoir' were often considered artful and elegant, photographs of me wearing Teenage Mutant Ninja Turtle boxing shorts didn't quite fall into the same category.

I was allowed to dress myself after all, and the others hovered at a safe distance until I was decent. Donning the boots, however, required teamwork and cooperation – I sat in a chair and pushed one way while Sally knelt on the floor and pushed the other. The photographer snapped away and Chris provided a helpful running commentary of our progress – which came to an abrupt halt when I got agonizing cramp halfway through, straightening my leg so fast I nearly kicked Sally across the room, then hopping around shrieking like I'd stood in a puddle of molten lava.

Oh, those boots were a bugger. I'd been over the moon when I'd won them on eBay; they were the most expensive part of my outfit, and the bit I'd been most excited about. They were knee-high black leather riding boots, exactly the kind that any self-respecting medieval squire would have worn. And I'm not admitting this influenced my decision in any way, but they were also worn by Han Solo in *Star Wars*. I'd specifically wanted the kind that didn't have a conspicuous zip running all the way up them, and they had to be the genuine article – I was fully intending on adding them to my regular wardrobe, hoping that they'd look funky and unusual when worn with jeans and a jacket.

Only, now I was having second thoughts about that part.

You know, the 'wearing them all the time in real life' part.

Because it took nearly half an hour to get the damn things on.

Then, finally bedecked in all my wedding finery, I stood up to show it off. It wasn't the most successful experiment. Between the tightness of the trousers and the inflexibility of the boots, I could hardly move my legs. I looked like a two-pin plug.

"Wow," Sally marvelled, "those are really... *impressive*. I know you like tight trousers, but you've outdone yourself there."

"What? I don't like tight trousers."

"Are you kidding? Tony, you were famous for it all through uni! You always wore super-tight jeans. Everyone knew which way you were hanging on a daily basis. There were *conversations* about it."

"WHAT?"

"You didn't know?"

"NO!"

"Oh, right. Err, maybe this isn't the best time to get into it."

"No, probably not."

"But interesting choice on the trousers. Can you actually walk in them?"

"I'm not quite sure…"

Official Vibes

I sent Sally and Chris off to mingle with the guests as they arrived in the garden. I armed them with a stack of paper cones and a bin-bag full of tree blossoms each.

"If anyone wants to throw something, give them this," I instructed.

"Are we confiscating eggs and rotten tomatoes then?" asked Sally.

"No, it's *confetti*. Environmentally friendly confetti."

She raised an eyebrow. "Where did you get it?"

"My aunty's back garden. There might be some small stones and branches mixed in with it, so try not to give those out."

"Fair enough."

Gill turned up to escort me over the road to the registry office, where the rest of my family were waiting. It was a grand old building, built in 1522 as a boys' grammar school. Ranks of carved stone window surrounds, narrow arched doorways and a miniature bell-tower gave it the air of a medieval monastery. At one point we'd given serious consideration to holding our main ceremony in the massive Tudor Hall, which took up one entire wing of the building. Since finding our secret garden, however, we'd downscaled our ambitions and booked the cheapest, simplest room they had for weddings; the ever-so-slightly more humble-sounding 'Small Room'.

I arrived outside the registry office building just before Roo did; the gleaming white stretched limo swung smoothly around the corner, sliding to a halt beside the stone entry steps.

Roo's window was down and she was smiling out of it, looking for all the world like a princess about to bestow her royal wave on the people.

The driver leapt out like his seat was on fire, and started pulling people out of the limo. "Quick," he said, "we're on double yellow lines here!"

It was a fair point. Wedding chauffeur he may be, but he would still get booked for illegal parking if the cops drove past.

People piled out of the limo, crowding the stone steps leading up to the registry office. I knew how many people could fit inside that car because I'd booked it, but it was still quite amusing watching them pop out one after another like they were emerging from the *Tardis*. Roo, her dad Gerrit, all three bridesmaids, Linda and her sister Irene, and of course little Saoirse, had been crammed in there.

As they assembled on the pavement, the sun came out in a flash of gold. Roo looked angelic. Her gown shone, diaphanous in the light; her tanned shoulders were glowing and her eyes seemed almost impossibly blue.

In all our time together, I'd never seen her wearing make-up.

Hairdresser Faye had outdone herself. She'd braided white roses into Roo's platinum-blonde hair, teasing it into a thousand delicate curls that cascaded down her back. Amazingly, she'd managed to do a similar job on all three bridesmaids – an epic feat, given her timetable of less than half an hour apiece. In their matching gowns of woodland green, Roo's sisters were stunning. They looked alike under ordinary circumstances, but all dressed the same and clutching matching bouquets they were almost identical.

I clomped down the steps as fast as my boots would allow me, and wrapped Roo in a make-up ruining hug. "You look incredible!" I told her.

"Thanks my love! So do you."

"How are you feeling?"

"A bit drunk," she confessed, "did you know we got free champagne in the limo?"

"No idea! It was kind of last-minute. I know I got to choose between pink or white ribbons."

As I said this, the driver was frantically ripping the pink bows off the car and dodging around the traffic to fasten white ones in their place.

"He's running late for his next job," Roo explained. "The motorway was hell."

I watched him edging carefully down the side of his car. He reached the boot, opened it, and wrestled Saoirse's buggy out of it. That act of selfless heroism used up the last few minutes of my hire, and he vacated the double yellow lines at top speed.

The photographer was busy by now, trying to capture the ladies while they looked their best. Linda and Irene were wearing their wings, of which Roo was very jealous. She *really* wanted to get married in wings, but decided it might look like she wasn't taking the whole thing seriously enough. That was why she'd bought the three-metre-long, faux-fur-trimmed cloak – not because it matched her outfit, but because she wanted to use it for fancy dress parties afterwards.

Always thinking ahead, Roo was.

Saoirse, in her a tiny purple fairy costume, was absolutely gorgeous. She was literally bouncing with excitement, twirling and jumping and burying herself in the train of Roo's dress.

"Look at her, she's going crazy!" said Linda.

"Too much champagne?" I asked.

"Don't get me started! She wants to do *everything* that mummy does."

"Oh God!" After spending a year in Thailand with Linda, I knew her better than most. "That's going to get messy…"

Roo and I presented ourselves at the office window, and an auburn-haired lady came out to show us to the registrar. She took us upstairs, through several sets of double doors, burrowing our way into the heart of what was essentially a government office building.

We stopped at a door much like the others we'd passed. From the outside, the Small Room was spectacularly unremarkable.

"And you've chosen to have no music?" the clerk asked.

"That's right, yes."

"Okay then. Follow me, please."

She led me into a small, wood-panelled room. It was as luxuriously-furnished and inviting as the average high-school staff room. No expense had been spared in decorating the place for nuptial ceremonies; an otherwise empty bookcase along one wall contained a small vase of fake flowers. There were two rows of straight-backed chairs for guests and witnesses, but only our immediate families had followed me in.

Roo waited outside in the corridor, accompanied by her dad – there would still be a ceremonial entrance and a symbolic giving-away, even though this was a strictly legislative procedure.

When the family members were seated, I assumed my position in front of the registrar. She was wearing a wig; it felt a bit like being on trial, only for a crime I was still waiting to commit.

"Are you sure you don't want any music playing?" asked the clerk. "We have some right here. Only, it'll be dead silent otherwise."

Ah, what the hell, I thought.

Suddenly, stood before that cheap wooden desk, the significance of the moment hit me. I might not consider this ceremony to be important, but the Law did – and no matter what else happened afterwards, officially this would still be the time and place of our marriage. Right now the background noise was 'people trying to be quiet' – our small congregation were wriggling in their seats, coughing, sniffing and clearing their throats, as their excitement ran full-tilt into the sombre atmosphere of the chamber. Doors banged in the distance, and even shifting my weight produced an audible creak from the floorboards. As always at these moments, I felt an uncontrollable urge to fart. Chances were, I wasn't the only one, and I really didn't want Roo to walk in to that.

"Dearly beloved…"

Paaaaaaaarp!

Even the thought made my diaphragm quiver; the threat of hysterical giggles was rising.

"Okay then," I relented, "let's have a bit of music."

Whatever they had on offer would be melodic and nondescript. Certainly better than the alternative.

"Marvellous," said the clerk, and she scurried over to the stereo. "Let's see what we've got on number one."

She pressed the button, and unleashed a torrent of angry sound. Men were screaming, in deep voices like the growl of an enraged beast, while guitars screeched in agony. It was some seriously heavy thrash-metal – *Slipknot* perhaps, or *Megadeath* – an indecipherable assault of noise and violence.

The clerk hit stop, just as I was reaching up to put my hands over my ears.

"Ooh, I'm terribly sorry," she said, "that won't do at all. I'll try the next one."

Her fingers dropped to the next button down; it was an old-school stacking system, with three separate CD decks on top of each other.

Why is that CD even on there? I wondered. *Who the hell gets married to that?*

People with no love for God, presumably.

Then the clerk pressed play on the second CD deck, and once again I was staggered. Insanely-fast rave music flowed through the speakers, a beat so rapid it could only be produced electronically. I don't know much about the speed-garage/house/trance music scene, as I spent most of my time in Thailand hiding from it, but this was definitely one of those. Techno? Happy hardcore? Your guess is as good as mine.

"Ah, let's see what's on number three," said the clerk, sounding confused.

I couldn't believe it. This stereo system existed for exactly one reason – to provide music for people to get married to. I'd thought my wedding was alternative, but there were must have been some pretty weird ceremonies in that room.

Third time lucky, I thought, as the clerk's fingers hovered over the play button.

There was a twang – and another twang – and then whole series of them.

This music had a slower pace. There was no backing track. It wasn't guitar music.

Was it about to develop into a country and western song? It had a bit of a red-neck vibe. I'd heard it somewhere before, actually. It was...

It was duelling banjos.

You have got to be kidding me!

The clerk looked over at me, spreading her hands in apology. *That's all there is,* she shrugged.

I shook my head in disbelief. But I was past caring. "You know what? It'll do."

Sorry, Roo, I sent out silently.

And so we were married to duelling banjos.

Roo processed into the room, arm-in-arm with Gerrit. Both of them wore furrowed brows, unable to ask the question that must have been killing them: What the bloody hell is this music? When did this become a hillbilly wedding? And are we supposed to finish with a 'YEEEE-HAAAA!?'

Thankfully, the volume was turned down during the ceremony. I met Roo's bewildered glance with a smile, and from there we carried on as normal.

It wasn't until afterwards, as we were signing the register, that my Dad said, "If I'd have known, I'd have worn my cowboy boots..."

"I can't believe anyone would get married to that crap!" I said. "I mean, even if you were really, really into it, it's just... not right."

"Maybe they weren't getting married to it," Roo suggested.

"But that's the whole point – they don't use this room for anything else!"

"Unless some of the staff snuck up here for a party..."

"Wow. I bet questions will be asked around the office tomorrow."

We posed for photos on a grand staircase of polished oak (which was nowhere near the Small Room), and a few more outside. It really was a lovely building, and its ancient stonework lent itself perfectly to our loose medieval theme.

From here we had only a short, glamorous walk – past the public toilets and across a car park – to reach the Castle Hotel, and the gardens where our guests would be gathering.

I struggled a bit with my boots on the cobblestones ("That's what you get for wearing heels," Roo said), and then we parted once more. Gill escorted me up into the secret garden, while Roo and her entourage disappeared into the trees.

No more rehearsals – this was it. Magic time.

It suddenly occurred to me that we hadn't arranged any cues or signals. I didn't have a clue how long it would be before Roo's party re-emerged from the foliage – and neither did they. We'd just have to make that bit up as we went along.

Come to think of it, a rehearsal wouldn't have been a bad idea.

Tying the Knot

This was it.

The guests were seated.

The harpist was playing.

I took my place before the giant chunk of tree-trunk, with Gill at my side – and waited.

Like an elven princess, Roo's arrival was preceded by the glimmer of white silk through the leaves. Sunlight dappled her path around the congregation, and I heard the rustle of people turning to look at her. I knew she'd made it to the tree opposite the altar when the harpist smoothly switched to *In Dreams*, a haunting instrumental from The Lord Of The Rings that we'd chosen to replace that gawd-awful 'Here Comes The Bride' racket.

A pair of butterflies danced above Roo's head as her sisters preceded her down the aisle, with little Saoirse skipping along behind her, holding onto her train. Arm in arm with her dad, Roo seemed to float down the aisle, though I could only allow myself a few sneaky peaks. And then she was there beside me, smiling in delight, radiating excitement, and more beautiful than ever before.

The ceremony started well enough. First Sonja came up to read a poem, 'Marriage is Like The Planting of Two Trees' by Moira Stuart.

Then Angela spoke up, thanking our guests for coming and for traveling such a long way. "And now," she continued, "we'll have a moment's silence for our loved ones who have passed away, who can't be with us today because… ah… because they're dead."

Must. Not. Laugh, I told myself.

Then Mum read a 'Above You Are The Stars', a piece drawn from an old Celtic hand-fasting ritual. After countless hours of internet research, debate, re-choosing, re-writing, re-printing and seeking approval, both readings were over in seconds. Each was a lovely addition to our ceremony, and both were delivered exactly as I'd imagined.

Can I Kiss Her Yet?

It was what came next that took me by surprise.

After briefly explaining the significance of nature in our spiritual beliefs, Angela asked everyone to stand.

From the beginning, we'd wanted pagan elements to be present in what was essentially a hand-fasting ritual, but always we'd been careful not to offend the staunch Catholics in our crowd.

I thought I'd done a pretty good job of distilling the essence of this ancient ritual, but our celebrant had a surprise contribution up her sleeve.

Actually it was tucked into the belt of her robe; I hadn't spared it a second glance, assuming it was part of the costume, until she snatched it forth and thrust it skyward like a loaded wand.

A maraca.

Facing the assembled guests, she started shaking the thing vigorously above her head, the distinctive rattle of the beans inside it almost drowning out her words.

Or maybe that was just the shock.

"I call to you, oh, spirits of the North," she chanted, as she shook the maraca in time.

My jaw dropped. Roo's nearly hit the floor.

Beyond a shadow of a doubt, the exact same thought was passing through both our heads. *What the hell is going on? Where did that maraca come from?*

I wanted to glance around, to see if our reactions were being filmed for some prank-based hidden camera show, but I was frozen in place.

I mean, I've nothing against maracas. I know that some cultures consider them sacred objects, but personally I've always associated them with Spanish flamenco dancing…

And hippie camp-fire sing-alongs.

Please God, don't let the bongos be next!

For a terrible second I thought she was going to hand me the maraca and ask me to sing my vows.

But then the rattle-swinging was over. Having called out for blessings to the spirits of all four cardinal directions, she placed the instrument on the altar and we were once again safe from the threat of a *Kum ba yah*.

Roo was grinning at me and shaking her head in disbelief. I knew what she was thinking; we'd spent hours going over this ceremony in the minutest detail, rearranging passages, sentences, even words. We'd discussed every aspect, every standing position, every prop.

The word maraca had never been mentioned.

But all that was now behind us.

It was time for the hand-fasting.

Angela took Roo's hands, placing them in mine, and began to wind the ivy-laced ribbon around our wrists. She did this slowly and solemnly, whilst speaking aloud the words of an incredibly poetic blessing I'd found online;

"These are the hands of your best friend, young and strong and full of love for you, that are holding yours on your wedding day, as you promise to love each other today, tomorrow, and forever. These are the hands that will work alongside yours, as together you build your future. These are the hands that will passionately love you and cherish you through the years, and with the slightest touch, will comfort you like no other. These are the hands that will hold you when fear or grief fills your mind. These are the hands that will countless times wipe the tears from your eyes; tears of sorrow, and tears of joy. These are the hands that will tenderly hold your children. These are the hands that will help you to hold your family as one. These are the hands that will give you strength when you need it. And lastly, these are the hands that, even when wrinkled and aged, will still be reaching for yours, still giving you the same unspoken tenderness with just a touch."

I was tearing up by the time she was finished, and then I realized we'd come to the point where we were supposed to exchange our vows. I also realized that we'd never quite got around to deciding what order we'd be doing this in.

Never mind!

I gave Roo a polite 'ladies first' kind of nod, and she responded with an almost imperceptible shake of her head. I waited patiently for a few moments, in case she was gathering herself to speak, but her eyes were growing wider by the second. Should I go first, I wondered? I didn't want to risk talking over her at a time like this. The silence stretched taut like a rubber band, destined to snap back on one or the other of us – and that's when I had a romantic revelation.

I knew Roo so well I could read even the tiniest nuance of her body language. As I gazed at her, she developed a slight set to her jaw which said to me, "If you don't open your mouth and start flapping it right now, I am going to punch you in the nuts in front of all these people."

That pretty much cleared up the confusion, so I cleared my throat and read the words I'd been struggling to memorize.

"Krista, since the beginning I've always felt at ease with you.

It was almost like I knew you already, like we'd been together before this time.

Our friendship was so effortless, so honest, and it grew into the love I've been looking for my whole life.
You are still my best friend, and will be forever.
And you are also the love of my life.
You are the most important part of me;
There is nothing that I do, that isn't for you.
I want to base my whole life around making you happy.
You are so beautiful, and magical; you are perfect to me.
I want to spend every day with you; while we are on this earth, and afterwards.
I want to be with you every single moment.
I will never leave your side.
I love you so very, very much."

Being a Man, and also technically an actor, I'd like to say that I stood there proud and strong, and projected this heartfelt declaration to everyone in earshot.

But I'm crap at acting, and not much better at being a man to be honest, so I descended into sobs halfway through and ended up with tears streaming down my cheeks. It would almost have been beautiful, if my nose hadn't started running too. That almost never happens when people cry in movies; just the delicate spilling of crystal drops from their eyelashes, whereas in reality there is a great deal more snot involved.

On the upside, my having made such a mess of things gave Roo the confidence she needed. *Can't possibly do worse than that*, she was thinking, but in a nice way – her smile was radiant, at once reflecting the happiness I felt whilst also thanking me for making this so much easier for her.

She closed her eyes and took a deep breath.

She was trembling as she glanced down at the paper in her hand. Bless her.

Then, softly, she began to read;

"Tony, you are my life, my love and my eternal soul-mate.

Every day I see you and fall more in love with you, and I know the rest of my life will be perfect with you by my side.

I am the luckiest girl in the world and I will treasure your love and companionship every second of every day.

I never dreamed of someone who could match me and share so many of my hopes, dreams and adventures.

I choose you, above all others every day for the rest of my life,

And if you will have them, my heart and soul will be yours

forever more.
　　I love you."
　　And it was perfect.
　　Everything was perfect.

As our hands were unbound, Roo and I shared a conspiratorial smile. The strip of scrap cloth, twined around with ivy that we had stolen the night before, was carried to the altar and placed ceremoniously atop it. The huge slab of tree-trunk, which had survived its journey there in the Micra's boot, had never looked more imposing. Whether or not the car had survived the journey remained to be seen.

Gill stepped forward bearing the wooden box that held our rings. *Two quid from a garage sale* I remembered – not the most romantic of notions to be dwelling on at that moment, but the ridiculousness of all the individual elements was starting to amuse me. Separately they were almost worthless, but together they became part of something far greater than all of them. There was a relationship metaphor in there somewhere.

Angela was speaking;

"The circle is the symbol of the sun and the earth and the universe. It is a symbol of holiness and of perfection and of peace. This ring is a symbol of unity, in which your two lives are now joined in one unbroken circle."

Roo and I took our rings from Gill, and placed them on each other's fingers.

It was time for Angela to wrap this show up.

"Tony and Krista, by the binding of your hands and the exchanging of vows and rings, you have promised before all those gathered here to love one another according to your highest spiritual intentions. It is therefore my delight and privilege, ladies and gentlemen, to present to you Mr and Mrs Slater!"

It was a line that built up in a crescendo, and there was a great rustle of clothing as everyone in the crowd prepared to celebrate.

But no signal was given.

A few uncomfortable seconds passed where no-one seemed to know what was expected of them. Applause? Hysteria? Mexican wave?

I looked at Roo, and then back at the celebrant.

Still smiling beatifically at the gap between our heads, she made a subtle 'shoo'ing gesture. Then, when neither of us moved, a slightly more emphatic one.

I traded confused glances with Roo.

Her brow was delicately furrowed. *Did she just 'shoo' us?* it asked.

I think so, I replied with a chin-shrug.

We stood in silence for several more seconds. It felt far more awkward than I hope it looked, but that was a temporary situation. I had to do something.

I cleared my throat again, as gently as I could, as pitched a stage-whisper at Angela.

"Um, can I, er, you know... kiss her yet?"

A look of shock passed over her face, and her hands flew to her mouth. "Oh! I'm so sorry! Yes of course, you may now kiss the bride!"

And that was the moment I'd been waiting for.

I gathered Roo in my arms and traded a kiss that skirted the bounds of decency for a public venue.

And the crowd went wild.

Angela recovered beautifully, and was a picture of calm authority as she bestowed our final blessing:

"May the blessings of Love be upon you,

May Love's peace abide in you,

May Love's presence illuminate your hearts,

Now and forevermore."

A wave of relief washed over me as she finished. *We'd done it!* Against all the odds, we had achieved it. Minor hiccups aside, the ceremony had gone fantastically. We were now married in the sight of Gods and of the Law, and all those months of planning and worry were over. All we had to do now was get through the rest of the day.

And that was bound to be the easy part.

We turned and waved to our guests, and walked back up the aisle hand-in-hand, surrounded by the clapping and cheering of our friends and relatives. I rode an overwhelming high, as it occurred to me that at that exact moment, every single person there was thinking happy thoughts about me. It was a strong cocktail of emotion and excitement, and it went straight to my head. I was giddy for a few steps, and felt as though my spirit was about to soar out of my body and fly a victory-lap around the castle.

Luckily, Roo brought me down to earth with a whispered warning; "Don't step on my dress!"

I looked down and saw miles of fabric beneath my feet, with hardly a safe place to stand. I was going to be playing *Twister* up the aisle at this rate.

But then we reached the back of the garden, and the big tree that we'd aligned the altar with. Suddenly we were mobbed by guests, hands shooting in from everywhere for a shake or a pat on the back. It no longer mattered that we hadn't figured out where to go from here;

knots of people blocked our path in all directions, and by the time we we'd accepted all their blessings and congratulations the whole party was scattered all over the place.

It was done. It was a triumph! And it was over.

Just the rest of the day to go, I reminded myself…

Freedom of Speech

We'd organised drinks outside the Winchester – by which I mean, one glass of champagne per guest, which Kaz had very generously included in the price of our dinner.

Most of the weddings I've ever been to seem to have been characterised by a lot of standing around; I was desperate to avoid this, as waiting is on everyone's list of least-favourite things to do. Thus, I conspired to solve the dreaded debacle of photographs ('Now the bride and groom with the immediate family. Now with just the men. Now just the bridesmaids and Great Uncle Ted because he won't shut up about it. And let's try everyone at the wedding in size order from small to large… with every second person doing a handstand…'). Firstly, I pretty much abolished the notion of large, orchestrated group shots in favour of more reportage-style photography. Secondly, I gave the guests a gorgeous natural environment, so they could run around the gardens taking photos of each other against the castle walls to their hearts' content. Finally, and most importantly of all, I dispatched Gill to start leading them across the castle grounds to the pub – where the bar awaited. Kaz was outside already, handing out glasses of champagne and bowls of strawberries from a silver tray; this was one of many small details which she pulled off brilliantly, unasked for, throughout the night. She was worth her weight in gold that woman, and really helped make the whole thing sing.

A glass of bubbly confirmed to the straggle of guests that they were in the right place, made them feel welcome, and (hopefully) provided a boredom-free transition from ceremony to reception. We only had to kill a few minutes while the photographer snapped Roo and I embracing against the backdrop of the castle, and then we too could traipse across to the Winchester to get our drink on.

Cheers greeted our arrival outside the pub, which gave me a lovely warm feeling – one I could definitely get used to! A random passer-by in a flat-cap leapt up onto the wall, introduced himself as a performance poet, then improvised a couple of verses for us on the spot. He was drunk of course, but the whole thing had the delicious tang of the truly weird; let's face it, no wedding of mine was ever likely to be *normal*. I was quite grateful for it.

The ancient wooden stocks from Taunton Castle were kept in the Winchester's courtyard, so inevitably I ended up in them, struggling to reach my mouth with a champagne flute in either hand. Then, as the last few guests found their way out of the gardens, the party moved inside.

Kaz had done a fantastic job on the décor. The wooden wall panels shone, harking back to a more grandiose era. The simple white table cloths perfectly complimented the clusters of candles and foliage in the centres; we hadn't had the time or the money for more elaborate decorations, but the dignified atmosphere of the eight-hundred-year-old stone building made the very best of what we had. Dinner was bubbling away in the buffet area, but it was still a bit early to eat. Luckily, we'd taken this into account, and had the perfect thing to plug the gap; speeches.

Ugh! I hate speeches. Everyone hates them. Especially wedding speeches – terrifying to do and a terrifying prospect to sit through; boredom, often to such a degree it should be banned under the Geneva Convention, is the lingering legacy of many a reception. I attended far too many weddings as a child, and sitting still interminably, listening to drunk old men ramble on about the meaning of true love, was the bit I feared most; I usually aimed to be drunk myself by then.

I'd pretty much said that anyone who wanted to make a speech was welcome to, and that no-one was going to be forced – we hadn't followed any of the common conventions, like assigned seating, in the hope that our guests would enjoy themselves much more in a less formal ambiance.

There were some givens, however; I would have to give a speech at some point, and I was pretty sure Gill had been concocting something to say. Recent proximity protected me from the dreaded toast joke, but Gill was nothing if not resourceful. I was sure she had something up her baggy medieval sleeve.

First up, Roo's dad Gerrit made a short, touching speech in which he welcomed me to the family. He told us Frieda would have been delighted to see her daughter so happily married, which brought a tear to the eyes of those of us who'd known her.

Then he yielded the floor to Sonja, who had a worrying gleam in her eye...

I was already bracing myself mentally for when Gill delivered her best man's speech. Traditionally, this was the opportunity to rip into the groom, pulling out all those embarrassing stories he'd rather keep under wraps and generally having as much fun as possible at his expense. Gill didn't need to do much homework; she'd known me as long as anyone could, and better than most ever should. But I'd become impossible to embarrass around the time I started telling everyone the gory details about my trip to Ecuador. I'd just launched a career based on re-telling the stupidest things I'd ever done and said, so I didn't have much to fear. Learning to laugh at myself had been easier than expected; after all, everyone else was doing it. So although I was still a tiny bit concerned, I felt I could survive anything Gill threw at me.

It never occurred to me to worry about Sonja.

She opened with the usual flurry of thank-yous, then mentioned that she'd known we'd be getting engaged way ahead of the event. Apparently, she'd read about it?

Eh?

Then, to my horror, she pulled out a crumpled magazine and smoothed its creases on the table. "I knew my sister had started dating him, but imagine my surprise when I saw this – a story, written by Tony, entitled 'Love In The Pumpkin Fields'..."

Oh God. Oh no! Oh please God, no!

"I'll just read you a little bit..."

NOOO! Anything but that!

And she was lying, because she read the whole damn thing.

My face glowed like a beacon. I'd written that article whilst camping in Margaret River, and to my shame, it was the first thing that I ever had published. It was in the cheesiest, trashiest of women's magazines – those ridiculously cheap, flimsy things you find piles of in dentist's waiting rooms. They'd been offering a prize of $200 for stories of true love, and we'd been desperate for cash. Telling no-one but Roo, I'd penned an awfully trite account of our courtship whilst working on a pumpkin plantation in northern Australia. I'd exaggerated a fair bit – every emotion was overwrought, and our love burned hotter than the surrounding bush-fires. Seeing no other option, I'd ended the piece with me proposing to Roo, both of us still plastered with mud in the middle of a pumpkin field.

Hearing it again – read aloud to me in someone else's voice – was agonizing!

Every cliché I'd abused, every torrid metaphor I'd pulled out – every pathetic, sappy word revealed... to the entire wedding party! Most of whom were in hysterics.

As the final, cringe inducing line approached, I slid down in my chair and put my hands over my eyes.

Sonja grinned at me over the magazine as she delivered the coup de grace; "And that's when I knew, I had found my true Australian Princess."

Oh. My. God.

Argh.

I think she got more applause for that story than I got for kissing Roo at the end of the ceremony.

All I could do, as the jeers and cat-calls rolled over me, was to make a brief plea to the crowd.

"In my defence," I said, "I was young, and I needed the money..."

My whole life, I thought I'd never see that article again. I honestly thought I'd gotten away with it.

The magazine has since been framed.

After that, my own speech passed in a breeze. I openly admitted that I'd been writing it with my teeth whilst driving to the wedding, and offered my scrawled and shredded notes as proof. They'd been in the pocket of my super-tight trousers since the Donning of The Boots, and consequently were now quite moist. Partly because of this, and partly because I was dying of shame inside, I kept it mercifully brief; I don't think I insulted anyone by accident (which is rare for me) and if I did, well, it was my wedding day so they probably forgave me.

Then came Gill's turn. After describing some of the ways we'd tried to kill each other throughout our childhood, she brought things bang up to date by describing how my relationship with Roo had begun.

"I knew they were going to get together," she explained, "because they spent more and more time play-fighting in the pool. Then one day Tony went for a shower, and Roo also went for a shower... and they didn't come back for *three hours.*"

There were groans from the crowd; they all knew where this was headed.

"And I *knew* they were in there, but I really had to pee. I mean, *three hours*, for God's sake! I held it for as long as I could, then I went into the toilet block stomping my feet and coughing as loud as I could. It was dead silent in there – apart from the occasional giggle – but sure enough, there were two sets of feet in the end shower stall..."

Thankfully, she left it there. Instead she moved on to give me some valuable advice – based, she admitted, on her having had vastly more experience of married life (three weeks and counting!).

"If you want a peaceful marriage – and this goes out to all the men in the room – you just have to practice these three little words: 'Yes, my Queen.' Come on, say it altogether!"

"Yes, my Queen," rumbled the men.

"Perfect! Let's try it. Honey, will you do the dishes?"

"Yes, my Queen," chorused the men.

"Honey, would you mind moving the couch back to where it was the first time?"

"Yes, my Queen."

"Honey, can you hold all my bags while I try those jeans on again?"

"Yes, my Queen!"

"Well done! See, it's not much to ask, really – just unquestioning obedience – and it will make her very happy. Which in turn will make you very happy. Because if she's the Queen, guess what that makes you?"

There was a spilt second of silence while her point hit home.

"The KING!" they cheered.

"So, without further ado, I'd like to raise a glass to the King and Queen – Tony and Krista!"

And finally, to thunderous applause, it was over.

Gill's speech had been witty, concise, and had skated just close enough to the borders of decency to embarrass me profusely, but no-one else.

Although Roo was still blushing from head to toe.

But Sonja? How on earth had she found out? Even writing about it a couple of years later, I still get snakes in my tummy. God damn you Sonja!

Well played.

Dirty Dancing

The food, now that its time had arrived, was another success. Only marginally more posh than regular pub food, it was still a revelation to the Aussies – they have bars and restaurants over there of course, but nothing to rival the traditional English pub. We had beef medallions, chicken breast stuffed with brie, salmon steaks in champagne sauce and some vegetable-based muck for the vegetarians. It was all beautifully presented, and Kaz once again exceeded her brief; we wanted plenty of food so our guests felt well-fed, and she'd managed to pull it off superbly. After our top table was served, everyone else queued up buffet-style – going back for seconds, and even thirds in some cases. The simple food was a triumph. Rather than forcing exotic dishes with names they couldn't pronounce on our guests, we'd given them what they'd most likely order themselves on a night out. My family aren't exactly connoisseurs of the finer things in life, so most of them were pleased they didn't have to spend half the dinner guessing which fork to use.

Champagne kept arriving at my elbow – typically by the bottle – so I rather enjoyed that leisurely hour of stuffing myself silly. Roo was just relieved she'd made it this far without passing out – over dinner she admitted that it was the first thing she'd eaten since the night before, having been too nervous for breakfast and too rushed for lunch.

Weddings, eh! Who'd have 'em?

Cutting the cake was a little different for us because of the cupcakes. They made a lovely colourful display in one corner, arranged on a many-tiered stand we'd bought on eBay. A special cake-cutting knife was one of the insignificant details that had never found its way onto our radar; Roo had the perfect alternative though, and drew the long, hand-forged knife I'd worn in lieu of a sword. I couldn't resist the temptation to lark around, so I held a cupcake in my teeth while she sliced it in half – both of us had been drinking by this point, as had the majority of the guests, which meant the trick was both far more dangerous and far more enthusiastically received than it would have been an hour ago. And then, as people lounged around munching their cakes, Gill told me it was time to get Roo onto the dance floor. For the first time in my life, I beckoned my wife to come to me. She'd been lucky enough to score a second cupcake, and made sure to take a bite out of it so that no-one else could steal it while she was away.

Gill gave me the nod, meaning the music was cued up. I strode into the middle of the dance floor, leading Roo by one delicate hand. I stopped and turned around, and it was only then, scanning the wall of expectant faces arrayed before me, that I realised I had forgotten something after all.

Every eyeball in the place was fixed on us, eagerly awaiting the start of our dance.

Only, we didn't have a dance.

I'd remembered to choose the music, as every couple appreciates the significance of 'their song' – but not until that moment had it occurred to me that every single guest at the wedding would be stood around in a circle, scrutinizing our first dance from less than three feet away.

Now, I may have mentioned that one of my defining characteristics is clumsiness. Unsurprisingly, this trait does not lend itself well to the mastery of dance; hence the reason I have never progressed beyond the level of the 'big-fish-little-fish-cardboard-box' type hand-jive. Well, I can do a rather exaggerated finger-point à la Saturday Night Fever, but this didn't seem like the right time to unleash that puppy. I was wearing knee-high leather riding boots, with slippery leather soles, a substantial heel and not quite enough flexibility to let me walk normally in them. And Roo was wearing flip-flops. The likelihood of her spending our wedding night with a broken toe loomed large in my mind.

We faced each other across the polished wooden floor, and I could see her expression mirroring the horror in mine.

Oh shit, it said, *how could we not have thought about this?*

It was like that dream where you realise you're naked in front of your whole school class – only this was real, and no amount of fancy clothes could conceal the fact that neither of us could dance if our lives depended on it.

But there was nothing for it – the crowd was seething with anticipation, and we had to give them something.

The music started, and the opening bars of Aerosmith's *I Don't Want To Miss A Thing* drifted out of the speakers.

Roo approached nervously, with a look that said 'this isn't going to end well.'

But it was too late to do anything about it, so I pulled her in close, wrapped my arms around her – and we waggled slowly back and forth for five-and-a-half agonizing minutes.

"Is it over yet?" she whispered, her lips only centimetres from my ear.

"No," I hissed, "they're still looking!"

"Oh crap. Keep waggling!"

And that is what I did, until Gill had mercy on us and faded out the music halfway through the final chorus. The thunderous applause that greeted us told me two things; that most of my guests were already drunk, and that they too were very glad the dance was over. It must have been almost as awkward to watch as it was to experience.

"Thank God that's finished," Roo said as the party music started cranking and the dance floor flooded with people.

"Hell yeah!" I agreed. "Right. I'm going to get a drink. And I believe that your next job is to dance with your dad, then my dad, then the best man... enjoy yourself!"

And I legged it off the dance floor as fast as my boots would carry me.

I spent the next couple of hours propping up the bar. Now that all the ceremonial stuff was over I was finally free to chat with my guests, some of whom were friends I'd hardly seen since university. I lost count of how many drinks I was bought that evening, but it was certainly more than I could have survived without a trip to hospital. Bizarrely, I drank almost none of them; I was so excited to catch up with my friends that I hardly touched a drop, nursing one bottle of cider for so long that at one point I had eight more drinks lined up waiting for me, and had to give them away to make room on the bar! Along with cider, people kept buying me champagne – only they seemed to do this in bottles, so that by the time Roo came to find me I was festooned with the things. It was a great excuse not to dance: I had champagne bottles protruding from every crevice I could stuff one in, and still they kept coming. Roo wasn't so easily deterred however, and hauled me off to the dance floor to visit the guests that weren't crowding the bar.

The Dutch contingent were having a great old time; they'd smuggled in a CD of folk music and convinced Kaz to put it on, and they were stomping around in some sort of traditional clog-dance. It was impossible not to join in, so infectious was their energy, and soon most of the wedding party had linked arms in a big circle and were rushing in towards each other like they were doing the *Hokey-Cokey*.

I was outside taking a breather when the fight kicked off – someone was dancing too enthusiastically with someone else's wife, and suddenly there were shouts and shrieks as a couple of the bigger blokes tumbled out into the courtyard trading punches.

But what's a wedding without at least one brawl, eh?

All too soon the festivities were winding up, and it was time to think about heading back to the Travelodge.

The trip was accomplished by doing two runs in the same minibus, thereby making the saving that had allowed Roo to arrive in such style. I was still amazed that everything had worked out so well, creating a seamless experience for the guests in spite of our modest budget. It had been a huge amount of work to make it all happen, but at the end of the night I decided it had all been worthwhile. We'd managed to have the wedding of our dreams for less money than some couples spend on the dress; Roo, bless her, had been as excited as I was every time we made a saving, and none of it would have been possible without her can-do attitude. I felt so lucky to have found her. I couldn't imagine anyone else complimenting me as much as she did. Any other woman would have told me to bugger off the second I suggested buying a wedding dress on eBay.

More Booty

Roo and I were the last to leave the Winchester. We'd have stayed the night if we could, but by then most of our guests were on their way to the Days Inn. There was enough booze stored there to keep the party going for the rest of the week, but it still felt like a wrench, leaving our reception. It signified that the whole thing was over, that all the energy we'd put into the dreaming and planning of this day was used up. It had been a spectacular success, but it was finished.

Tomorrow would be just another day; the first one of the rest of our lives, as the saying goes.

When we reached the Days Inn, we let our guests check in first, as we didn't want anyone else to be last. The receptionist was doing a staggeringly crap job of organising all the rooms, greeting every member of the group with confused questions, almost as though no-one had told him we'd booked out half the hotel.

When our turn came, I figured there couldn't be too many problems. By now there should only be one room left.

"Double room, please," I said, putting on an encouraging smile for the bloke.

His reply was less than encouraging.

"I haven't got any double rooms left. There's a big wedding party in tonight, so we're all booked up."

I sighed, and put my arm around Roo. "Look, I know this sounds crazy, what with her standing here in a wedding dress and all, but we are part of that wedding party."

"Oh. So you're in the 'Slater-Reynen Wedding Group' booking, are you?"

I was fighting to keep the sarcasm from my voice. "Yes. Yes we are."

"Okay. What name, please?"

"Mr and Mrs Slater-Reynen."

"Hm… Slater… Reynen…" He was actually checking the listings. "I don't think I've got you down for a double room."

"I'm a hundred percent sure that you have, because I made the booking myself. I made it very carefully over several weeks, and it is itemized exactly. And in case you haven't noticed, we are the bride and groom. We've only been married for eight hours, so we *really* don't want to be sleeping in separate beds."

"Well I can have a look if number four's a double, but I don't think so..."

He started rooting through his desk for keys. I was contemplating strangling him with his own tie, when two of my teenage cousins burst in, looking for me. I recognized the look of panic on their faces straight away. I'd last seen them getting on the bus, escorting their younger sister who'd been doing what I did at weddings when I was her age – drinking everything I could lay my hands on.

"Oh-oh. Is she okay?"

"She's not very well..."

Roo stepped up to the desk. "Don't worry, I'll sort the room out. You go and make sure she's alright."

"Thanks love."

I left the world's dumbest receptionist to his blundering and followed the girls through the doors to the stairwell. "So, what's up?"

"Thing is, she's actually not too bad now, but she, er... she made a bit of a mess..."

I looked down as we climbed the stairs. There was a small puddle of vomit on every second or third step, as though she'd been struggling to contain it all the way up – and then, on reaching the landing, it had finally proved too much for her. A vast pool of spew saturated the carpet, lapping gently against the fire-door. Chunks of mushroom floated on a sea of alcohol; she'd had the capsicum stuffed with wild rice, from the look of things.

This was a bit of a worry. My cousin was going to feel pretty rough tomorrow, but that kind of goes with the territory the first time you get wasted; she'd either learn to love it, or learn to hate it. The problem was the idiot on the desk – he was bound to go walkabout at some point, inspecting the building or checking my guests weren't getting too rowdy. If he saw this before we could get it cleaned up, there'd be a monumental bill waiting for us when we checked out. Rock stars wreck hotel rooms all the time, but I wasn't quite there yet; a six-figure salary leaves enough leeway to smooth over this kind of issue, but my book earnings to date were a measly £120. I didn't want to start my marriage in debt to the *Days Inn* for God's sake!

"Right, you go and make sure she's still okay," I said to the girls. "Try to get her to drink some water." They nodded, looking glum, and sped off down the corridor.

Glancing around, I spied a cleaning closet. There was an old vacuum cleaner inside, but I had a feeling it would do more harm than good. There wasn't much else for sucking up spilled stomach contents, but on the top shelf I discovered one of those industrial-sized rolls of flimsy one-ply toilet paper. This would have to be my salvation. I lugged the roll outside and tore off several handfuls, wadding them up around the edge of the vomit to stop it spreading further. Then, ripping off another few lengths, I rolled my sleeves up and got stuck in.

Ten minutes later, another trio of my cousins arrived, rushing up the stairs in crisis-response mode. They rounded the corner and froze in horror, staring at me as though they'd caught me molesting a dead donkey.

"Hi guys, I said cheerfully, "bit of a mess I'm afraid."

Sarah, leading the pack, chose her words wisely. "Tony, it's your wedding night, and you're on your hands and knees in the corridor, mopping up vomit. Are you *sure* you don't have *anything else* you should be doing?"

"Ah... that is a good point..."

"Yes, quite. We'll take it from here."

And they surrounded me, relieving me of vast amounts of soggy bog-roll, and shoed me back downstairs.

"Give me a shout if you need a hand," I called from the landing below them.

"No, we won't!" came the reply.

Roo was waiting for me in my friend Mark's room, where the after-party was just kicking off. I apologised for being late and explained the situation. Mark, a snowboarder friend I'd met while stranded in Méribel, summed it up in the appropriate vernacular: "That is *fully sick*," he told me.

"Did we get a room?" I asked Roo.

"We did," she said. "It's opposite your Mum and Dad's room I'm afraid, but it's a double. Actually it's a disabled room. I'm not quite sure why we ended up in there, but it's got a double bed in it, so I didn't bother asking."

"Ah! That sounds fine." I poured myself a drink from the crowded minibar that had been created on the TV cabinet. It held all the booze we'd brought from home, plus several bottles that people had sneaked out of the Winchester. It was a very tempting spread, as I'd somehow made it through the entire reception without getting even remotely drunk.

Now, at last, surrounded by my closest friends, I could relax.

At least, I could once my damn boots were off.

"Anyone want to give me a hand here...?"

Sally took charge. Perhaps because she'd helped me put them on, she had some idea of what to expect.

"Right!" she shouted, above the general cacophony of drunken hilarity. "You three, hold him down."

Three of my guests obligingly pinned me to the bed, leaving only my legs and my head protruding from the man-pile.

"Now you lot – grab that," she ordered.

More hands fastened themselves around my boot than could feasibly hold on to it. Enthusiasm was trumping common sense, which is not unheard of where large amounts of drink are involved.

"Brace yourself Tony," said Sally, "this might get a bit uncomfortable."

I didn't have the breath to answer her, so I nodded.

"Okay, NOW!" she bawled.

With a many-throated roar the pulling team heaved back on my boots, fingers digging in wherever they could.

"ARRRRR!" I cried, more from surprise than pain – my pullers were doing a particularly savage job, dragging me half out from under the pile of sweaty bodies. "It won't work! It's too tight!"

A deep voice at the back yelled, "WE NEED LUBRICANT!"

And everyone dissolved into fits of laughter.

At that point it occurred to me to wonder what our neighbours thought of us. On the other side of that flimsy partition wall was a couple, or perhaps a family on holiday, innocently partaking of their night's accommodation. A call for lubricant was the last thing they wanted to hear from next door.

And I bet they could hear every word.

Just as I decided to mention this, Sally reached a conclusion of her own.

"We can't do it like this," she said. "We can't get the right angle." She called to the lads holding me down. "You lot – get off him and flip him over."

"No, no!" I yelled, "just give it up!"

"Aww, are we hurting you?" asked Sally. "Do you want something to bite down on?"

"No, I mean—"

"Right, hold him tight!" she yelled.

"OWWwww!"

"Oh, don't be a baby," said Mark, "it'll only hurt for a minute."

It hurt for longer than that, but the party carried on unabated. I bowed out less than gracefully at around 4am, because I had a wife to take care of. This was our wedding night, after all. I left the room to promises that all traces of the party would be cleared away by morning – and to the credit of my guests, they were. Personally I blame Sally and Mark, who managed to dispose of all the remaining alcohol by themselves. I think they finally stopped drinking at around the time I was getting up again, but they were as good as their word – the room was spotless. The same was true of the rest of the hotel. You'd never know there'd been a party at the Days Inn at all – well, except for the drying patches of vomit on the stairs. Oh, and there was one other minor detail...

Off to A Flying Start

On my first morning as a married man, I was faced with the same series of dilemmas most newly-wedded males encounter. Chief amongst these was my intense desire to stay in bed with my wife, something I couldn't do on account of having guests that needed attention – and because we were going to be kicked out of our room in ten minutes anyway.

The next issue may be more familiar to the female half of most couples, in that I had simply *nothing* to wear. My wedding outfit was a screwed-up ball of sweat-stained shirt and skin-tight trousers; it was about the least appealing thing I could think of wearing to breakfast with my entire extended family.

Unfortunately, I had no choice. The rest of my clothes were still where I'd left them – in the Grand Ballroom of the Castle Hotel, in the centre of Taunton.

My shoes were with them.

My focus on the events of the day itself had been so complete, I hadn't spared a single thought for the next day; the result of this was that I hadn't even brought a change of underwear.

Which didn't matter, as I never wore underwear anyway.

I was kind of wishing I'd brought a toothbrush though.

Or socks.

Or anything other than a skin-tight, quasi-medieval costume that I'd still been partying in five hours ago.

"What are you going to wear?" I asked Roo, as she began to stir.

"Good morning, husband!" she yawned.

"Oh yeah, good morning my wife!"

We shared a giggle at the absurdity of that notion.

"We're *married!* How weird is that?"

"I know!"

Then, as Roo reluctantly swung her legs out of bed, I broached the topic again.

"Are you wearing your... outfit again?"

"No, course not! I'm putting my shorts on."
"Oh! You brought clothes?"
"Of course. What, you didn't?"
"I had a lot on my mind yesterday!"
"I bet you're glad I brought clothes then."
"Yes! Well done, love. What did you bring?"
"I told you. Shorts and a singlet."
"No, I mean, what did you bring for me?"
"Why would I bring clothes for you?"

Donning my wedding shirt chased away any vestiges of sleep; it was cold and clammy. *Still moist*, I thought. *Yummy*.

That done, I eyed the boots wearily. Half an hour and at least three assistants would be required to get them on, and I just couldn't face that twice in twenty-four hours.

Barefoot, then. Hell, it wouldn't be my first time.

Strolling across the car park in her short-shorts, long blonde hair loose around her shoulders, Roo looked a bit like Daisy Duke. Holding her hand, bedraggled and shoeless, I looked more akin to a contestant on *Survivor*.

Our wedding crowd were choosing their breakfasts from the café. The Days Inn had done us a great deal; for an extra £5 with our accommodation, we'd each been given a voucher for £8's worth of breakfast. By some amazing coincidence, the cheapest thing on the menu was also £8, leading some to believe there was a cleverly-orchestrated scam going on. But never mind – the food was surprisingly good, and all the more welcome after the night of dancing and drinking. No-one batted an eyelid when I explained why I was barefoot – after all, these were people who knew me. There was some concern over where my parents were though, as no-one had seen them all morning.

When they did show up, Dad was looking sheepish. I could just tell that something had happened, so I tackled him straight away.

"What's wrong?"

"Oh, nothing to worry about," said Mum.

"Really?"

"Well, you know they put us in the room opposite yours?"

"Yes?"

"When we checked in last night, the man on the desk said he was giving us that room because we were responsible and sober."

I stifled a snigger. "Sorry. And?"

"Well, he warned us that there was no spare key for that room, so we had to be extra-careful that we didn't get locked out of it."

"And what happened?"

"We got locked out of it."

"What? How?"

"Oh, ask your dad. He had to take the damn dog for a walk…"

"I thought she was in the bathroom," Dad explained. "I told her I was going out with Cassie…"

"Only I wasn't in the bathroom, was I?" Mum chipped in.

"…so I shut the door, and then met Mum in reception."

"Ah."

"But don't worry," he finished, "they've got a bloke working on it right now."

"Oh dear. I'll go and see what's happening."

"No," said Mum, "no need for that. Finish your breakfast!"

"I'm a married man now," I reminded her. "You don't need to tell me to finish my breakfast! I've got man-things to do."

As I set off back through the car park, I could almost feel her shaking her head in despair.

Crouched by the door to my parent's room, swearing copiously, was a short bloke in overalls. The corridor around him was littered with tools and liberally sprinkled with wood-shavings.

"You alright, mate?" I asked him.

"Just tryin' to drill the lock," he said, pausing to wipe the sweat off his forehead with a rag, "but she won't budge."

He'd pulled away the faceplate from the locking mechanism and removed the door handle, but all that had left him with was the barrel of the lock firmly embedded in the door.

"They're security-bolts y'see, with a metal plate on the other side. Might have been easier to pick it, but…" he waved a hand to indicate the ruined keyhole, chewed up by his power drill. "Don't know what I'm going to do, to be honest. Think I'll have to call the boss."

He didn't sound too thrilled about that.

Instantly, I knew this was my moment. Being married was already doing all kinds of worrying things to my confidence.

"Stand back," I told the bloke, "I'm going to kick it in."

"Eh? You're welcome to try, but there's not much room."

"Don't worry – I'm staying in the room opposite!"

I produced my keys and opened the door to my room. I don't know if it filled him with confidence or not, to realise I was related to the idiots who had caused this problem in the first place.

"Are you sure you wanna do this?" he asked.

Hell yeah! I wanted to say. But I was afraid that might make me sound a little unhinged. I mean, who doesn't want to try kicking a door down, given the chance? A *security* door? With permission!"

"Yeah, I'll give it a go," I said, struggling to keep the excitement from my voice.

The bloke scraped his pile of tools out of the way as I retreated a few steps into my room. "Don't hurt yourself," he warned.

"I won't," I promised.

He glanced down at my feet. "Um... are you going to put some shoes on first?"

"Nope."

And then it was time. I advanced a step, sprang forward another, and unleashed a front-kick that was aimed ten inches beyond the door. My foot slammed into the polished wood with even more enthusiasm that I'd expected, and with a mighty CRACK! the door burst inwards. A split second later there was a clang from the far side of the room, as the steel reinforcing plate shot across it and bounced off the opposite wall.

Broken lock components tinkled to the floor as the door quivered in its frame.

"Fuckin' 'ell! Well done lad," said the maintenance man.

"No worries," I told him. "Not my first time."

"Ahh."

"So, are you okay with this?" I asked.

"Oh yeah, I'll sort it out. Thanks for yer help though."

"Any time."

I strode off down the corridor, and waited until I was out of sight around the corner before I stopped and looked at my foot.

It looked normal.

Which didn't explain why my whole leg felt like it was about to drop off at the hip, but I guess that was to be expected. Slowly, the wave of pain subsided, and I dared to put my weight on the offending foot again. It hurt – but I could walk.

Kind of.

As I limped back to the café, my parents were just finishing their breakfasts.

"Did you help him get it open?" Dad asked.

"Oh yeah. Smashed it."

"That's great! How did you do it? With the drill?"

"No." I slapped my leg, eliciting a wave of pain from my joints. "I actually smashed it."

"Oh?"

"Yeah. You, ah, might be getting a bill..."

It was a long time before the partying died down.

Some guests left straight away, driving back up north or taxiing to the airport. Most notably Sue and Phil, long-term friends of Roo's family who have been traveling the world since before we were born, hitch-hiked out of there.

Despite our hotel being on the motorway services.

Their loose plan was to pick up a lift from somewhere, heading somewhere else...

Now that's the kind of travel planning even I admire!

But most of my new Australian family stayed on at Holly Cottage, and due to the vast quantity of champagne we'd amassed over the course of the wedding, we drank the stuff with breakfast, lunch and dinner, every day for a week.

It was a really great time, with constant comings and goings and a carnival atmosphere that never seemed to end. Roo and I didn't get much alone time however, and when we did it wasn't the sort of *quality* alone time that newlyweds crave – after all, we were still sleeping in the tent.

One by one our guests departed, until Holly Cottage was empty once more. Sonja was the last to leave, having spent her final evening in the country helping Roo dye her hair into pink and turquoise stripes; honestly, I think Roo was done with being a grown-up. Gill and Chris had gone back to stay with his mum in Hampshire, leaving Mum, Dad, Roo and myself to figure out what would happen next.

Nothing much, seemed the obvious answer.

But unbeknownst to us, Dad had a plan.

Without warning, in a spontaneous display of generosity, he booked us a honeymoon in Spain. We were staggered. Perhaps Mum had been nagging him about grand-kids? She'd certainly been nagging me.

Hell, she'd been nagging me from the moment I met Roo.

Before we were together, even.

"But Gill and Chris got married first..." had become my stock response.

Dad had decided to take the bull by the horns, seeing as how we clearly weren't going anywhere under our own steam. He was from a generation where, when you got married, you moved out straight away. The same night, even, carrying your beloved across the threshold of the home you had prepared for her. Whereas I was a poster child of the current generation; in some ways I'd moved out years ago, but at the same time I'd never left at all.

Perhaps buying us a holiday was his idea of a subtle hint?

The Honeymoon in Spain

We arrived in Torremolinos, and immediately began ███ Then we ███ after which we were ready for ███ Later on, we ███ But it wasn't long before Roo ███ And then she ███ as we ███

Later still, ███ and ███ and even ███! ███, ███ with an elongated egg-whisk! ███, ███ bizarre bull statue with an anatomically correct anus… ███ And ███ "I'm going for an ice cream." ███ sand in every crevice ███ said Roo.
"Yeah," I agreed, " I think it's broken."
On our last day we ███, ███, and ███!
And before we knew it, we were on the plane home.

Departure

Gramp passed away a few weeks later.

He'd been in pain for some time, and was taking a cocktail of pills every few hours to control it. Then one night, dozing on his sofa, I had a dream about my Nan. She'd visited me in my dreams for months after we lost her, until finally she'd told me that she couldn't stay any longer, and had to move on. I hadn't dreamed about her in over a decade, but suddenly she was back, walking through the house, opening drawers, touching different objects and peering around as though searching for something. She looked completely different, with someone else's face, but I knew instantly that it was her.

"What are you doing?" I asked her.

"I'm looking for the missing part of me," she said.

The next morning Gramp was admitted to hospital.

I'd like to say he passed peacefully, but that wasn't the case. There was very nearly a stand up fight between my family and the nurses over the quality of care he received. On admission I'd been given an 'All About Me' form to fill in on his behalf. I spent a good thirty minutes painstakingly describing not only his medical conditions and his physical and mental states, but answering questions about his favourite foods and TV shows.

So Dad got a bit of a shock the next day, when an orderly from the hospital called him at work to ask why Gramp was having so much difficulty walking.

"He can't walk! He's been in a wheelchair for months!" Dad said.

"Well he says he can walk," came the response.

"That's because he's suffering from dementia, you bloody idiot! If you ask him where he is he'll probably tell you he's in Berlin as part of the Army of Occupation!"

I won't go into more detail as it was a very upsetting episode for all of us, but Gramp went into hospital with a stomach ache, and less than twenty-four hours later he was comatose.

Leaving Roo at home to dog sit, Mum, Dad, Gill and I spent a long, long night by Gramp's bedside, powerless to do anything but watch him sleep.

Nothing changed.

I'd been getting some funny looks from the nurses, and couldn't figure out what was wrong until Gill pointed at my t-shirt. I hadn't thought about it, just grabbed the first clothes to hand – consequently I was stood in the middle of a hospital wearing a t-shirt that read 'I DO BAD THINGS'.

When Gramp's breathing quickened, suggesting he was in pain, a syringe-driver was called for. Gill and I shared a grin, as she wondered aloud whether a burly bloke in a hardhat was about to show up, piloting a truck with a giant needle on the front of it.

In actual fact the syringe-driver was a tiny plastic device, powered by AA batteries, which automated the process of gradually pushing the plunger on a hefty dose of morphine. Gramp was nearing the end of his struggle now, and after variously dozing in chairs, sitting by his side and holding his hand, we were struggling ourselves. We'd rushed into hospital at 4am; it was now after 2pm, and Gramp's condition hadn't changed. We were exhausted, emotionally drained, hungry, thirsty and suffering from cabin fever.

Figuring that the next ten minutes was unlikely to be any different, Gill and I nipped out to fetch some food from the supermarket. I drove Gramp's Micra, and the world outside the hospital was bathed in sunlight, a gorgeous afternoon utterly at odds with the storm raging inside me. I was speed-choosing sandwiches to take back to the hospital when Mum rang; Gill took the call, nodded once, then grabbed me by the shoulder.

"We've got to go *now*," she said.

Flinging aside armfuls of sandwich packets we sprinted for the entrance, scattering incoming customers like ninepins. We leapt into the car and cursed as I crawled through the endless succession of speed cameras leading back towards the hospital. Ignoring the parking meters we barged into the building, charging up three flights of stairs rather than wait for the lift. We skidded around the corridor corners and into the room – just as Granddad breathed his last.

Mum looked up at us. "You made it," she said, "he was waiting for you."

And all four of us broke down in tears.

An hour later it was all over. We'd collected Gramp's few meagre possessions, and his earthly remains were in the care of the nurses. Now began The Process, which as anyone who's lost someone will know, involves an awful lot more than time and grieving. First, there was paperwork. Then there was more paperwork. There was a funeral to organize, venues to book, lawyers to be called, wills to be read, taxes to be paid, fees to be paid, and paperwork, paperwork, paperwork.

Even dying isn't easy.

There was also the small matter of Gramp's flat – and the lifetime of accumulated stuff he'd brought with him from Scarborough. We had a scaled-down version of the same job to do here as we'd done there, only this time every discovery was tinged with sadness, and for the most part it was achieved in a sombre, uncharacteristically quiet manner.

It couldn't last, though. Gramp had always been pragmatic about death, having spent the last few years expecting it at any moment. He'd often said to us "I could pop off at any time, you know!" – quite cheerfully, as though he'd long since lost any fear associated with it.

So it was that I found myself laughing again – at Gill, as usual – as she tried to get a handle on her irrational fear of a doll left in Gramp's flat. We'd both grown up seeing this doll on visits to Scarborough – it had spent most of the time in the living room, gazing lifelessly out at us. I thought it was hideous, a big plastic lump the size of a small child, with frizzy ginger hair.

Gill, however, was scared shitless of the thing.

She wouldn't touch it, wouldn't even go near it, and she now recounted a fear of the doll stretching back as far as she could remember. It *really* freaked her out when she walked into Gramp's bedroom the following day and found the doll had dropped its pants. I refused to comment about my involvement in such shenanigans, but I did move the thing around occasionally just to mess with her.

The doll was one of the last things for us to get rid of; partly because it was iconic, and partly because I was having too much fun scaring Gill with it. When it came time to take it to the charity shop, Gill recoiled as I carried it past.

"I though you liked that doll!" Mum exclaimed.

"What? No way!" Gill shook her head vehemently. "I hate that friggin' thing!"

"I though you loved it, because when you were a baby, Nanna used to stand it in your cot at night to watch over you."

Gill's mouth fell open. "Oh for God's sake!" she said. "So I've been shit scared of that thing for three decades, because it used to terrorize me as a baby? Who puts something like that in a baby's cot? It's three feet tall and looks like a dead thing!"

"So, now you know," I said.

"Bloody hell! Yes, now I know."

"So," I held the doll out to her, "kiss and make-up?"

Gramp's small bathroom wasn't in the best of states, so cleaning it fell to me. He hadn't been able to use the shower for several months and the place was crammed with half-used bottles and products, many of which I suspected had come with him from Scarborough. One by one I prized the tops off, tipping the contents down the toilet before chucking the crusty bottles into a bin bag. The effect on the toilet bowl was striking; psychedelic, as though assorted aliens from Star Trek held a projectile vomiting contest in it.

It wasn't until I decided to flush the multi-coloured goop away that I realized my mistake; despite not actually having a bath in that room — or perhaps because of it — a significant proportion of what I had just emptied down the toilet was bubble-bath.

In seconds, a tsunami of bubbles exploded from the toilet, overwhelmed me, filled the bathroom and advanced down the hall towards Gramp's bedroom. Compounding my first mistake was my second; I'd been kneeling on the floor in front of the loo when I'd reached up to flush it, and consequently I was now up to my ears.

When I could open my eyes again, I retreated to the kitchen. There I found my mother on her hands and knees, her head buried in the cupboard under the sink. It must have been quite a feat of contortion getting into that position, with the kitchen being as narrow as it was. I had to step over the protruding portion of her (which I occasionally referred to as the more intelligent part) to get in.

I found a disgusting mess of pulped herbs swimming in the sink, which was rather inconvenient. "I want to wash my face," I moaned.

"I thought you were in the bathroom?" she responded.

"Yeah... you might want to avoid the bathroom for a bit."

"What did you do?"

"Nothing. So what's all the crap in the sink?"

I started to dig the nasty muck out of the plug hole.

"It's rosemary. I was steeping some in wine to give Granddad, when he was first diagnosed with Alzheimer's. It's supposed to be really good for improving memory."

"Did it work?" I asked.

"I don't know. I forgot to give it to him."

I took over in the kitchen for a bit, while Mum went off to investigate the rest of the house. I was still scrubbing away an hour later when there was an almighty crash, followed by some fairly course swearing. I decided against asking what had happened, but Mum filled me in anyway; "I've found the worst thing in the world to drop," she shouted.

I couldn't resist. "What have you dropped?"

"A crate full of light bulbs!"

I was impressed. She really had discovered the worst thing to drop.

But that wasn't the best part. The comedy came when she tried to explain what had happened. From the direction of the crash I could tell she'd been in the under-stairs cupboard, but that's not quite how she put it.

"I was rooting around in the glory hole..." she started.

Now, I've never heard it called that before. She assures me it is a very old, and completely legitimate, name for such a place. I've heard the phrase before of course, but usually in reference to a particularly depraved place in a sex club – for those of you who haven't, I shall leave it to your imagination. As for how I know – well, research of course! It's a writer thing. Honest.

And now I can practically feel your fingers crawling towards Google...

Don't do it. Trust me.

But Mum's best clanger came a few days later. In circle-of-life-esque fashion, shortly after Gramp passed, one of my cousins in Manchester became a father for the first time. It was a ray of light in what was otherwise a fairly dark time for our family, yet Mum, fighting to keep pace in an ever-changing world, brought a steady stream of laughter into our lives.

"Hey guys," she said to us, "come check out Dale's baby on eBay!"

"Uh, Mum," I replied, "I know times are hard in Manchester, but I think you *might* mean Facebook."

A Grand Adventure

The loss of Gramp left an eighty-three-year-old man-shaped hole in our plans. Suddenly, instead of basing our lives around looking after him, we had large quantities of free time that we simply didn't know what to do with. My parents and I had been taking turns sleeping on Gramp's sofa, making sure there was always someone there to help him to the toilet in the middle of the night, and to get him up, washed and dressed in the morning. I didn't mind it one bit and was glad to be of some help, but it had pretty much taken priority over everything else in my life. Now, with Gramp hopefully enjoying a well-earned rest upstairs, I had the opportunity to do something other than sit watching infinite re-runs of *Only Fools And Horses* with him.

But what to do with this new-found freedom?

And perhaps more importantly, what to do with the £1,000 that Gramp had left me in his will?

The idea came whilst driving through Glastonbury.

Roo was behind the wheel of Gramp's Nissan Micra, which I had also inherited – despite not being legally able to drive it – on the grounds that Mum and Dad already had four cars and a camper van between them.

Being Australian, Roo didn't have much appreciation for how history has shaped our fair isle.

"Who put that crappy house there?" she complained, as the road threw an abrupt dog's leg to avoid a crumbling building. "It's in the middle of the bloody road!"

I rolled my eyes skyward. I'd been defending England's quirks since our arrival, and sometimes it seemed like a full-time job.

"My love," I said, "that house probably existed before the road. Lots of places were built before we had cars, which is why all our streets are so narrow."

"But why didn't they just knock it down to make room when they built the road?" she said. "It's not like it's any good. That place was so old it was disintegrating."

"Well, we English are very proud of our heritage. Even if it does get in the way a bit."

"We're proud of our heritage too," she retorted.

"My love, you're Australian. You don't have any heritage. My house is older than your entire country." Which, strictly speaking, was not quite true, but I loved to press her buttons.

"That's bullshit! Australia has had an indigenous population for tens of thousands of years!"

"Yes my love, but so has France. We don't consider *them* civilized, do we?"

I figured I'd made my point, but Roo wouldn't leave it at that.

"We have history," she declared. "We have ancient colonial buildings still around from when the first settlers came to Australia."

"The convicts, you mean?"

"Yeah, so?"

"So you have old prisons."

"Yeah, but they've been renovated! You can do tours of them. We look after our ancient buildings just like you do."

I gave an overly dramatic sigh. "Roo, something has to be a lot older than two hundred years to be considered 'ancient'. Otherwise my mum would qualify."

This gave us both a chuckle.

"You should see if they'll award her National Trust status!" Roo suggested. "You could make some money."

I remained silent on that. I love to take the piss out of my mother, but there are lines that should not be crossed; charging people £12.50 for entering her was probably one of them.

Our constant bantering about English history (or the Australian lack thereof) masked an obsession both Roo and I shared. Since we'd first started looking for a wedding venue, she'd developed a fascination with castles and tumble-down, ruined farmhouses – especially when she wasn't having to detour around them. I've always had a keen interest in the old buildings that litter the English landscape, and I spent half my childhood clambering around every castle my parents would take me to.

This became the genesis of an idea that grew more attractive the longer we thought about it. We could take a trip around England in this little car I'd inherited. We could use the money that had come with it, and see how far we got before it ran out. It would be like an extra honeymoon – one that was more 'us'. I could show Roo the best bits of our declining national beauty, and take a last, lingering look around the country of my birth – before I emigrated to hers.

Because the way things were going, by the time I got back most of it would be covered in 'affordable housing'.

My parents seemed to think that blowing my entire inheritance on a one-off jaunt around the UK was a great idea. I guess I'm just lucky that way.

"How long will you take?" asked Dad.
"Dunno. See how far we can get on the cash, I suppose."
"Not very, is the answer to that!"
"Are you going to write about it?" Mum wanted to know.
"Dunno. Maybe."
"You can call it your Grand Adventure!"
So. That was settled, then.

We planned to travel as cheaply as possible. We're backpackers at heart and happy that way; we just had a slightly bigger, bright blue backpack made of steel. With an engine in it. To celebrate this, we stuffed the car every bit as full of random shit as we usually do our rucksacks. Then, because Roo is incapable of treating a car as, you know, *a car*, she named him 'Bubble', and decided to decorate him all over with stickers designed for a wheelie bin.

I knew she'd secretly harboured a desire to do this since we first started driving him, but until recently he'd been technically on loan.

The last time we'd driven Gramp up to visit relatives in the north, I'd made the mistake of telling him we'd be going in 'my' car.

"I think you'll find it's my car," he'd said without missing a beat.

I can't imagine he'd approve of us covering the thing in dolphins.

Gods, I missed him.

Once the car was suitably bedecked in garden gnomes, ice creams and cartoon octopus, Roo added one last touch; a plastic dragon cable-tied to the grill. She explained it to me like this; "We have to have a plastic dragon on the grill or no-one will notice us!"

I held my tongue. I couldn't fault this logic. I didn't even want to try.

We were almost ready to go. Only one thing was missing (well, unless you count my dignity) – we had no concept at all of where we were going.

It is because of this issue that I have decided to create a 'Guide To A

Grand Adventure', which I will be sharing with you as we go along. This seems like an appropriate juncture to lay the first part on you:

The First Step in a Grand Adventure:
Plan the Grand Adventure. At least a little bit.

This is how we went about our planning. We got out our Road Atlas of Great Britain. This venerable document was on loan from my Dad, and had been our companion through many a difficult journey. Unfortunately, it had a tendency to make those journeys even more difficult, because it was complete bollocks. Entire motorways had been known to emerge in the physical plain right in front of us, despite there being absolutely no warning from the trusty road map. Only one page was missing, but no matter where we went it was *always* that page we needed. Or the one on the back of it.

I flicked to the contents page, as the front cover had long since crumbled to dust. I had my suspicions, but travelling at sixty miles an hour towards Spaghetti Junction – when you're desperate not to be – never seemed like the right time to be reading the small print. Now, having gone to the extraordinary lengths of bringing the map into the house, I wanted to check one tiny detail.

And there it was. Ha! That explained a few things. It had been published in 1994.

So I threw out our Road Atlas of Great Britain and stole my sister's instead.

The reason behind the surprisingly archaic atlas is that when driving, my Dad relies on some mystical sixth sense to find his way. Seriously – the guy is part pigeon. He can do amazing things like – when caught in a motorway traffic jam a hundred miles from home – come off at the nearest exit, know full well where he is, and create an alternative route spontaneously. Based on the fact that he 'visited a customer not far from here in July 1982, and it's still mostly the same...' An almost eerily good memory for complex road systems, combined with years working as a traveling IT salesman, has turned my Dad into a human Sat-nav. Google spent thousands of hours, millions of dollars and the odd supercomputer figuring out their journey-planning system around the UK. All they really needed to do was ask my dad.

My sister Gill, however, has a far more pragmatic approach to reaching her destination.

She looks it up, and follows directions carefully.

Or she would do, if she still had her map.

I thought about planning our route according to the sights we most wanted to see; I took into account Dad's sage advice on all the country's worst traffic hotspots, and any other places I specifically wanted to avoid. Finally I made a mental list of all the cities we could stay in for free, with friends and relatives who had offered us a bed, sofa or back garden for the night. It was shaping up to be a tricky task, reconciling all these variables into a coherent strategy. I never had to do it though, because Roo had ideas of her own.

She spent a quiet morning with the map and a pink highlighter, chuckling to herself and colouring in all the places with the silliest names.

When she was done she displayed her handiwork, proudly flipping the pages of the map for me to see. "Let's to go to these places!" she said.

So that is what we did.

Supply and Demand

We bought a tent that was small enough to carry if we did any hiking. We put it up in my living room using books and piles of camping gear to hold down the guy ropes. Then we crawled inside, the thing collapsed on us and we both suffocated to death.
The End.

Okay, so we didn't die. We did decide that it was a bit too small – the rule, I've come to appreciate, is that all tent manufacturers are full of shit. If the tent can fit one person and a bread roll, they feel justified in calling it a two-man tent. It's like an accepted thing. How do they get away with it? Have you seen the size of men lately? I mean, I'm a bit weedy and Roo is built like a twig, but neither of us could have fitted comfortably in that tent, let alone both of us. The pile of camping gear we'd inadvisably bought at the same time as the tent would fill it – in fact it was a pretty good size for a shopping bag. Maybe if we both cut our arms off and top-and-tailed it, we could just about slide in. But then we'd have to fasten the zippers with our teeth, we'd never be able to get out again and if I got an erection it would tear through the tautly-stretched nylon and pin me in place like a harpoon. It'd probably make a nice perch for a bird though.

So we repacked the tiny tent and returned it 'unused' (declining to mention to the shop staff that we'd been forced to cut our way out with a plastic spork).

We bought a bigger tent, which we still felt we could carry – until we got to the car with it. By then my arms were shaking and I was having serious doubts about the proposed hike.

One of Roo's recently acquired ambitions was to walk the length of Hadrian's Wall, the Roman ruin that spanned England at the narrowest point from Carlisle to Newcastle. She'd done a bit of research and discovered that it could be done in a week with a following breeze, and that the best way to attain a following breeze was to walk it from west to east. For this reason we would be driving north towards Carlisle, via Upper Piddle, Lower Piddle and any other kind of Piddle you can mention, plus 'Dorking', 'Limpsfield', 'Three cocks', 'Knucleass', 'Fingringhoe' and my personal favourite; 'St. Mary's Hoo'. And calling in on various relatives on the way.

But there are limits to what a thousand pounds will let you do. We could never have bought a car; even Bubble, with his top speed of fifty-five-and-a-half miles an hour, was worth nearly that. So as we packed for the journey ahead, instead of a spending spree we had a lending spree.

Mum furnished us with cooking pans. We took the spare duvets off every bed in the house. Tinned food came from the neighbours (who I'm sure thought we were going off to die in the wilderness) and one of them even handed me a bottle of champagne (presumably to celebrate the fact that we were going off to die in the wilderness). It was the beginning of September, so we gratefully accepted bobble hats and gloves and hoped we wouldn't need to sleep in them. Most exciting of all though, was a slim stack of membership cards. My parents donate to almost every charity on the planet, from building houses for Muslim rhinoceroses in the Sudan to Christians who weave school clothes for Bangladeshi orphans from their own body hair. Amongst such worthy causes they also support both 'English Heritage' and 'The National Trust', meaning they get into all sorts of historic buildings and monuments for free. And now, since we were also called Mr & Mrs Slater, so would we.

This freed up the 'Entrance Fees For Castles' portion of our meagre budget, and had the happy side-effect of enabling us to set off with a few bottles of cider bought from the farm behind my parents' house.

It was Saturday evening, so we figured we'd have one last day to psyche ourselves up, and set our departure date for Monday. The next morning we saw the papers.

'HURRICANE UK', read the headline. 'It's called Katia... it's 500 miles wide and it's heading for Britain on Monday!'

It looked like we were going to our deaths after all.

The border country between England and Scotland, where we were heading, was set to be the epicentre of the huge storm. The highest and most exposed areas were said to be the most dangerous to be in – which kind of threw out our plans of hiking across the moors. I'd been a firm advocate of the following breeze theory, but these winds could spread the buttocks of a wildebeest. I wasn't mad keen on being followed by something stronger than I was, so we thought long and hard, and made the painful decision to chill out at home for another couple of days while the weather cleared. Life can be tough sometimes.

We weren't completely idle though.

Okay, I was completely idle.

But Roo wanted to make the most of the delay, so she set about raising some money by selling bits and pieces on eBay.

Amongst the more unusual items I'd inherited from Granddad were two sets of lawn bowls – his own, and a matching set which had belonged to my Nan. He'd bequeathed them to me in one of his more lucid moments, stating that he was "a bit past bowling now." Come to think of it, it may have been one of his less-lucid moments, as I was even less likely to use lawn bowls than he was – but they'd been expensive items back in the day, and I figured the technology involved in bowls was unlikely to have changed much.

Roo put them up for sale, listing them as 'used, in good condition'.

The first set sold for rather more than we'd expected – almost £80! We were super careful, wrapping them several times and spending over a tenner just on postage.

It seemed too good to be true, and it was.

The buyer wasn't happy. The bowls, it seems, had 'scratches all over the surface'. I very politely pointed out that this occurs almost immediately in the life of a set of bowls, largely because the aim of the game is to send them crashing into each other. A bowl without scratches is certainly not a 'used' one. This didn't help. It seems I'd missed a series of emails requesting a discount, then threatening to return the bowls, then finally one telling me they were on their way. It looked like he'd been angling to get some of his money back whilst still keeping them, and I had inadvertently called his bluff. We took return delivery of the bowls and repaid his money, less postage. A couple of days later he was back in touch; the bowls hadn't been all that bad after all (presumably because he'd seen the price of new ones) – and would we send them back in return for half the money?

Ha! I think not.

The second set went for a more modest sum to the owner of a courier company. He said he needed them immediately; the money was in the bank almost before the auction was over. I've seen men this desperate for several things in my time – women, drugs and alcohol more than anything – but never for lawn bowls. He even sent one of his staff to collect them personally! The courier arrived, labelled the package and off he went.

They didn't get there, of course. I got a call from a nervous sounding Scottish lady at lunchtime: "Hello Mr Slater, I'm the secretary for Mr BigCheeseSandwich. Did you give the item to the courier?"

For a minute I thought I *was* in the middle of a drug deal.

She rang me again a few hours later.

"Sorry to bother you, but you *definitely* gave them to the courier?"

Understanding must have come only when Mr.BigCheeseSandwich took delivery in his office of something that quite blatantly was not a set of lawn bowls. The courier had mixed up two packages – his only two packages, by all accounts – despite the fact that one of them was going to the Managing Director of his own firm. It can't have improved his career prospects.

Just when I thought Roo had had enough of eBay, she discovered something else to sell underneath our bed.

It was a sleeping bag my sister had bought in Australia, before our last major hike – a thousand kilometres through pristine bush-land, carrying all our gear including up to ten days worth of food. I'd convinced her that a child's sleeping bag would be suitable, as Gill shares our Mum's rather gnomic heritage. It meant she could afford to buy a kick-ass technical sleeping bag, the adult version of which was way out of her price range – and the bag would be smaller, so there would be less weight to haul around for two months.

On my advice, she'd bought the bag. It didn't fit. Not unless she carried something else with her to drape over her nipples. So amidst much wailing and gnashing of teeth (from Gill – and raucous laughter on my part as she struggled in vain to pull the thing up past her waist), the thing had been abandoned. It was an internet purchase and it didn't go down too well when I tried to explain the problem.

'Dear Supplier, I'm poor so I tried to buy a children's sleeping bag and now I can't fit into it.'

'I'm sorry sir, our refunds policy doesn't cover cheapskate idiots.'

The return postage to Asia was more than the bag was worth, so it had hung around in wardrobe after cupboard after wardrobe, gathering dust on at least three continents, before it occurred to Roo that we could sell it.

"Should I list it as new?" she asked.

"Well, yeah, I guess so. I mean, Gill never slept in it. It only came up to her navel."

"Okay, new... Hang on! Didn't we take it with us on that camping trip a few months back?"

"What camping trip? Oh yeah! Ha. I'd forgotten about that. We didn't sleep in it though. It would barely cover my ankles. I guess there could be some grass on the carrying sack or something..."

"Nooo!" she hissed. "We DID use it. Just not for sleeping."

I thought hard. Of course! We'd laid it down as extra padding, to cushion our knees from the ground and to protect our own sleeping bags while we... Ah.

"Ah," I said.

"Yes! See what I mean? We can't call it 'new', can we? It might be... *stained*."

I had a horrible feeling that it was.

"Imagine the feedback we'd get if we sold someone a sleeping bag that was... you know, *soiled!*"

It was a good point. But as I read the auction listing over her shoulder, something far worse occurred to me.

"Holy shit Roo, it's not just soiled – it's a *children's* sleeping bag! If we sell that to the wrong person, we could end up in prison!"

And so, later that day Roo listed our last two items for sale;

'One set of lawn bowls – relisted due to a time-waster', and

'Children's sleeping bag – used once, and thoroughly washed...'

Bureaucracy

We didn't leave that week.

In fact we nearly didn't leave the next week.

An unexpected problem had arisen in the Slater household, and Roo and I were caught up in something so distasteful that I shudder to repeat it here. Without warning we were consumed by the most diabolical aspect of the civilized world, that most despised, most railed-against, most universally-hated contrivance:

Red tape.

Damn, I hate red tape.

The trouble was, I was in the middle of applying to emigrate to Australia. That was to be the grand adventure after our Grand Adventure – although it was destined to cost considerably more than a grand...

Three months had seemed like a reasonable enough time-frame for processing a visa, so shortly after Roo and I returned from our honeymoon in Spain I'd used my credit card to buy cheap flights for the pair of us to her home city of Perth.

Then I'd busied myself getting ready for the trip around England, figuring I'd drop my Australian Visa application in just before we set off, and return to find it all organised.

So with the car packed and half our stuff still selling on eBay, I took the chance afforded by the severe weather warning to look into the emigration situation.

The first piece of advice on the visa application website was 'DO NOT book your flight to Australia until this visa has been processed.'

Oops! Still, at that point I had nearly three months.

The second piece of advice was this; 'Visas will take a minimum of six months to process from the date of submission.'

Ah. That was a bit of a bugger.

It was at this point that I started to take things a bit more seriously, and decided to do some research. The more I read, the more I realised that – in terms of setting off on a Grand Adventure in the morning – I was about as screwed as a person can get. And then some.

For anyone thinking of emigrating to Australia, I have this piece of advice:

Don't even think about it.

Seriously!

Jumping off a bridge is a quicker and considerably less painful way to enter paradise.

The first thing I needed to do was book an appointment to have a Visa Medical. There were only a handful of places in the country where this could be done, and most of them were depressingly swanky-sounding Harley Street clinics in London. I finally found one in Cardiff that would take my call – presumably the others had some sort of screening software fitted to their phone system, which warned them that the caller was too broke to be worth talking to.

I managed to book my medical appointment for a few days hence, and threw up in my mouth a little when the receptionist told me it would cost £380.

Then I discovered that the fee to apply for the visa – none-refundable of course – was £2,000.

The Second Step in a Grand Adventure:
Become completely and utterly penniless.

Okay, that step is optional.

I printed the application form. It was only thirty pages long and had just over ninety questions. I got stuck in straight away, and had filled in nearly half the form when I came to a fairly innocuous question: 'Is your wife an Australian Citizen?'

Why yes, of course she is! Otherwise it'd be a waste of time filling the bloody form in, wouldn't it?

"Please let me come and live in Australia."

"Why, is your wife Australian?"

"No, she's from Blackpool, but we really like the look of Australia…"

I looked for the box marked 'Sarcastic Reply', but there wasn't one.

What there was, was an instruction directly underneath the question:

'Please attach a certified copy of your wife's birth certificate.'
BOLLOCKS!

Her birth certificate, of course, was in Australia, packed up in storage with everything else we couldn't bring to England. According to some lightening-fast checks of the Aussie government's website she not only needed the certificate – she needed it copied, and the copy had to be witnessed by someone who knew her, and signed by a judge...

In Australia.

And of course, she had to be present for the entire process.

I placed a quick call to Perth, to Roo's twin sister Sonja.

"Sonja, you know all that stuff in the garage... yes that's right, the boxes and boxes and crates and bags that have been in there for the last two years, stopping everyone from parking their cars in it... well I've got a favour to ask..."

Luckily for me, Sonja was equal to the task. She dug through half a lifetime's worth of crap and discovered the document. Took it to work and got it copied. Took the copy to her doctor and received assurances that he was allowed to certify it. Being an identical twin, it was then comparatively easy for her to pose as my wife for the purpose of said certification. I'd only recently learned to tell the two girls apart, and apparently this was a skill even their doctor had yet to master. Finally, triumphantly, Sonja posted the precious document to me in England...

Where I'd just discovered I had to get signed, witnessed statements from at least three Australian Citizens, swearing that my relationship with my wife is genuine.

So.

It was back to Roo's sisters, who took it in turns in front of the judge to swear their oaths. They each wrote an essay about how long they had known us, how we'd gotten together and how 'real' our relationship seemed to them. To prove they were who they said they were, they also had to provide copies of their passports, which they first had to get certified...

This was starting to get old.

The last few questions of the application form held another surprise: it wanted to know every country I'd visited in the last ten years. Now, for some people that's not too difficult; England, the World of Warcraft, and possibly a week in Ibiza for their best mate's stag do. Alas, I have been known to do a spot of traveling. Suffice to say that, in the last ten years I'd visited almost thirty countries, some of them several times...

and I needed the dates for every single trip.

Then I had to list all the countries I'd spent over a year in – luckily just England, Australia and New Zealand.

And I had to get a police records check from all of them.

My heart skipped a beat. Actually it skipped an afternoon's worth of beats. I realised that if I'd stayed in Thailand for another month and a half, I'd have had to do the same thing there.

During my time on the paradise island of Koh Phangan I'd had three run-ins with the police; the first was when I'd been in a bike accident, which was clearly not my fault. The Thai being Thai though, had given the benefit of the doubt to the other driver – who was Thai. The second time I'd been pulled over for running a red light (the only one on the island I hasten to add, which had been broken for the previous six months). The third time I'd saved them (the police) from a marauding monkey, for which they had gratefully agreed to wipe the slate clean. You can do this sort of thing in Thailand – both tackle enraged primates AND embrace police corruption in the space of a single day. It's one of the things I loved most about the place. But what records they did keep, assuming they kept any at all, might not be up to the standard expected by the Australian High Commission.

It was a close call.

But it still left me with a few issues. Phone calls to London, Sydney and Wellington revealed that I could get the Police Records Checks by mail order – all for about £70.

Except.

The Australian Federal Police would only accept payment in Australian Dollars – forty-three of them to be exact, and nothing as distasteful as cash. Nor would they accept bank transfers – I called Australia again and the solution was made abundantly clear. An International Money Order was the only way forward.

Which was bizarre. In this world of internet banking and wire(less) transfers, I wasn't even sure that money orders still existed. The concept seemed archaic, like asking for a telegraph, or a message in Morse code.

Nevertheless, Lloyds bank informed me that they could still process such a transaction, and that it could only be handled in an appropriately obsolete fashion – by post.

So I set out for my local branch. A friendly lady behind the counter rooted around in their stockroom and produced a dusty form for me to fill out. Half an hour later I'd arranged to buy the Money Order – at an additional cost of £20 – and it would take a full two weeks just to be delivered to me.

Arse-biscuits!

I was rapidly losing all hope of becoming Australian.

On the upside, I'd written my essay; sixteen pages of A4 paper on the history and nature of my relationship. It started when we first met, included details of every significant event, descriptions of our rapport, how the relationship had developed, our shared plans for the future, how we were supporting each other financially and *emotionally*... And Roo had done the same. Then we'd printed out every raunchy email we'd ever sent to each other, dug out tickets for flights we'd taken together, found a couple of old tenancy agreements and harassed the banks in three different countries for proof that we once had shared accounts.

We'd done about everything we could.

And then I noticed a new 'check list' available to download from the Immigration website, designed to ensure that applicants didn't miss out on a vital piece of evidence. It looked like we had everything on the list, except for one thing – 'A Completed Copy of Form 80'. This had me a little concerned – until I had a look at Form 80.

Then it had me a lot concerned.

It was comparatively short, only eight pages, containing several questions about my family.

Then, out of the blue, Question 28 asked: 'Please list every address you have lived at during the last 10 years. If you have periods without an address, please explain why...'

Oh God.

Again, for most people this would not be a problem. It was a bit of a nightmare for me though – I've lived for weeks in hostels, for months in a tent, slept on beaches, public monuments, trains, hammocks, sofas... I must have had a hundred different addresses in that time, and I didn't know any of them.

But it was Question 30 that really took the biscuit: 'Please provide a complete employment history since leaving school, including all sources of income during any periods of unemployment.'

Oh... *Shit*.

I've worked cash in hand. I've sold my body to medical science. I've taught things I've no qualifications to teach, in countries I'm not allowed to teach in... I've worked for my keep, picked fruit for it, cleaned hostels for free accommodation, sold stories, sold weed, sold blood, sold... no, I won't go there. Suffice to say, a complete employment history would take many, many pages and would probably lead me straight to prison.

At the very least, it was unlikely to endear me to the Australian government.

I now had less than two months before I was due to fly to Perth, and absolutely no chance of even applying for the visa in time, much less being granted it.

Roo found me sitting in front of my laptop, my head in my hands.

She placed a consoling arm on my shoulder. "Um… how's it going?"

I shrugged. "Well, I believe the technical term for someone in my situation is 'buggered'."

"Oh. Sorry, love."

"I mean, it's almost like they don't *want* me in Australia…"

"That's only because they don't know you like I do."

"Ha! If they knew me like you know me, then they *definitely* wouldn't let me in."

"Yeah… true enough. So here's a thought; how do you feel about, you know, *lying?*"

Expenses

The next morning, Roo drove me across the border into Wales. This wasn't the start of our Grand Adventure, though she suggested it could be; no, this wasn't D-Day. It was M.D. Day – I was going to Cardiff to have the medical check-up that could make or break my emigration to Australia.

"If we counted this as Day One of our journey, it would blow our budget for the first half of the trip," I told Roo.

"It feels good to be going somewhere though," she countered. "It's like we're off on our adventures again, rather than sitting inside staring at our computer screens and filling out paperwork."

I knew what she meant. The last few days had been frustrating. We both wanted to be gone, but there was always something else rising up to block us. Part of me wondered if I was allowing this, sort of an unconscious sabotage mechanism, derailing our trip before it started because I was scared of how much effort would be involved. And scared of the inevitable hardships, the potential for disaster and, of course, the big one – watching our last thousand pounds dwindle into nothing.

We found the clinic without too much difficulty and parked Bubble, stickers and all, next to some of the most expensive cars I've ever seen in Wales. There were several Porsches and a Maserati, flanked by a variety of gigantic four-wheel drives. In the middle we left our tiny blue Nissan Micra, with dents in the doors and a cartoon sperm whale giving us a cheeky grin from the bonnet.

I walked in, up to the reception desk and opened my mouth. "Hi there! I'm here for a visa med—" And that was as far as I got.

In a terrifying burst of efficiency the receptionist demanded, accepted and processed the payment before I could utter another syllable. It was the fastest I had ever been deprived of £380 in my life.

Before I knew it I was sitting in a comfy armchair with no recollection of how I got there. Roo was sitting in the chair next to me, looking concerned.

The quality of those chairs told me two things:

1) They could afford nice chairs here. No shit! And,

2) They needed nice chairs here. To cushion people like me, who are so shocked at the speed with which their credit card is maxed out, they don't even remember sitting down.

That receptionist was brutal. I was clearly not her first victim.

But those chairs reassured me. That tasteful décor reassured me. It said, 'This is an okay kind of place. These people know how to take care of you. They aren't just lining their pockets with your money and driving Ferraris to work...'

Or maybe they had that playing on a subliminal loop tape? I could almost hear it beneath the soft elevator music. If I listened really hard...

"MR SLATER!"

It was my turn already. My ass had barely made an impression on the seat! Jeez these guys were fast. Their turnover must be... my mind shied away from the calculation – both because I am crap at mental arithmetic, and because my money had now entered that equation. I decided not to think about it any more, and followed a grey-haired nurse into the x-ray room.

I took off my shirt; I'd felt compelled to dress smartly, as though this was an interview. Why? Well, big money makes me nervous. These people would be judging me I knew, and expecting to see me in skanky jeans with holes in, and a curry-stained t-shirt. They *knew* I was a backpacker, here as part of a one-time deal because the Aussie government had me over a barrel. They could tell I didn't belong in a posh private clinic...

Or perhaps I was being paranoid?

Roo would be rolling her eyes at the very mention of it, I knew.

She tended to be a bit more level-headed than me. When she wasn't day-dreaming about unicorns.

Which was why she was allowed to drive and I wasn't.

The x-ray machine did nothing. I'd expected a 'clunk'. Obviously these private places could afford machines that don't need to go 'clunk'.

Seconds later I was back in the comfy chair, explaining the mystery of the missing clunk to Roo, when a familiar cry rent the air;

"MR SLATER!"

What had I done wrong? I Instinctively knew there was something.

But it was only my lungs, which I can't really be blamed for.

They were too big to fit onto one x-ray it seems, a legacy of my year as a professional diver in Thailand. The process was repeated focussing on the bottom bits of my breathing apparatus, and it was back to the chair again – for less than a minute – and then into the nurse's office for the rest of my tests.

The way this was going, I'd be out of here before the Bubble's engine had cooled.

So far it had taken less time than I normally spend on the toilet.

"Your blood pressure is a little high," the nurse told me. "Have you been rushing to get here?"

"A little."

"Are you nervous?"

"Um... a little. I guess."

"Are you stressed at all?"

"Well, a bit! Mostly about how big my credit card bill just became! You must get that a lot though," I joked.

"No." She said it in a slightly frosty tone, as though daring me to deny that £380 was pocket change to most rational adults.

It was definitely time to let that go.

She asked me to lie down and started opening all those little sterile packets that hold the component parts of a syringe.

"Now, there's nothing to worry about. I just need to take a little blood. You're not afraid of needles, are you?"

"Ha! No, I..." and here I did a very rare thing, for me. I stopped myself, on the brink of saying something very, very stupid, and gave my mind time to engage and consider the situation. If this happened all the time I'd have a lot less trouble in my life. But then my stories would get rather boring. On this occasion, however, I was pretty grateful for the save.

'No, I've had *lots* of needles,' was my stock response – the one I'd come dangerously close to giving. That could have opened up a whole bag of worms...

Instead I took a deep, calming breath.

Disaster averted.

"No. Not afraid of needles," I said, and left it at that.

The rush of endorphins was a reward from my brain, for letting it get its own way for a change. I lay there on the gurney, thinking how close I'd just come to undoing all my careful work.

At all costs I had to avoid mentioning my career as a human guinea pig.

She didn't need to know that I'd supported my travels around half the world by going into hospitals on three continents and letting them pump me full of untested medicines.

Perhaps no-one would care. Perhaps the visa medical was just another way of testing our resolve, an obstacle we applicants had to overcome to prove how much we *wanted* to become Australian. And of course, they were checking to make sure I wasn't highly contagious or already dying.

But what would they think if they knew I'd spent more time, in more different hospitals, than most octogenarians ever will? Would it muddy the waters slightly, to know what I'd allowed the pharmaceutical industry to put inside me?

To know that I'd been deliberately exposed to certain pathogens; that I'd been intentionally tortured with pain-causing chemicals? That I'd been routinely overdosed on a wide variety of experimental medicines, several of which had never made it through to production on account of being deemed too dangerous for human consumption?

Nah, probably not.

But I decided to keep it quiet just in case.

I explained the near slip-up to Roo as she drove me home, only a handful of minutes later. Overall it had been the quickest visit to a doctor's office I'd ever had – if you didn't count the two-hour drive either side, of course. I couldn't stop myself trying to calculate things – perhaps it's how I deal with shock. Anyway, my fretting brain informed me that my time inside the clinic had cost me a little over £27 per minute.

"So what did you tell the nurse?" Roo asked.

"Nothing! Nothing at all."

"Good. Did she ask though? Anything... dodgy?"

"Nah, she just went through the usual. Y'know, have I done drugs, do I smoke, have I ever smoked..."

"Whew! You lied about all that too, I'm guessing?"

"Indeed."

"So it's all okay then?"

"Yup. The way I see it, it probably wouldn't have mattered. It's just better not to mention it, in case it means extra paperwork."

"Oh yeah! We could do without any more paperwork. *Ever.*"

"True story! It's like that question on my visa application form. You know, the one that says 'Do you have any Weapons or Explosives Training'. Of course they want to know if I've done any of that, because it could be important, so they'd want to follow it up with more paperwork. I just ticked 'No.' It makes it so much easier. I mean, I was only in the Territorial Army for six months, and yeah we learnt how to build Molotov cocktails and did rifle shooting and throwing grenades and stuff. But I don't think they need to know about all that. It only complicates things."

"Yeah! They'd want to see your discharge papers, at the very least."

"Yup. And of course I don't have any, because I'm technically still AWOL…"

"So just better not to mention."

"Yup."

Roo and I, for once, were in total agreement.

Getting Off

The sun dawned on the day of our departure, as it had many times before – only to be scuppered yet again by the arrival of the morning post.

There was an issue. Yes, it was Australian-visa-related. Yes it would take time and more paperwork to sort out, cost more money and quite likely give me a migraine. Dark clouds threatened once more.

And so we thought, bollocks to it, we're going anyway. Because honestly I was getting a bit nervous about the whole idea. It'd been quite a while since I travelled properly, and that vague fear of the unknown that makes leaving home so hard to do in the first place was starting to reassert itself.

"We should just jump in the car and go, wherever it takes us," Roo told me.

"I've been home so long, I'm forgetting how to jump," I admitted.

And so, sticking a jovial English two fingers up at the demands of the Australian government, we jumped. Into the car, and into the loveliest part of the British countryside. Within minutes, the sun came out again. The uplifting of the sky mirrored my mood, which grew lighter with every mile we drove. This was it! We were finally on our way, with no fixed abode or agenda; just Roo, the car and me (in order of importance). It felt… liberating! It always does, once you get past the initial fear. It surprised me to realize just how much I'd secretly dreaded setting off on this trip – the likelihood of getting hopelessly lost, of spending long, sleepless nights in the car, of trading home-cooked meals for cold beans and crackers – it had all weighed quite heavily on my mind. Now, having faced those fears and set off anyway (mostly because of Roo pushing me), I was sliding down the back of that wave of emotion, feeling the excitement and anticipation of those exact same situations. To be lost was to discover new places; the comedy of eating instant noodles in the shadow of expensive restaurants appealed to me again; all the memories of times I'd overcome this kind of adversity came flooding back. Sleeping on a park bench in Paris, subsisting on stolen food in Méribel in the French Alps; I'd survived a lousy situation or two before this. And this time I'd be in my own country! What could possibly go wrong in a place as harmless as England?

A few pleasant hours winding around the fields and forests of Somerset ended in a surprise campsite near Wells. We arrived in daylight, pitched the tent as only two seasoned backpackers can, and spent about an hour sorting through all the crap we'd managed to fill the car with before leaving. Every so often one of us would hold up something unexpected – like an electronic photo frame, or a plastic bag containing a pirate costume – and say, "What the *&@£!! is this?"

We ate a huge meal in a nearby pub to celebrate our survival thus far; we only ordered a normal-sized meal, but when it arrived I found there wasn't a single part of it which would fit into my mouth. The joys of good old English pub grub were already looking like they might be a regular feature on this trip.

And then, with full stomachs and a warm tent awaiting... well, a tent that we would make warm, with vigorous generation of body heat... we were happy. Living with my parents throughout the planning, execution and aftermath of our wedding had been a life-saver as well as great fun, but it had afforded us very little in the way of privacy. And we were a married couple now...

Not counting the gigantic meal, the only money we'd spent so far was on fuel: £30.01 (This was down to Roo. She has a theory that our local petrol station's pumps are rigged to always add a penny onto every transaction. I think she spends too much time day-dreaming about unicorns when she should be watching the counter. The debate continues.)

Oh, and the campsite: £12.00 ("Jess' gi' us twelve squid," said the man in the site office, as though he was doing us a favour. Was he? No. That's their regular price. But we couldn't resist his authentic West Country accent, and the red hot showers were worth every penny.)

The Grand Adventure was now officially underway.

The next day brought some exploration of strange and unique buildings (including a turret-shaped 14th century toll-booth that had been converted into the smallest house I'd ever seen). It also nearly resulted in a four-car pile up when Roo drive past a sign that said

217

'Book Barn'.

It was my fault – I was doing that thing where I automatically read out every sign we passed. Then I did a double-take.

"Look, that sign says Book Barn!"

"Says what barn?"

"BOOK-barn!"

"*Book-barn?* Really?"

Roo slammed on the brakes and slewed the car around in a spin. Other vehicles screeched and swerved, smashing into each other at high speed and somersaulting through the air. Roo stepped hard on the accelerator and we were gone, leaving a pair of flaming tracks in our wake…

Well, that's how it happened in my mind. In fact she found a nice, quiet farm entrance to do a three-point-turn in, but the fact remains that Roo and I share one major obsession (beyond each other) – and that is books.

Ahhh… books. I love them so much! I have hundreds. And hundreds.

The vast majority of which I'd be leaving behind in a few weeks when I moved to Australia – this was the current tragedy in my life, and I was trying hard not to think about it.

So the idea of a barn full of books – all for sale at 'super-low discount prices' was almost too much for us to take. Despite the fact that anything we bought would most likely also be staying in England. Rational, logical thoughts rarely take precedence where books are concerned.

The Book Barn was the size of a football stadium. There must have been tens of thousands, perhaps hundreds of thousands of books in there. The lure of all that reading material was so hypnotic that I got run over in the car park by an electric vehicle (in my defence, the damn thing was completely silent. How was I supposed to know it was reversing right over the top of me?).

What saved us from blowing the budget in one fell swoop was our mutual disappointment. Ninety-nine percent of the books crammed every which-way onto the Book Barn's mismatched shelves dated back to that golden era of publishing between 1955 and 1980. There were piles of cookbooks fronted by women in oversized glasses and big woolly jumpers; tomes entitled Wonderful Science that made wacky predictions like, 'One day, man will walk on the moon'. The vast majority of the barn's contents were obsolete non-fiction, and whilst some of it was worth acquiring purely for amusement value (see above) – most of it was destined to stay where it was, slowly disintegrating amidst the stacks.

In the end we bought less than fifteen books each, which wasn't bad considering I'd set our budget at £10.

We hadn't stuck to it, but what do you expect?

It may have been a tad anticlimactic, but it was still a Book Barn.

According to the map, our route was about to take us past a Stone Circle. There are literally hundreds of these things dotting the English countryside, and whilst they're not all as impressive as Stonehenge, they don't cost £30 to enter and aren't surrounded by crowds of Disneyland proportions. Stonehenge, whilst being truly magnificent, falls into both of these categories and had been disqualified from our itinerary for that reason. Plus, I'd already been there about fifteen times, because it *is* absolutely epic.

This smaller stone circle took some locating, and turned out to be in a farmer's field on the outskirts of a tiny, unassuming village. As I climbed the stile over the fence, Roo was reading the information board next to it.

"Fourteenth century," she informed me, "that's over six-hundred years old!"

"Yeah, I can see it from here. It's just a bunch of rocks though."

Roo shot me a look. "Don't break anything!" she warned. Then she looked down at the dubious quagmire we were about to walk into. "And don't step in any shit," she added.

Back in the car, bumbling around delightful country lanes, we noticed a disused viaduct in the distance.

"There's got to be a way to get closer to it," I said.

"Why?" Roo asked.

"Because I want to climb it."

"No." said Roo.

And as she was doing the driving, that was that.

But she found a convenient lay-by to pull up in, with a view of the viaduct to enjoy while we buttered bread on the dashboard.

For anyone that doesn't know, viaducts are incredibly vast, brick-built railway bridges, designed to span valleys a hundred years before high-tensile steel suspension bridges were available. Columned arches, sometimes hundreds of metres high, reach up from the bottom of the valley, creating a level bed across which the track is laid. This was the old-school, industrial-era approach to problem-solving, and it almost defies belief – for sheer audacity, they are amongst the most impressive structures in the country, and probably the most underrated.

It occurred to me that if we were looking for the essence of Britishness — at least as other countries see us — then we'd just about discovered it.

Sitting in our car, eating crisp sandwiches, looking out at the railway line.

I was one cup of tea and a scone away from sticking a live ferret down my trousers.

But Roo was never going to let me climb that viaduct.

Adapting

As we pushed on towards the Somerset Monument (something we only knew existed because it was marked on the map), the road climbed up and down a series of hills, passing through small chunks of forest between endless fields of grass. Often the trees lining the road met overhead, and we were driving down a tunnel of foliage dappled with sunlight. It made my heart sing, and Roo was also moved by the beauty of the scene. This green and verdant landscape was the thing I would miss most about England, once I was gone.

The Somerset Monument was an impressive tower with a balcony at the top. It was not, however, in Somerset. It was surrounded by a garden and separated from the road by a low stone wall. There was no footpath and no obvious way in without hiking back up the main road, so we leapt comfortably over the wall and wandered up to the base of the obelisk.

We were debating whether or not it was hollow with stairs inside when a brusque voice came over the back hedge.

"Is somebody there?" It was a suspicious, accusatory voice; female, but not at all welcoming.

"Good evening," I said to the voice. "We're just here admiring the monument."

"Monument's CLOSED," came the voice, bellowing as though its owner meant to do us harm.

"Oh! Sorry! We didn't realise."

"How did you get in?" The voice demanded. "Did you climb the wall?"

"Yes, indeed we did!"

"You can't do that!"

"I think you'll find we can," I replied. "But we're happy enough to go back again. Good evening!" And we strolled back towards the car, ignoring a tirade of abuse unworthy of the guardian of a piece of England's heritage.

It didn't bother us in the least. We were young and free! We could go where we wanted and climb what we wanted, because we had respect and intelligence, and that woman was clearly the kind of person that other people crossed the street to avoid. Bring positivity into this world if you're going to bring anything, that's what I say; and if your monument is closed and some young couple are keen enough to climb a low wall to have a look at it, well then; be grateful they're not the other type of young people who'd piss all over it, set fire to it and then break into your house and do the same to you. This was rural Gloucestershire – not exactly The Bronx, at least not yet – but some people still have trouble being happy.

Not us.

Our first night under canvas had passed so quickly and smoothly, we hardly knew it was there. The only thing missing was power – we went to bed with the sun because there was sod all else we could do. But as I promised Roo, that was about to change.

"I'm going to find us a campsite with power. Loads of them have electric hook-ups. It'll cost a few quid more, but it'll be so worth it! We could snuggle up in bed and watch a movie on the laptop."

"Hey, we should look for a site with a TV room!"

"Uh… yeah, that's never going to happen, I'm afraid."

"Oh. Alright. If we find one with a kitchen then, we can charge the laptop while we cook dinner."

"Love, do you remember me explaining the difference between English and Australian campsites?"

"What, you mean they don't even have ones with kitchens here?"

"No."

"Oh. I guess we could make do with a gas barbeque then."

"Ahhh…"

"Oh, you've got to be kidding! What the hell do people cook on?"

"That's why we brought that little Bunsen-burner."

"I thought we brought that for when we were hiking!"

"And for camping."

"But we're going to be camping the entire time!"

"Ah… yes, I'd imagine so."

She was horrified. "But… we've got to cook *all* our meals on that?"

"Yes."

"But you can't cook on those things! Not proper food!"

"We managed alright on the Bibbulmun Track."

"Tony, we ate nothing but instant noodles for two months! Even I lost weight. I was so hungry I nearly ate you!"

It took most of the evening, following signs with caravan symbols down narrow, twisting lanes. By the time we came across a place with electric hook-ups, it was already closed for the night – but they didn't have a barrier, so we drove Bubble into their back field and resolved to pay for our pitch in the morning.

I'd spent the last hour reminding Roo that it would be all worthwhile, once we were cosy in our sleeping bags with a light to read by and a laptop full of films.

So I was less than pleased to discover that electricity came in the form of a giant blue socket, requiring an equally giant round plug to go into it. I should have known; caravanning as a kid, we'd always taken an adaptor. Those sockets were heavy-duty waterproof ones, and were a standard design throughout the entire country.

Which was a bit of a bugger.

"Oh yes, you'll need an adaptor," Dad informed me cheerfully, when I called him.

"I just discovered that."

"They're not too hard to come by. Should only cost you ten or twelve quid. But you'll need to find a specialist caravanning shop. Ordinary camping shops don't sell them, because no-one uses electricity when they're camping."

"No. That seems to be the case."

"It's a shame really. I've got three of them right here."

"Yes, thanks for that."

Not to be deterred, we pitched our tent with the last of the light and settled down to cook in total darkness. It was about now I wished I'd brought a decent torch – all we had was a tiny wind-up key ring thing which Roo had bought from Poundland! For some reason it just hadn't occurred to me that we'd be camping in the dark. What is this, the middle ages?

It then emerged that the other thing we'd forgotten to bring was any food. Oh, we had plenty of snacks – a crate in the back of the car filled entirely with crisps and chocolate, Peperami sticks and Snack-a-jacks – the legacy of sending Roo out to do our grocery shopping. Sadly, a close investigation revealed nothing remotely resembling dinner. The contributions from our neighbours were also less useful than I'd realised, consisting mostly of tinned rice pudding and fruit salad. It was almost as though they'd given us the crap from the back of the pantry that would never get eaten anyway…

Then, just when all seemed lost, I discovered the small stash of tins I'd stolen from Mum's kitchen. They'd been on the top shelf, so it's not like she'd have been able to eat any of them before I got back.*

Amongst the canned horde were Heinz beans and a tin of ASDA's finest spaghetti bolognaise. The two seemed destined for each other, and for our bellies, so without further ado Roo mixed them together in a pan, blasted it with our Bunsen-burner stove, and that was dinner sorted. It made me quite proud, to think how well we were looking after ourselves in the wild.

(*I believe I mentioned that my mother is a gnome. She has to stand on two copies of the *Yellow Pages* just to reach the bottom shelf.)

Life Under Canvas

We'd pitched our tent under a group of trees, without realizing just how many birds were living in them. The dawn cacophony was magical and deafening at the same time, and utterly impossible to sleep through. A few ducks added their over-enthusiastic quacking, and were joined by the deep bass rumble of what Roo tentatively identified as a T-rex.

The rumbling got closer and more threatening, right up to the point where we cowered in our tent, convinced that the rapture was approaching; in fact, it was a gigantic, caterpillar-tracked excavator which the campsite owners, in their infinite wisdom, had decided to unleash upon us all at 7am. What was it doing so volubly, that simply couldn't wait another hour? Why, it was trimming the hedgerows of course. And then dredging the streams that bordered the site. Obviously a full day's work had been scheduled for the 300 decibel behemoth, so we gave up any thoughts of sleeping in, and got the hell out of its way.

Our first stop was the toilet block. For those not familiar with camping, this is the communal toilets/showering facility – pretty much the only amenities they do provide on UK campsites, unless you include the rusty tap sticking up in the middle of the field for filling water bottles.

Rocking up to the loo block first thing in the morning, toothbrush and towel in hand, is a bit of a ritual – and not quite as wholesome as you might imagine. For starters, most of the other male campers are OAPs. Most of them are fat, hairy and distinctly unashamed about it. And most of them eat more baked beans during a week's caravan holiday than they do in the rest of the year. So as I queued for a shower cubicle behind a sizeable portion of body-bearded man-blubber, it was to the tune of a procession of seventy-plus-year-olds taking it in turns to void their irritable bowels explosively. Never before in the field of human history have so few toilets taken such a beating from so many bloated backsides. The seats had become uncomfortably warm by the time my turn arrived.

The shower seemed more welcome by the minute. Feeling much less violated once the hot water began to flow, I lathered up while humming a half-remembered song. I'd hardly even noticed I was doing it, until the bloke in the next cubicle took up the tune. That scared me a little. Then, as someone a few stalls up joined in, the memory clicked – God knows why, but I was humming 'Once in Royal David's City' – a Catholic hymn and Christmas carol from my childhood. Oh. Oh no. I suddenly wanted to leave very quickly, before a half-naked octogenarian could tackle me about my dedication to Jesus. I showered at high velocity, and luckily there wasn't anyone waiting in a towel outside my cubicle to ask me for a 'Hallelujah'.

Roo found this hysterical, of course. According to her, the female contingent of the campsite underwent their ablutions in complete silence.

"Apart from the occasional 'oops, sorry!' when someone got in your way, it was quiet. The only sound was running water."

"What, no flatulence?"

Her eyes went wide. "Of course no flatulence! We're *ladies!*"

The Third Step in a Grand Adventure:

Choose your ideal campsite. I recommend that you:

Find a campsite before dark. Ideally before it's closed.

Find a campsite with fewer birds – or birds that are quieter.

Find a campsite that isn't a Bible Camp.

Find a campsite with power.

Find a suitable way to harness said power.

Find a campsite with fewer giant diggers (None at all would be nice).

As we grudgingly paid for our pitch, the manager mentioned that there was an outdoor superstore on the road to Tewkesbury. I'd never been to Tewkesbury, but it sounded like a nice place to visit so we made that our goal for the day.

Why not? We had ultimate freedom, and with ultimate freedom comes ultimate difficulty in deciding what to do with it. For now, I was happy enough to trust our direction to fate – and more specifically, to the chance of getting my hands on one of those damn power adaptors.

The place we'd ended up in turned out to be called Slimbridge. There was a Wetlands Centre just beyond it which was apparently quite famous – presumably amongst people who actually know what a Wetland Centre is. All the signs praised the biodiversity of the area, and listed hundreds of species of birds which could be observed there. We felt we'd seen enough birds for one day, had in fact spent most of the morning trying to sponge vast amounts of their shit off our tent, so we chose not to dig deep for the rather excessive £10 per person entrance fee.

Instead we got free entertainment watching the drivers get riled up when they had to wait for the Slimbridge's slim bridge to swing back into place after letting a boat through. The mechanics of such things have always fascinated me, but not so the occupants of the cars opposite, who were positively incensed at the five-minute delay to their journey.

Where the hell were they going in such a hurry? This quiet, rural road led to the dubious attractions of the campsite and the Wetlands Centre – nothing else. Why was anyone so desperate to get there? A lot of people seem to struggle with waiting, but you kind of get used to it if you do much travelling. I take advantage of the time to marvel at the audacity of man, that we'd create not just a canal, and not just a bridge over a canal, but a bridge that moves at the push of a button. Staggering! And here, in the most out-of-the-way spot, where it can't possibly benefit more than fifty cars a day. Yet someone deemed it important enough to spend the time and money required to construct a minor engineering marvel. And these things are scattered all over the country, hundreds and hundreds of them! We might be burning through our ozone layer and poisoning the oceans with our rubbish, but we've achieved a few good things in our time.

Anyway.

Our next stop was for a slightly older engineering marvel.

The Long Barrows were recently discovered Neolithic burial sites – 5,000 year old tombs predating all recorded history in this part of the world.

We crawled inside one, and were amazed by the way they were built. Huge stone blocks divided the central passageway from several separate graves on each side. The whole thing was roofed over with carved stone slabs bigger than Bubble, which were then covered with mounds of earth.

We were in awe.

I've been to the pyramids in Egypt, and the scale of those things blew my mind as well. But there are legions of scholars arguing about giant ramps, about wooden rollers and barges, and every so often evidence is discovered of enormous camps the size of cities, where labourers and craftsmen lived for decades whilst devoting themselves to the project.

These were different. A soggy ridge in the middle of England somewhere, and a bunch of people making a family tomb. They didn't have the whips of the Pharaohs, or ten thousand labourers at their beck and call. Yet somehow they'd made and moved blocks very nearly as impressive – and all to cover up a few dead bodies.

How? And why? When a hole in the ground would have sufficed, and taken quite a bit less effort. Prehistoric people were awesome. They really liked to go big with their monuments. I wish I had their motivation – they could probably have chiselled this book onto stone tablets faster than I'm typing it. Of course, they'd probably bury someone in it. That does seem to be pretty much all they did. But hey, who am I to question my ancestors?

Continuing the theme of ancient monuments, we stopped next at a 11th century church – one of the few still standing in Britain. Odda's Chapel had been built over nine-hundred years ago for an Anglo-Saxon earl – right next door to Fred's house. Okay, it might not have been Fred's, but it was someone's house – built into the other half of this historic structure was a regular dwelling, complete with satellite dish. It still maintained the insanely bowed wood-and-wattle walls, with tiny windows squished between the heavy black beams. Surely the floor inside followed the contours of those beams – it'd be like living in the middle of a hump-backed bridge. And I can't imagine they were allowed to alter the crumbling building; a fresh coat of paint, or a nice set of patio doors leading out onto a balcony would be right out of the picture.

Still. Over nine-hundred years old...

Roo and I were insanely jealous.

"You see," I said as we drove away, "there's a building that really IS older than Australia."

And then came the most anticipated stop of the day: the outdoor superstore.

And it was vast.

We sat in the car park, staring at it. I was trembling. "Okay, we get straight in and straight out," I said. It was like we were planning a bank robbery. "We have ten pounds or less to spend and we need a outdoor power socket adaptor. Say it!"

"We have ten pounds and we need an adaptor thingy..."

But I could tell her mind was somewhere else. Roaming the aisles of what must have been the biggest outdoors shop either of us had ever seen.

Now, I do like gear. We both do – but I have an almost unhealthy obsession with the stuff. I love it almost as much as I love taking the piss out of people who buy it – the vast majority of whom will do nothing more extreme than wear it round Tesco.

Unfortunately, outdoor gear is ridiculously expensive, the clothing in particular. That's one of the main reasons why people buy it, assuming it must be super-fashionable because of the insane ticket price.

It's not.

Those trousers might be wind, water and mosquito-proof from fifty degrees below zero to fifty degrees above it, but they don't look nearly as good on your arse as a pair of jeans. That's why charity shops are full of the stuff.

So this was going to be our challenge. Get in and get out without blowing our budget... which I'd set at £10. Because realistically either one of us could spend the whole grand in this shop – probably before we got anywhere near the electrical adaptors. For shoppers on a shoestring like us, this place was enemy territory. High-priced, highly desirable items lurked on every side; it was touch and go whether we'd make it out solvent.

We were doing well. We got inside without incident, and past a pyramid of boxes displaying the very latest in Gore-Tex hiking boots – when off to one side a blur of colour caught my eye. Roo's head was also turning towards it... and lo! We beheld the amazing new Airbeam Tent from Vango – a self-inflating tent, with channels of compressed air sewn into the lining in place of tent poles! You literally had to chuck the thing on the floor, plug in the compressor and press go.

Before I even knew it, my credit card was in my hand. Roo saw the tell-tale flash of silver and dived on me, wrestling me to the ground and grabbing for the plastic. I twisted away just in time and launched myself through the tent's back door, thinking to lose her amidst an aisle of hanging sleeping bags. But Roo was too quick for me; I was cornered before I could escape the Vango exhibit. She blocked my path to the tills, brandishing a foam roll-mat with grim determination.

I tried to beat her off with a canoe paddle but she ducked behind the advertising stand and retaliated with a promotional leaflet. This blow struck home; I was transfixed by the specifications of the

Airbeam, and rendered powerless to resist as she pried the credit card from my fingertips. A spell had been cast over me and I lumbered along behind her, zombiefied by the information I was ingesting.

Muttering things like "Sewn in groundsheet..." and "mmm, Tension Band System..." I was easily steered through the product displays to the electrical section.

When I came to, we were back in the car. There was drool on my chin. Roo plucked the leaflet off me and I reached for it like a baby for its dummy.

"No!" Roo smacked my hands away. "Bad Tony! No Airbeam for you!"

I did the only thing I could do in such a situation.

I cried.

"But look what I've got here for you," she said.

And before my eyes she dangled the familiar shape of a caravan power adaptor.

It was new and shiny, so I reached for it.

"There you go!" said Roo. "You can play with this, if you want, while I drive us home."

The Difference A Plug Makes

It was delightfully sunny as we rolled into Tewkesbury, guiding Bubble down streets lined with half-timbered buildings and the occasional stone church.

The campsite we were aiming for was right in the shadow of Tewkesbury Abbey; much better than being way outside town in a field full of diggers.

"And are you both members?" asked the site manager, when we'd finished explaining our needs to him.

"I'm afraid not."

"No problem at all," he said, and his smile widened. He was right, it wasn't a problem – for him. He charged us £25.

I tried not to look too gutted as I handed over the cash. To most people, twenty-five pounds for a night's accommodation was hardly a disaster. I just have an in-built accountancy package which is constantly processing raw data and throwing up interesting facts, like how short this trip would be if every night in a campsite cost us £25, and the likely price of a double bed in a nearby Travelodge being only £5 more...

But at least we would have power.

Power! Ahh... the possibilities! It meant we could plug in our lamp. Which meant we could read after dark, which in England, in September, meant after 7pm. It meant we could find food in the town, then come back to our cosy little place and actually enjoy our evening, instead of going straight to bed. Our options were always going to be limited, because we were living in a tent; we wouldn't be hosting a late-night table tennis tournament for example, or doing a thousand-piece jigsaw. Not unless we wanted to sleep on it. But being able to do anything at all with our evenings would be a bonus, particularly for me. With power in the tent I could hook up my laptop, deny Roo's fervent request to watch a Ryan Reynolds movie on DVD, and buckle down to get some serious writing done.

And maybe then watch a Ryan Reynolds movie. Because otherwise she'd never shut up about it.

Now, we did have a few other electrical appliances with us.

My Dad is addicted to tea; he drinks at least twenty cups a day, more than anyone else I've ever met. However, he refuses to believe that anyone else does any different; thus, he wouldn't let us leave home without a kettle. He'd tried to get us to take two, in case one packed up of an evening and we were left cup-of-tea-less and 'gasping' for a whole night – his worst possible nightmare. I'd had to do a bit of careful negotiating, and had managed to convince him we'd never be too far from a 24 hour ASDA. The result; we'd only had to bring one kettle, which was probably still working as we hadn't been able to use it yet.

We both had phones that needed charging, and I was keen to try using mine to create a wireless hotspot, to see what was going on in the wide world of the internet.

Alright, if you must know, I wanted to check on my book sales.

We writers have been known to do that, from time to time. Or every five minutes, internet permitting.

But I didn't want to get my hopes up. Surely that was too much to ask for?

It was.

I plugged the collection of cables into each other, stood facing Roo in the deepening twilight, and intoned the fateful words: "God said, Let There Be Light…"

And I threw the switch.

Nothing happened.

The next half-hour of dialogue I won't recount, save to say that God still featured heavily, along with a wide variety of mostly four-letter words.

Nothing I tried would work. Roo retired to the tent and resigned herself to another early night, but I wouldn't let it lie. I stomped back and forth between the tent and the glowing power box, tugging on the cables where they connected.

"There's nothing… nothing to stop it working! The bloody thing MUST be broken!"

"Is there anything else you need to do? To switch it on at the post I mean?"

"NO! I've done EVERYTHING right. You just plug it in! I've used these things dozens of time – hundreds! All over the country. All my life! I could plug the caravan power in when I was six. They're all EXACTLY the same, except for this bastard thing which is broken."

"Well, the shop was open 'till eight tonight... we could always take it back?"

"Alright then. We bloody well will," I fumed.

So Roo very calmly got in the car and drove for half an hour back to the Outdoors Mega-store. She'd even persuaded me to relax by the time we pulled into that enormous car park.

The store was still open, though seemingly deserted.

After the near-disaster last time, Roo threatened to leave me in the car.

"I'll be good," I promised.

"And NO GEAR."

"Okay love. No gear."

She still made me lock my wallet into the glove box.

It was a quick trip – the shop was closing and the staff, concerned with the loftier matters of high-tech tent display, had little time for mortals like us. Roo collared a cashier and presented the adaptor plug. The young lad explained that they had no way of testing it in store, what with the store being indoors and all. It was a stalemate – we couldn't prove the thing didn't work and he couldn't prove it did. In the end all Roo could do was tell the guy we'd give it another go. Then she must have looked around and realised that I wasn't there any more – but with zero spending power on me, she wasn't too worried. Eventually she rooted me out in the camping utensils section, where I'd amassed an armful of fascinating gadgets.

"We're not buying them," she said.

"Just one."

"We can't afford it. And you've got no money."

"But this one..." I held up a scrubbing brush that resembled the cartoon octopus on our car. "Look! You fill the reservoir at the top with soapy liquid and press this plunger..." I demonstrated the plunger. Roo wasn't particularly impressed. Well, I'm sure she was *secretly*, but she was trying not to show it for my benefit.

Such is the strength of Woman.

"It's only £4," I pleaded.

"We don't have £4."

"I do!" Fishing in my pocket I produced a handful of coins. "I've got it!"

So we escaped almost entirely unscathed. One octopus-shaped scrubbing brush with liquid chamber and plunger was added to the pile of gear in the back of Bubble.

"You won't use it," Roo warned me.

"I will," I said. "I'll wash the dishes with it tonight!"

But we ate at the oldest pub in Tewkesbury that night. The Black Bear Inn furnished us with a meal so delicious I quickly lost any desire to clean plates, and that was the last time I thought about that little scrubbing brush. I haven't used it since.

I still maintain that it's very, very cool though. I heartily recommend you buy one. And while you're at it, get another one for me; you can never have too many of something so useful!

Rather less useful was the power adaptor; the damn thing still didn't work. I was past cursing the thing, so we went to bed and snuggled, leaving further reprisals for the morning.

It was as we were packing the tent to leave that I made the discovery. The power pole was a squat grey bollard with a light on the top. It was bright enough in half-darkness that it had obscured everything else on the post, so I'd had to plug us in by feel alone. During my temper tantrum I'd felt every inch of the power box, searching for some kind of switch or button amongst the cobwebs and insects. I'd found a few protrusions, pressed them, tried every possible combination of pushing, pulling and wiggling. Now, revealed in the daylight, they were mostly indicator lights which didn't press or wiggle. One though, was a tiny plate with a notice printed on it. It was entitled 'Instructions for Use'.

1) Insert plug.
2) Twist plug to activate power.

"You've got to be shitting me."

I twisted the plug.

In the tent the lights came on, startling Roo as she was sitting on them.

Twist the frigging plug.

"I'd thought you'd used hundreds of these things," Roo teased. "All your life, you said!"

"Well they don't twist. EVER. Never ever before in the history of bloody anything! Why would you twist a plug? What the hell kind of stupidity is that? It's not a frigging safe lock. Nothing twists! Name one damn thing that you have to twist to get it to work."

"Yes dear. Very strange I'm sure."

I was a little placated. "Well at least we have power now."

"Yes, that's lovely," she agreed. "Now unplug it and let's get out of here."

The Fourth Step in a Grand Adventure:

Twist it. Even if you've never, ever had to before. It's a big world out there, full of many strange surprises. Trust me. Twist it.

Posh Nosh

Tewkesbury, we loved. The main street was lined with old buildings in myriad architectural styles; had Kevin Macleod from Grand Designs been with us, he would surely have read the history of the whole country written into the subtle nuances between one period feature and another. Unfortunately I know bugger all about architecture, so was reduced to pointing at a pub across the road and saying "Oooh, that one looks really old!"

Luckily Roo, being an Aussie, isn't a connoisseur of heritage architecture either, so she mostly just agreed with me and then did the same thing at the next old building we saw.

"Cool, it almost looks like a castle!"

"Look at the old beams, how they bend!"

"I love those tiny windows!"

"See how much that roof is sagging?"

Yes, it's safe to say we enjoyed Tewkesbury.

I've read a few travel books, of the 'miserable old bugger roams England, moaning about how it's been ruined recently' type. They bore the shit out of me. Everywhere changes; some people love it and some hate it, but it happens. Otherwise we'd still be pointing spears at each other.

I believe in being positive. Bitching about how much better everything used to be in the Good Old Days achieves only one thing – it makes you sound like a bitter old man. Which, as we all know, is everyone's favourite demographic.

So – Tewkesbury was a ray of sunshine for me, because it showed how a thoroughly modern town could thrive inside the shell of an ancient one; how high street shops and chain-stores could flourish while maintaining the character of the buildings they took over. Yes, it would be nice to wander down a genuine medieval street one day – like everyone else on the planet I am eagerly awaiting the invention of time travel. But I don't reckon many people would last longer than a day before they missed the little things, like underground sewage systems instead of puddles of poo in the road, and the ability to nip into a shop and buy a packet of painkillers when their head hurts, or a cheap umbrella when it starts to rain. I love being able to go down the road to the corner shop and buy a pint of icy-cold milk in the morning, instead of having to trek miles through muddy countryside to squeeze a cow. And it's so convenient to shop for, let's say, a jacket, without having to knit one from the hair you shaved off a goat you spent the last three years raising.

I love life in the 21st century and I'm not ashamed to admit it.

Even if it does mean we have to put up with Justin Beiber.

We spent an hour exploring the abbey (it was free!), and as always I was staggered by the audacity of the people who'd designed and built such a monster. It was truly beautiful, breath-taking even, and utterly epic in scale. For all the elaborate carving and complexity of the exterior, inside it is mostly one gigantic open space. Looking up, I could see tiny doors and catwalks amidst the ornate moldings. There were hidden ways within this building, I could tell; secret staircases within the walls, galleries and passageways high above our heads, that ordinary people never get to see. Whenever I see a door in an odd place, I always want to open it. Doesn't everyone? Sadly, here they all had security alarms. But the mystery and the magnificence of the abbey was well worth a visit, and well worth a donation. I put my change in a box by one of the many side-altars, lit a small candle, and prayed to the powers that be to take care of my granddad.

Lunchtime found us in Worcester.

Lunch itself, however, was a different matter.

I was starving, which meant that Roo, with her racehorse-like metabolism, was almost literally starving. When this happens, she has a tendency to pass out, and that's almost never a good thing when she's driving a Nissan Micra through the middle of a bustling city. So we parked up, I put an arm around Roo just in case, and the pair of us went in search of an affordable bite.

We didn't find one.

There's something I'll never understand about inner-city eateries, and it is this: why don't any of them serve simple, reasonably-priced, edible food?

The UK is in crisis. Our economy is crumbling like a thin slice of madeira cake, but if there's one kind of business that can survive in times like these, surely it's the food-providers? Because no matter what else happens, we've still got to eat.

So what do our cash-strapped citizens need most of all? Why, legions of cheap cafés, of course! Good food at honest prices, common and plentiful for the poor person on the go.

But we haven't got any of that.

Instead we have posh, swanky cafés – millions of the bloody things, lining the pedestrianized streets with their quaint, old-fashioned chalk boards that have almost nothing in English written on them. Places that only serve things you have to put on an accent to say, like pâté and soufflé. There's a rule I've discovered: if the menu lists three or more pieces of information about an ingredient in a sandwich, I can't afford it. Either the ingredient or the sandwich.

Prime (?), Free-range (1) Lincolnshire Pork (2) and Columbus Leek (3) sausages with pan-fried (1), lightly-seasoned (2) King Edward (3) potato slices.

Or, sausage and chips to you and me.

The difference is that sausage and chips is worth about £3.50, whereas the remarkably similar meal above would have set us back more than £12 per head.

At a café. Where you sit outside, on garden furniture. Because apparently that's what rich people do?

Pah. As far as I'm concerned, a canapé in England is that frilly bit of awning outside the front of the shop.

I don't need to know the origin and variety of every single component of the snack I'm about to consume. I'm going to eat it. I'm going to shove it in my gob, chew the crap out of it, swallow it, and ta-da! Just like that, it's gone – in considerably less time than it takes some marketing genius to write a sonnet about it. Next time I see that meal I'll be squeezing it out of my ass, and I'll care even less about what Greek province the olives came from.

"Can't we just buy a cheese sandwich from somewhere?" Roo pleaded.

"I'm trying," I promised. "This place does a 'Roasted Portabella Mushroom served in a wholemeal seeded roll with fresh tomato, spinach, Dijon mayonnaise & red onion marmalade'. I mean, at least we know they use fresh tomato, right? None of that powdered shit."

"Can we afford it?"

"Well, we could buy one and share it. And camp in a field tonight to recoup our losses?"

"Ugh!"

The next sign we passed boasted coffee that was 'biodynamically produced'. I thought this was a step too far – they were clearly making this shit up, and I was onto them. 'Bio' meaning a living organism and 'dynamically' meaning movement – well, that'll put all those people selling still, dead coffee beans right out of business.

But they also sold fruit lassies and masala-chai lattes, so they obviously knew more about the beverage industry than I did.

Poor Roo was struggling to stay upright by this point.

"Hey love, do you fancy a homemade focaccia stuffed with black kalamata olives marinated in apple cider and red wine vinegars, Italian panacetta and blue-veined Somerset Stilton cheese?"

"I dunno. What is it?"

"Well, it looks like a ham and cheese sandwich, only the bun has knobbly bits on it."

"How much is it?"

"Erm... nearly eight pounds."

"Then no."

"Sorry love! We'll find something..."

By now we'd passed more than a dozen ridiculously pretentious cafes, all mostly empty of customers, and still couldn't find anything we could afford to eat. Hell, we were struggling to find anything I could read out in one breath! Every corner, every shopping-centre entrance was festooned with the places, selling seeded organic wholegrain rye bread with free-range, dairy-free, wheat-free, gluten-free... I'd never seen the word 'free' used so much in a place that charged five times the going rate for everything.

I was crying out for a bacon butty.

Eventually, down the furthest end of the main street, way past where it ceases to be shops and becomes all that other crap that's been forced out of the pedestrianized area by their low profit margins, we found food.

A fried chicken joint that sold a bewildering array of edibles – all of it junk, like pizza, chips, kebabs and burgers – but we could recognise all of it, and we could buy half the menu for the price of one soy-cheese and seaweed brioche from the nearest Vegan Bistro.

I bought a pizza for £3.50. It was bigger than my head.

Roo had a burger and chips, and we went wild and ordered onion rings which neither of us could eat. We got a can of Coke each, too. The whole bill came to £8. No wonder they couldn't afford to rent a shop next to Marks and Spencer.

But by the time we finished eating, the queue was out of the door.

Functions of the Body

We pressed on to Kidderminster, which was tentatively on our list of comedy place names. However, a quick drive through showed the place to be remarkably normal. I'm not quite sure what I expected – people walking around dressed as clowns perhaps, or penguins, or streets paved with marshmallows – but Kidderminster was extremely ordinary. Most of the amusingly-named towns we'd passed through had exhibited similar levels of normalcy, which was unfortunate as I'd been hoping to write a book about them. Most of them were perfectly nice places, but still – perfectly nice can be perfectly boring, as anyone who's dated a Hare Krishna devotee will know.

So, choosing not to stay there, we pressed on – hoping we might have more luck with Monkhopton.

First though, a small brown sign caught our eye and directed us to the 'historic town' of Upton on Severn. It really was a charming place, about as close to a still-medieval town as you could find in England. The solitary main street was squashed between opposing rows of half-timbered buildings, their projecting upper stories sagging visibly from many centuries of existence. Amazingly, one was for sale – for £100,000! It must have been the cheapest house in the country at that time, presumably because whoever bought it would be struggling to keep it standing – along with the houses either side, which were leaning on it quite heavily.

"That's the trouble with all this historical stuff you've got," Roo pointed out. "It's beautiful, and it's fascinating – but it's too damn old."

"That's deep," I said.

"Huh. True though. If no-one buys that house, half the town will collapse."

"Guess that's why it's still for sale."

Upton turned out to be the birthplace of Formula One racing legend Nigel Mansell, but more interesting to me was that John Dee, magus to

Queen Elizabeth the First had once lived there. History, crumbling though it might be, lay thick on the town. A hotel called the White Lion had been a fixture since before the English Civil War, and apparently soldiers from both sides had gathered there, happy enough to throw off their rivalries for the sake of a good pint. Just standing in the foyer was to feel ghosts breathing down my neck. This was a building that must have seen every imaginable act and aspect of the human condition – love and marriage, adultery and betrayal, birth, death by means both natural and most foul… violence and revelry, hope and fear, the myriad minutiae of life for thousands and thousands of individuals who had passed through its doors – almost all of whom were now long dead.

"Wanna stay the night?" asked Roo.

I did. And I probably would have, had they been charging sixteenth-century prices.

Instead we pointed Bubble in the direction of Monkhopton, anticipating cloisters full of robed and tonsured old men all bouncing around on one leg, and set off.

Alas, Monkhopton, if it even existed, was so small we couldn't find the place – and the campsite we were heading for turned out to be for caravans only. As did the next one we visited, after following a series of signs from the main road.

"Let's go back to that 'Bridgnorth' place we passed through," Roo said, gunning the engine. "There's bound to be more signs, we pass them often enough."

And yet, the next set of signs led us to a site that didn't even allow touring caravans – only the monstrous static varieties, with their giant lounges and en-suite bathrooms.

We were getting desperate… or to be more accurate, Roo was getting desperate. The sheer quantity of junk food we'd put away had taken its toll on her digestive tract, with predictable results; she was now driving with her legs crossed, and producing the kind of noises I was led to believe that ladies didn't.

Digging around in the back seat I discovered a phonebook-sized directory of campsites which Dad had lent us, along with his membership card to the 'Camping And Caravanning Club'. It was a bit of a stretch, as I didn't think they had any members under fifty, but an explosion was imminent – at this stage anything was worth a try.

"Take this turn," I told Roo, and she swerved off onto a narrow country lane.

Bubble swung around the bends, a tight fit between two tall

hedges on either side, winding further and further away from civilisation. A gap in the hedge was our only clue that we'd arrived at our destination; a club-owned site, that I fervently hoped would let us use their toilet.

A handful of vans were strewn around the edges of a large, sloping field. A gnarled old fellow approached us as we pulled up beside a portacabin labelled 'Site Office'.

I hailed him while he was still a way off.

"Hi there! I'm a member, but I only have a tent and my wife really needs a poo," I shouted.

"I'm afraid all members have to provide their own bathroom facilities," he called back. Just as I'd feared. "We only provide a chemical-toilet emptying point."

"I knew that of course, being a member," I told him. "So there's no place to poo?"

"No, no poo," he shook his head sadly.

We were back on the road again minutes later. The book showed us one more possibility. It was a very basic site and it wasn't super-close, but Roo was pushing Bubble up to speeds that made him quiver like a dog getting its favourite ear scratched.

A contact number was listed, so I typed it into my phone, mentally rehearsing my request and crossing my fingers that they had space.

The conversation went as planned, until the woman on the other end of the line said, "You sound young. I have to ask: how old are you?"

"I'm thirty-three."

"Oh." There was silence for a few seconds. "Well. I s'pose that's okay then. I'm not keen on having youngsters in tents y'see. They're more trouble than they're worth. They annoy the other campers. You'd better not get up to any mischief, or I'll be sending you on your way again."

I was suddenly quite glad I hadn't opened with 'Hello, my wife is busting for a shit...'

"I live on site too," she continued, "so I'll be watching you."

"Don't worry, there'll be none of that from us," I assured her. "We're quiet and mature. And sensible."

"And full of shit," Roo added, proving that women can multi-task. If I was concentrating on keeping my bum clenched as hard as she was I'd have been reduced to single syllables along the lines of 'Uuuuuuurrrr!'

"How far is it?" she asked as I hung up.
"Not far. Maybe ten or fifteen minutes."
"I think I can make it."

I borrowed a piece of advice my sister had once given me in the same situation, and deployed my best Obi-Wan Kenobi impression. "Use the sphincter, love."

With my phone on the dashboard, I dug the laptop out of the bag by my knees. I was going to rely on the miracle of modern synergy; phone and computer seamlessly integrating to give me unfettered access to the information super-highway. Google would be our saviour – their maps would guide our way, even whilst doing 80mph in a car that had been shaking itself apart since 60.

"If nothing else, our technology will make us look like grown-ups," I pointed out. My sleek new MacBook Air, wirelessly tethered to a nearly new HTC Desire smartphone, was sure to impress someone who lived full-time in a field.

Roo was still a little concerned. "I hope she doesn't expect us both to look 33…"

It was a good point. I hadn't taken into account that Roo was only 25, and blessed with a childlike complexion that recently resulted in her being ID'd in ASDA whilst trying to buy superglue.

It probably wouldn't help that she had pink and turquoise hair, either.

"That's okay love. We're good people. We're dressed tidy. I'll use some big words…"

"Is that before, or after we roll up in a car decorated with cupcakes and octopuses?"

It's not often I'm grateful for arriving at a campsite in the dark. In fact, I think this is the only time it has ever been an advantage. The owner still gave us a good look over as we unfolded ourselves from Bubble's seats. Roo sprinted straight for the toilet (there was only one), which left me free to placate the woman. Yes, we're young, but married, exploring the country with a tent and an inheritance… I think I made it sound quite romantic.

Then Roo was back to help me pitch the tent, and our efficiency in accomplishing this in near total darkness explained more eloquently than I ever could just how sensible and disciplined we were.

I even stopped myself from spanking Roo with the fibreglass poles, rolling around wrapped in the groundsheet as though it was attacking me or narrating the entire process like it was the FA Cup final. For the first time ever!

And when finished, I refrained from inviting the rest of the campsite to come and admire my erection (as had been my habit until then).

Instead, we crawled inside the tent, safe from critical eyes, and then at last we could relax.

"Ahhhh!" I sighed. "Glad that's over."

"Yeah!"

"Did you...?"

"Yes, thanks."

"Oh. Good."

"Yes it was."

"Thanks for that."

We were silent for a while, luxuriating in the freedom to do absolutely nothing. If there's one advantage to being hopelessly lost in the deepest, darkest countryside, miles and miles from anywhere, it's the peace and quiet.

"Um... Tony?" said Roo.

"Yes love?"

"I'm a bit hungry..."

Strange Folk

The next morning we woke up to find a deluge of biblical proportions had happened overnight. Against all the odds, the tent had remained waterproof – everywhere except the bits where our bodies touched the sides. Because this was a three person tent in name only, a midget couldn't sleep in the foetal position without at least part of him touching the walls. Consequently Roo's feet were soaked, and I was soggy in any number of places because I thrash around like a dying fish when I sleep. I guess we should count ourselves lucky the tent was still up, instead of shrink-wrapped to our skin.

Our first order of the day was to eat breakfast, which we did in rare style – there was left over pizza from a takeaway I'd discovered last night, and an ill-advised (but irresistible) purchase of frozen cheesecake now proved fortuitous. We were far, far from civilization and had very little desire to navigate the back roads into town on an empty stomach.

Instead, we lounged on our camp chairs and watched the guy next-door oiling his tepee. No, that's not a euphemism for something indecent – he had a pile of twenty-foot long poles laid out on the floor in front of his decrepit caravan and he was rubbing them vigorously.

After a while he noticed us watching and gave us a friendly wave.

"I like your wood," I told him.

Well, what would you say?

"Thank-you," he replied. "You're camping, eh?"

"Yes," I said, redundantly, as I was sitting in front of a conspicuously moist tent.

"Terrible rain last night."

No shit. I surveyed the pond which had formed on my flysheet and decided it was too early in the morning to be sarcastic.

"I know. I'm wearing most of it."

"Did it wake you?"

"No, we slept through it. And in it, actually."

"Not the best weather for camping, this time of year."

"Is that right?" My resistance was wavering.

"S'why I bought the van," he explained, jerking a thumb at the shittiest example of a caravan I'd ever seen. It didn't look substantially more waterproof than our tent.

"It's nice," I lied.

"Yeah, keeps the rain off our heads," he said. Which I doubted. "We'll all be dead next year anyway."

"Mmm," I agreed, before I'd fully processed his statement.

Roo's eyes went wide as she looked at me.

Oh no, I thought. *Not again.*

I think everyone, at some point or other, starts to think they're attracting nutters. Maybe it's because the nutters outnumber the rest of us? Or maybe it's because each nutter can latch onto many different people in the course of one day. Nutters aren't known to be fussy. But I *really* attract nutters. Roo thinks it's because I'm too nice, and I can't bring myself to be rude to them. I just sit there, making hints, and it's common knowledge that nutters are completely immune to hints. Personally though, I think it's because I have a missing component in my brain. Where most people have a built-in nutter-detector, or even the hyper-sensitive run-like-fuck-ometer, I just have a big blank card that reads '404 Error – item not found'. Consequently, I'm often well into conversation before it dawns on me that the person I'm talking to is a few teddy bears short of a picnic.

"Oh, you mean that whole Mayan Calendar thing," I said.

Roo was moving her head from side to side very slowly. *Stop encouraging him!* she was warning me.

But it was too late.

This nutter looked to be in his late fifties; he was stripped to the waist, but even without a linen smock he radiated 'hippie'. His girlfriend was a surprise, when she emerged from the caravan with a cup of chai; she was about twenty-five and Swedish. Swedes are normally too pragmatic to drink the Kool-Aid, but this chick was built like a brick paver and had more body hair than I do. Perhaps her brain was as fuzzy as the rest of her? At any rate, she seemed eager enough to spend the morning polishing her sugar-daddy's wood.

As we couldn't escape further than our tent without major effort, we ended up chatting amicably about the end of the world coinciding with the last days of the Mayan Long Count Calendar in December 2012. Our neighbour explained that an upcoming planetary alignment would mark the beginning of the end, as the stresses it put on our fragile planet would destabilize Earth's magnetic field. Presumably this was the reason why he'd abandoned his wife of thirty-odd years and the business they ran together selling alternative clothing, and was living in a field with a Swedish chick half his age varnishing his ridgepole.

"It only cost eight grand," he said proudly of his tepee. "Should have cost over forty, but I got it for eight because it wasn't finished."

Wealthy, shacked up – as nutters go, he wasn't doing too bad for himself. But for a hippie, he seemed like a bit of an jerk.

Later that day I navigated back to town (which meant it took substantially longer than it should have). We found the hippie's ex-shop, complete with his ex-wife, and Roo bought a patchwork skirt from her out of sympathy. I wanted to tell her that when the world didn't end in 2012 his new life would fall apart. He'd loose his mystique along with his mission, most likely loose his disciple too, would run out of cash to feed his bong and would come crawling back to her. But who knows? He seemed pretty determined. And maybe he had a thing for Ewoks.

We returned to the site well after dark, to avoid any more close encounters.

The next day we rose early (for us), and considered the lengthy task ahead of us. In order to leave, we had to pack up the tent – and to accomplish that, we first had to dry the thing. It was utterly soaked from our second night of rain, and to be honest we weren't much drier ourselves. A few hours of blazing sunlight would have made our job much easier, but at that point I think we had more chance of the tent growing arms and shaking itself dry. I picked up our one sodden tea-towel, which was still ringing wet from wiping out the inside of the tent. It wasn't much bigger than a handkerchief, and seemed spectacularly unequal to the task.

"Good morning!" An elderly lady poked her head out of the only other caravan on site. "You must have had an awful night with all that rain. You poor things!"

"Good morning," I replied cheerfully. "We're fine actually. We're used to it!"

"You must be freezing cold! How about a nice cup of tea?"

"Oh! Well, why not. Thank-you very much."

"Ah, not for me, thanks," said Roo.

She tut-tutted at that. "Have you got a cup?"

"Erm..." I glanced back towards the car.

"No bother! I've got a spare cup right here." She poured tea into an old enamel mug and carried it over to me.

"Thank-you!"

"Oh, don't worry about it! You poor, poor thing. Are you sure you don't want one?" she asked Roo.

Roo shook her head.

"Do you want to borrow the kettle? Then you can make yourself another cuppa later on. You can keep the cup for now."

"Er, thanks, but we've actually got a kettle in there somewhere," I jerked a thumb towards Bubble.

"Oh! Would you like some milk then? No bother, I'll pour you out a little bottle."

And she scurried off back to her caravan.

When she emerged, she was also carrying a packet of biscuits. "Here you go, loves," she said. "I feel so sorry for you! Are you sure you won't take the kettle?"

"No, we're good, thanks. We're actually thinking of leav—"

"I know what you need!" she declared, eyes bright with triumph. "A hot water bottle!"

Roo shook her head. "Is it you that attracts these people, or me?"

Although camping in England in late September is kind of an endurance sport, I felt we were coping rather well with it – but nothing could persuade this woman that we were happy with our lot. She kept disappearing back into her van and emerging with some device she felt we needed, like a toaster or an electric blanket. When we politely refused each loan, on the grounds that we had no bread anyway and didn't want to electrocute ourselves if our tent lost its capacity to withstand the elements, she shook her head in pity and returned to her van to see if she had anything else which could make our lives less miserable.

"Better get out of here before she tries to lend us a gas fire," I said to Roo.

"It's your fault," she replied, "you shouldn't have told her it was our honeymoon!"

The kind woman's husband came into the bathroom as I was brushing my teeth in the sink.

"Don't mind if I use the facilities?" he asked me.

I had a foaming mouthful of toothpaste, so I couldn't answer him one way or the other. He decided I'd be okay with it, so he squeezed past, turned his back to me and took a piss.

Then came another of those awkward camping situations. He wanted to wash his hands, but not while I was hovering over the sink about to spit. So he hung around beside me and tried to make casual conversation while he waited for me to finish.

"So, where are you and your wife from?"

I thought about this for a second. Clearly he could see I had my mouth full. Maybe it was rhetorical. I ignored the question and brushed on.

"Are you staying here long?" he asked.

I Mmm-Mmm'ed a negative.

"So, where did you get married?"

I gave a shrug and pointed at my mouth with my free hand, and he fell silent for a couple of seconds.

"So, what made you want to go camping for your honeymoon?"

I looked at him. My cheeks bulged like I was about to blow a giant raspberry. I had a sudden urge to spit a great gob-full of toothpaste all over him before calmly answering his question, but I didn't. I'm nice like that.

"So, where did you two meet?" he asked.

I gave up, emptied my cheeks into the basin and spoke to the cold tap. "America."

"Ah! So where'd you get your tent?"

"Millets."

"How long you had your Micra?"

I realized then that he wasn't going to stop. He didn't care about my answers. He wasn't even listening to them. He probably didn't even want to wash his hands. What he wanted was human interaction, presumably because he'd been alone with his wife in a field for longer than is healthy, and he wasn't going to stop until he'd had his fill.

"It's my Granddad's car," I told him, "and he's dead."

And I fled before he could ask why an octogenarian had owned a car with garden gnomes all over it.

"Forget drying the tent," I said to Roo when I got back, "We've got to get out of here! I've just met her husband, and if he starts talking to us before we leave we might not be able to.

"Okay," she said, "but first, please will *you* return these? She literally wouldn't take no for an answer."

She held up two matching knitted jumpers, one with a cat on it and one with a dog. Then she pointed at the door flap to our tent. Just inside were two identical pairs of slippers. I reached in and pulled them out. Inside one nestled a rolled up scarf. Inside the other was a thermos flask.

"And whatever you do," Roo added, "DO NOT let her give you that air-mattress."

Training Day

When I discovered that Bridgnorth had a cliff-lift, or Funicular, I had to take Roo on it. My Granddad had spent most of his retirement years driving the Scarborough cliff-lift, which I have since discovered is the oldest one still operating in the UK at almost 140 years old. For anyone who hasn't seen one before (there's only about 20 left in England), they are vertical railways, with small carriages that are pulled up and down a cliff on very steep rails. Normally there are two cars, and one rises as the other descends, counterbalancing each other. This one had originally been powered by filling a water tank beneath the top car until it was heavy enough to pull the bottom one up, then pumping the water back up and repeating the process. We got a great view over the town and surrounding countryside as we descended, though a glass roof would have improved this considerably. It was a quaint and charming way to visit the lower part of Bridgnorth, and we made sure to check the timetable for the last trip back – getting stuck at the bottom would mean a truly epic climb up the stairs.

We explored the ruins of Bridgnorth castle, which consisted of one enormous chunk of tower leaning at a crazy angle over the surrounding gardens. How it's still standing is a mystery, but apparently it's angle of 15 degrees gives it four times more lean than the famous Tower of Pisa.

Our next trip was taken in honour of my Dad. The Severn Valley Railway is a heritage line which runs restored steam trains – another bastion of British history that Roo had never been able to experience in Australia. The powerful locomotive was noisy and smelly, gushing steam at deafening volume and letting fly with a shrill whistle at regular intervals – Roo loved every minute of it! We spent most of the sixteen-mile journey back to Kidderminster with our heads hanging out of the windows, shrieking like kids when a gust of wind blew grey smoke right into our faces. We got off halfway to see the museum, and stood on the footbridge while the engine shuddered past underneath us.

Then we bought ice-creams. Because that's also quite British.

We came back on the last train of the day, happy and knackered, and collapsed into Bubble. It was already getting late, and the least-favourite part of the day was still to come; the inevitable twilight mission to find somewhere to camp.

But then Roo had a brainwave. "Why don't we treat ourselves to a night in a hotel? We could look online to see if there's any last-minute discounts, and drive to anywhere that has a good offer."

It was a stroke of genius. It could mean a longer drive, but there'd be no tent to set up in the dark when we arrived – that alone made the idea appealing.

The last place we'd packed the tent away had been in the Field of Nutters. We'd set up there (inevitably) in the darkness, and had been more focused on convincing the owner it was safe to let us stay than on finding the perfect place to pitch.

The result was that we'd camped out right on top of a big pile of shit; we'd tried to wipe the worst of it off the bottom of the tent before putting it away, but again we'd been distracted – this time by our impending doom as the procession of the planets sought to tear the fabric of our world apart. What's a little cow poo compared with the threat of cosmic annihilation? After all, isn't the smell supposed to be good for you? Now though, faced with the prospect of unpacking the tent to see what kind of a mess we'd made by rolling it up, a hotel didn't seem like such a bad idea. If we were lucky, it might only cost double the price of a campsite. And there were other double features to consider, like the bed…

I hooked the phone to the computer and browsed LateRooms.com. This website had been our saviour many times in the past and today was no exception. A few clicks and a swift hunt for my credit card and we'd bagged ourselves a bargain: an Executive Suite in a hotel promisingly called 'The International'. Wow! A £130-per-night room which we had snuck into for less than £30 – that had to be a record, even for natural-born scroungers like ourselves. Whatever the case, we weren't going to turn it down, so Roo piled on the gas and we blazed a trail for The International before they could spot their mistake and rectify it.

I had two fears; one, that we'd show up looking like a pair of homeless vagabonds and be refused entry, and two; we'd show up to find a total shithole and look like we belonged. Both seemed equally possible, but in the event this deal was every bit as good as it seemed. We parked Bubble a safe distance from the hotel and walked around the block first, so that no-one in the building would associate us with the car.

I rooted through my rucksack to find a clean shirt for check-in; Roo, to my eternal delight, looks damn sexy in almost anything because she *is* damn sexy. And no, you can't have her. Her tight jeans and flip-flops took the focus away from my lower half, which was good because it was covered in soot and food. This is not unusual for me, but it only becomes a problem when I try to check in to insanely expensive hotel rooms – not something I have to do very often. So far, so good. We'd made it to the front desk, and our cover was still intact.

Should I tip the concierge, I wondered, like they do in movies?

Or would he be insulted with the paltry amount I could offer? He was impeccably dressed in a stylish blue suit. He probably earned more than I did.

What the hell was I on about? I'm an unemployed starving writer. There are ten year old orphans working in Vietnamese sweat shops that earn more than I do.

So we just paid for our room and took the lift, sneaking back later to bring our rucksacks up. The same guy was still on the desk and he had a laugh when we dragged the over-stuffed backpacks through his marble-tiled lobby. "Camping out are we?" he joked.

If only he knew.

For a minute I considered telling him the truth; that we needed somewhere with enough floor space and free toilet roll to wipe a two-day old turd sandwich off the bottom of our tent... and we'd just found it.

£30 well spent, I say.

After the first trip we couldn't resist bringing the rest of our gear up. The receptionist had a sense of humour, even if he seemed to be laughing *at* us rather than with us; so we brought up our food crate, our spare clothing bags, our computers... although Roo drew the line at Dad's kettle. "There's one in the room," she pointed out.

"But it's tiny!"

"How many people are drinking tea?"

"Just me."

"Well then."

I took the octopus-shaped scrubbing brush though. Just in case.

After the tent was cleaned, the gear re-packed, and we'd sorted through our clothes and laundry, we took it in turns to abuse the bathroom. After campsite toilet blocks it was pure luxury to take an extra-long shower, safe in the knowledge there wasn't a semi-naked, bible-bashing pensioner waiting outside the door. We made good use of the power sockets to charge everything we could find, and good use of the bed for… well, it was a bed. Let's leave it at that.

Dinner time came around and we both had quite an appetite. We could go out and look for food of course, but we'd already spent £30 on the room. It was shaping up to be an expensive day, what with being charged full price for the train tickets. Roo, however, had an idea. "We've already got our food up here, and our cooking gear."

"What?" I was staggered by the depths of her cheek. "You're not really suggesting we set up our camping stove and cook in the room."

"Why not? It doesn't make any smoke. We've got tins left. Tonight should have been…" she glanced into the crate beside the bed. "Beans. Baked beans and… macaroni cheese?"

As ideas go, it had it's possibilities.

"Beans and mac-and-cheese it is then."

So we sat there cross-legged on the carpet, cooking a tasty one-pot meal on our little gas burner, chuckling at the ridiculousness of the situation.

It was another thing I decided not to mention to the man at the front desk.

Afterwards, I washed the dishes in the bathroom sink and dried them on thick white hand towels. I didn't use the new scrubbing brush; somehow it looked too clean and new, and I didn't want to ruin it.

I'd love to know what the staff thought of us the next day, when they came to clean our room. No-one had seen us emerge from the room all night, and in the rubbish bin were empty bean cans, a gas canister, the last of our cheese, milk and butter (all of which had gone off), several stones (Roo picks them up everywhere we go, and if I don't get rid of them fairly regularly the car would be knee deep in them), several pairs of stinky socks which we deemed too far gone to wash in the sink, and acres of soggy toilet paper encrusted with thick mud and cow shit.

As a parting joke I stripped the bed and laid out the bedding on the floor, Crocodile Dundee-style.

I don't know if they do those mega-cheap room deals anymore, but somehow I doubt it.

Abridged

The breakfast spread at the International Hotel was so exciting I felt a little pee come out. An endless table laden with serving platters stretched off towards the horizon; it was so long that the far end vanished into mist like the other side of a rainbow. Honestly, you should go there sometime.

Roo sidled along behind me, still acutely aware that everyone else in the room was dressed for business. Having pink and turquoise striped hair did make her *slightly* more conspicuous. I hung around, shielding her from prying eyes while she filled a plate with hash browns and scrambled egg.

Then, after escorting her to a table, I came back to attack the buffet.

When I sat down opposite her and tucked into my bowl of corn flakes with relish, Roo looked aghast. "Tony, you have that for breakfast every morning! We've got a box of corn flakes in the car!"

"Oh, don't you worry," I told her, "I'm just getting started."

We stayed at that table for two hours.

Roo was getting quite embarrassed by the time we left.

In addition to the corn flakes, I ate a full cooked breakfast, two croissants, a yoghurt, a muffin, a bowl of fruit salad, several pieces of toast with jam, and some unchristenable Danish pastry-type thingummy. I washed it all down with five cups of coffee and an apple juice, and we stole four pieces of fruit, two more croissants, several tiny packets of butter and jam and a little box of Kellogg's Frosties.

Each.

There have been times when I've criticised Roo's penchant for gigantic handbags, but I take it all back; anything that can smuggle a complete picnic lunch for two people in it has to be worth having around. It also comes in very handy for sneaking snacks into the cinema.

Our plan that day, after making our escape from The International, was to visit an intriguing spot Roo had discovered on the map. It was labelled 'Secret Bunker,' which seemed a bit conspicuous if you ask me. I mean, I know there's this thing about hiding in plain sight, but surely some kind of line had been crossed here? Like issuing a floor-plan of Guantanamo Bay and leaving 'Torture Chamber' marked on it. Whatever the case, we had to investigate.

Leaving Telford (where the hotel was), we first visited Ironbridge, a town known for – yep, you guessed it – a bridge made of iron. We'd picked the place because it was on our way, but it proved my point that there's chunks of history crammed into every nook and cranny of the UK. This particular iron bridge was apparently the first in the world, and it was still standing in spite of a recent flash-flood which tore down several other bridges over this stretch of the River Severn. The 235-year-old structure comprised over 1,700 individually cast components, every one of which was different. It looked incredibly complex, like a steam-punk take on a bridge. Oddly, the road atop the iron archway sloped up on both sides to form a peak in the middle, rather than being flat; it looked kind of precarious, like a bit too much weight on that central section would cause the whole thing to fold in on itself and fall into the gorge.

Which was probably why they didn't let cars drive across it.

The minds of people who dream up this sort of thing astound me. Personally, I'd have been inclined to think 'Ah, building a bridge out of thousands of cast iron components sounds a like a lot of work. There's already a bridge a few miles up the river. I'll just use that one.'

Our lunch stop was the result of a fairly epic left-turn, which added nearly 200 miles to our route courtesy of the Northern Welsh countryside. Our target was a World Heritage Site – one of only three in Wales. I believe this is partly because of the place names, which are so damn unintelligible UNESCO must dread having to talk about them. This site, the last to be added, was called Pontcysyllte – and before you ask, no, I have no idea how to pronounce it. And I lived in Wales for five years.

It didn't stop me trying though, and a short way into our journey Roo had to ban this practice because I was covering the windscreen in spit.

"It's a guttural sound, the double-L," I explained to her, "it's made way back in your throat, like *CGH*—"

"Eww! You're cleaning that up right now!"

"I think we need the next left," I said, ignoring her. "There's a

CAN I KISS HER YET?

sign that says *Pont—*"
"*Stop saying it!*"

Pont-whatever-the-fuck-it-was is an aqueduct – which I appreciate makes it sound about as sexy as a tube of haemorrhoid cream. But let's break it down; this is not Ancient Rome. We have indoor plumbing nowadays – well, apart from the Welsh. So, if we get our water from a system of underground pipes, what use is an aqueduct, right? Well, this might make it sound a tiny bit cooler – an aqueduct, at least these days, is a bridge for boats.

Venice may be famous for the beauty of its canals, but in the UK we have over 2,000 miles of them. Because boats can't sail uphill, locks are used when the level of the water changes from one canal to the next. Locks are operated exclusively by old men with huge beards in late-night documentaries on Channel 4. 'But what happens when a boat needs to cross a wide valley?' I hear you cry. Well, then it's buggered. Or that would be the answer I'd expect to hear.

But a long time ago, some very clever people came up with a plan to make an enormous bridge, fill it with water, and float boats across the top of it. I'm not sure everyone at the time thought of them as clever – phrases like 'complete bloody lunatics' spring to mind – but they did it anyway. And the fruit of their labours is what we were going to see... and hopefully walk across.

We parked Bubble and strolled along the towpath (so called because before they had engines, the barges were towed along by horses). The canal was just wide enough for Roo to demand I not try and jump across it – and yet narrow enough that, once her back was turned, I made the jump by the skin of my teeth. Twice.

Roo was not best pleased with my athletic display, but I knew that deep down she was secretly impressed.

The aqueduct was quite possibly the least-likely construction I have ever come across. Remember me waffling on about viaducts? Well this was one of those – nineteen stupendous columns towered up from the valley floor below, built of stone mortared with lime and ox blood. The columns gave rise to a series of graceful arches, across which the water flowed – in a cast iron trough, like the world's longest medieval bath tub. The whole thing seemed impossibly narrow. The channel for boats couldn't have been more than ten feet wide, and there was no guard at all between the edge of the metal trough and the plunging drop. We followed the towpath, which necessarily continued all the way across. It was just wide enough for us to walk single-file; a skinny metal railing was all that separated us from a drop of well over a hundred feet down into the valley below.

Walking across the thing was awe-inspiring, because of the incredible view along the lush green valley in both directions – and pant-wettingly scary, because when the wind blew (and we were a hundred feet up in the air, remember) – there was nothing to do but cling onto the safety rail and pray it would stop long enough for us to get to the other side. For boat pilots it must have been truly terrifying, as their decks would stick up well above the height of the water-filled trough. They could literally step right off the boat into fresh air, almost forty metres above the ground. Clearly not a good place to drink and drive.

An hour's drive to the north, Secret Bunker proved surprisingly difficult to locate. Perhaps the scale of our map was to blame; we'd failed to find entire towns before now, on account of the town name being substantially larger than the pin-prick denoting it's position. Eventually, as night fell, we came across a subtle clue in the form of a large green sign that said 'Secret Bunker —> 200 Yards'. A note along the bottom of the sign informed us that this was a 'Temporary Sign' – presumably they were trying to come up with something more ironic to replace it. The Secret Bunker itself was closed, which was not unexpected, but we were thrilled to find out that we could come back and explore it during working hours. That's the hours people work, by the way – not the Secret Bunker, which had been decommissioned and turned into a museum. Of a bunker.

Is it just me, or has that word lost all meaning?

For no immediately apparent reason we leapt around like goons in the darkness, pretending that some mysterious government agency was watching us. If they were, they must have thought we were a pair of complete idiots. In which case, they were right – but we were hungry idiots, so we soon abandoned our capering and went in search of sustenance.

As we hadn't paid for our breakfast or our lunch, we totally splurged when it came to dinner time – and went to McDonalds. Yes, I know, most people wouldn't count that as splurging, but Roo and I have very simple needs. And nutrition, apparently, isn't one of them. I'm shamed to say, our first date was at McDonalds – it was all I could afford on a pumpkin pickers' wages. And the place was only half-built too, so there were boxes of light fittings and ladders all over the place. We loved it, as we love each other; our compatibility is almost too good to be true, and this sort of event is the proof of that. What other girl could I take out on a romantic date to a fast food outlet, and still expect her to be talking to me at the end of the night?

Would any of you folks be happy with this kind of scenario?

Thought not.

Even now, three years later, we're not substantially better off – but Roo doesn't seem to mind one bit. She would say that she's part Dutch, so frugality is built into her DNA, and that nothing else really matters so long as we have each other.

I would say I'm fortunate that she has such low expectations.

I count my stars every single day that Roo continues to put up with my shit.

I'm a lucky, lucky man.

But I'm giving serious though to stepping up my game.

Next time I'll take her to Burger King.

Variation On A Theme

It was late when Roo guided Bubble into the confusing mass of motorways that surround Stoke-on-Trent. We were here for two reasons; three actually, if you count it being in our way. I had relatives here that had agreed to put us up for a couple of nights, and the biggest and best theme park in the UK just happens to be on their doorstep.

I tend to visit these relatives quite a lot.

Stoke-on-Trent is one of those places steeped in a local industrial tradition – in this case it's the home of The Potteries, the huge factories where the best English crockery (like Wedgewood and Spode) was made for generations upon generations. Until this one, when the people in the posh suits figured it was cheaper to make the stuff in Indonesia.

Stoke hasn't really recovered from that yet. It has raging unemployment, an identity crisis and a handful of remaining factories that run guided tours to prop up their ailing pottery businesses.

People who are born there rarely leave. This creates a rustic, small-town feel, where everyone knows everyone else and extended families are spread out with only a mile or so between all of them.

I couldn't do it. I mean, I can see the appeal of making life-long friends (and/or enemies) with your neighbours, of being on first-name terms with your milkman and the paper boy and the vicar. But don't they ever wonder what life would be like on the other side of the world? Or, you know, the other side of their county?

Perhaps I should be thankful that I'm in the minority. If everyone had my wanderlust, there'd be legions of people roaming the world with rucksacks, writing about their adventures. Then I'd be really screwed.

We bought microwavable curry from a supermarket on the outskirts of town, and also spotted an assistant marking down all the sandwiches that were getting close to their sell-by date. Score! We bought the lot.

So many in fact that our chances of consuming them all before they went bad were minimal – but then, I've never let a simple thing like mould stop me from eating a sandwich. Roo is not quite as hard-core as me in this, being of an altogether more delicate physiology, but all that meant was more cheap nosh for me. And possibly a bout of Salmonella, but I'd cross that bridge if I came to it.

Aunty Sylvia welcomed us into her home, which was warm and bright and comfortable. It even had a small piece of carpet on top of the toilet lid, much to Roo's amusement. "What is it?" she asked me.

"It's a toilet... erm, cover thingumy. I don't know if there's a word for them. But everyone has them."

"No they don't! I've never seen one before in my entire life! Who needs a hat on top of the toilet? What does it do?"

"Well, it... sort of protects... well, it means you can sit on the toilet, when it's closed."

"Ridiculous."

But we passed a pleasant evening there, in spite of the confusing accessories.

Roo convinced me to call my parents. Not because she thought they'd be worried about us, but because she wanted to check on the hamsters. Dad reported that the hamsters were fine, if a bit sullen. He then told me that a Money Order had arrived from Lloyds Bank, made out in the amount of seventeen Australian dollars. Did I need anything doing with it?

Well, yes, was the answer to that. I needed it crumpling up into the spikiest possible shape, and inserting rectally into the arsehole that had sent it. Seventeen dollars? What the hell was I supposed to do with that? *Forty-three dollars* was what I needed – no more, and no less. It was clear what they'd done – despite precise instructions to the contrary, they had taken the fee for issuing the Order out of the value of the Order itself, rather than simply deducting the fee from my bank account. If I hadn't been royally screwed before, I was now; another Order would have to be paid for, issued and waited for, before it could be posted off to the Australian Police. Yet another month had been added to an emigration timetable that didn't even have a day to spare. But what can you do, really? Banks control the world. They can do whatever they want, and we, their precious customers, can do not one single thing about it.

I'd have been quite bitter about the whole state of affairs, were I not so excited about the trip to Alton Towers in the morning.

Right then. Listen up, all you fun-lovers! If you really want to have a kick-ass day out at pretty much any major theme park, there are some easy ways to ensure you get maximum enjoyment for your dollar. Alton Towers is not only the best in the UK, it's also the most expensive; £49 ($82!) per ticket, single admission, one day only. Jeez, man! Why, a family of four-and-a-half people could go to the Slimbridge Wetlands Centre for that!

What, no takers?

My Grand Adventurer's Guide To Theme Park Exploitation:

1) Simple, really. Go in the middle of the week, so the only kids there are yours (who have been pulled out of school legitimately for reasons of personal bereavement); kids belonging to parents who have no respect for the educational system; kids who are skiving of their own volition and live close enough to walk (I believe most schools in the area are fairly wise to this practice); and kids on organised school trips.

2) Go on all the famous rides first – the school groups won't arrive until halfway through the morning, as most of them don't leave their school until around the same time the park is opening.

But by far the best strategy of all is:

3) Go when bad weather is forecast! It's really bizarre, how much people in the UK worry about the weather. I mean, we've all grown up with it. We all know it's crap. But surely by now we can deal with that? Apparently not. With rain scheduled for most of the day, Alton Towers was deserted. People coming from a decent distance away must have chosen not to make the trip and risk ruining their enjoyment. Pah! Suck it up, I say; human beings are, for the most part, waterproof. I once walked through the rain for two solid weeks – and yes, it was amongst the most miserable experiences of my adult life. Even watching the Star Wars prequel movies paled in comparison.

But I survived, damn it! I even wrote a book about it.

So, can I sit on a rollercoaster and still enjoy it, even though I'm getting a bit wet? Hell yeah!

Roo and I donned ridiculous yellow body-condoms, bought for the princely sum of £1 each, and prepared to have the time of our lives.

And you know what? It didn't even rain.

The sun cracked through the clouds as we paid our entrance fee, and we spent the rest of the day skipping merrily through the park, dodging puddles and being grateful we weren't getting sunburnt. We rode all the biggest rides twice, then found and experienced every single ride in the place (except for the teacup merry-go-round, which Roo decided was too undignified). Oh, and we didn't ride the log flume; having stayed dry all day, there was no point in pushing our luck. We ate our cut-price sandwiches in one laughable excuse for a queue – after walking half a mile through the barriers, passing signs bearing ominous warnings like 'Queue Time From This Point: 1.5 hours,' we arrived to find less than thirty people waiting for the ride. Hell, it took me three goes on it just to finish my sandwich!

The only ride we had to wait more than a couple of minutes for was the infamous Nemesis – Europe's first inverted rollercoaster, and the parks biggest, baddest ride at the time. As we stood in line on a pitted steel walkway, a huge shower of sparks erupted from the railing right next to us – perfectly timed to make the whole queue jump about a foot into the air. The atmosphere was charged and the setting was done perfectly; rumbles and crashes came from brutal-looking machinery, rusty chains and hooks dangled, blood stains and gouges covered the steel-panelled walls and artfully-piled tools littered the ground, encrusted with gore. Then, from the mist obscuring the empty queue gates behind us, emerged a figure. Gigantic and lumbering, the man moved steadily towards us, mumbling and twitching. His costume was perfect, and he was really selling his performance; I'd done the same job for a brief summer In Granada Studios, and knew how much fun it could be. He lurched closer, twitching with every step; all that was between him and me was the skinny metal railing, and I had a horrible feeling he was looking for a victim to make a scene. Swathes of his brown, threadbare jumper hung off him like a mummies' bandages and in one hand he clutched... *something*. Was it a rusty cleaver? I love a good fright, but for some unknown reason I scream like a girl – it's one of the few things that has the power to embarrass me. Roo thinks it's hysterical, and she was still sniggering from the shriek I'd let out when the sparks had gone off. I always get picked on by character actors in theme parks and I always end up screaming – much to the amusement of everyone else in the queue.

And it was about to happen again.

Up came that enormous hand, filthy and thick-fingered. The guy's gaze was fixed on the floor and he was moaning slightly as he lunged closer. His beard covered most of his face and bristled dramatically in all directions – it was a masterpiece of prosthetics, I thought, and must have taken hours to apply each day.

He surged closer, moving now with greater urgency – and then carried on past us, down the empty queue gate to terrorize some other poor bugger.

Or... not?

As I was breathing a sigh of relief I saw him raise his hand to steady himself on the railing. In it he was clutching... not a cleaver! A carrier bag? Full of snacks, it seemed...

"My God," said Roo, "he's not in costume. He's a customer!"

It was true. The filthy, ragged giant had staggered all the way down the empty queue gate – bothering no-one, at least not intentionally – and climbed onto the ride.

He wasn't a heavily made-up staff member on a mission to scare ten shades of shit out of the customers! He was here, just like the rest of us, for whatever passed for enjoyment in that addled brain. He'd even brought a picnic.

Over the next twenty minutes, as Roo and I queued patiently, the freakish bloke passed us a further five times. His gait and overall hairiness put me in mind of a Yeti. He was here by himself, clearly quite stoned, and was using the 'single rider' lane to lap us over and over again, getting several rides in the time it took us to get one.

"He's pretty clever, for a drugged-up yeti," Roo remarked.

And a yeti that was fixated on riding The Nemesis as many times as was physically possible in one afternoon. Well, he was getting his money's worth out of his clothes – it looked like he'd hadn't taken them off for at least a year – so it was only natural he'd want to make the most of his day at Alton Towers. All I wanted was a photograph, to prove this behemoth existed; I already knew there would be sceptics amongst my friends. But, like his namesake, this creature proved impossible to capture on camera – partially because he moved so fast, albeit awkwardly, that he was gone before I could turn the camera on – and partially because I was afraid to draw attention to myself by being more obvious about it. There was still a slight chance that he had a rusty meat cleaver in that bag...

Over thirty rides later, we called it quits. Not by choice; the park was closing, and rumour has it they're allowed to hunt you if you try to stay.

Our mood as we left Alton Towers was summed up beautifully by their traffic lights – which, to Roo's delight, had smiley faces on them!

To round out the day nicely, the manager of the 'Man In Space' pub told us to BOGOF; that's, 'Buy One Get One Free', on our evening meals. Full to bursting, we snuggled up in a real bed in Aunty Sylvia's house, with the comforts of home all around us (by which I mean, we didn't have to sprint across a muddy field to visit the bathroom).

"Can we do this again?" Roo asked, sleepily.

"We certainly can, love. Same time next year?"

"I was thinking about tomorrow…"

But tomorrow would be a totally different story. Because Roo's stated intention was to walk clear across England, one-hundred and eighteen kilometres from Carlisle to Newcastle, following the line of Roman Emperor Hadrian's Wall.

Sooner or later, we were going to have to get serious on that score.

I was fine with later.

Homes and Castles

Staying with relatives beats the snot out of camping.

Seriously. Free food, no site fees, and they almost never expect you to sleep on gravel. Plus, there are those little luxuries you don't even notice until you've lived in a tent for a few days; things like bedsprings, ample headroom, and soft carpets underfoot; the ability to move when you sleep, and not be rewarded with a face full of cold, soggy nylon.

It does make it slightly more awkward when you're caught in the nude on the way to the toilet in the middle of the night – but those are the kinds of things families can laugh about afterwards. Over breakfast.

And breakfast, at Aunty Sylvia's house, meant Staffordshire oatcakes.

Ohhh, oatcakes! I've never found them anywhere else in the world.

Like a thick, savoury pancake made from oatmeal, they have a distinctive, wheat-y flavour. Of course, you don't notice that so much when they're grilled, buttered, filled with bacon, sausage and cheese, rolled up and stuffed into your mouth whilst still steaming hot! They are absolutely delicious, more so than I could ever make them sound – but you'll just have to trust me, as the chances are you'll never get to eat one. Oatcakes were the fast-food of the eighteenth and nineteenth century in Stoke-on-Trent, but for some reason they never spread to the rest of the country – much like the people, I guess. Maybe that's why no-one wants to leave Stoke? Maybe a life without oatcakes would be too much to bear?

My Dad was born in Stoke – the exception that proves the rule – and he goes back every couple of months to stock up. As I write this, sitting in a rental house in Perth, Australia, I can tell you without a doubt that there are Staffordshire oatcakes in my Mum's freezer in Somerset.

"There's something familiar about this, I can't quite put my finger on," said my aunty as she handed me a plate. Atop the oatcake, several rashers of bacon had been artfully arranged in the shape of a man – with a solitary sausage hanging down between his legs. I must have blushed, because everyone else in the kitchen cracked up.

"Next time we go travelling," Roo said, "and we're planning on staying with people, could you at least *consider* buying some pyjamas?"

With the finest breakfast of the whole trip already under out belts, it was all downhill from here. We still planned to check out that Secret Bunker, although now it would mean considerable back-tracking. Maybe we were delaying the epic Hadrian's Wall hike on purpose? Subconsciously sabotaging our chances of ever reaching the starting post, let alone the finish? It was, after all, quite a long time since either of us had done any hiking. Neither of us were in the best shape physically, as we'd discovered when our wedding photos came back. A long-distance hike with a seriously heavy backpack could be just what we needed to kick-start our bodies into exercise mode – or, quite possibly, it would knacker us.

According to our hastily-prepared schedule, we had three days to find out.

Seeing as we were heading back South anyway, we took the chance to check out an iron-age hill fort that we'd been too late to visit last time around. I didn't really know what to expect, other than the traditional signs of archaeology – a bunch of holes in the ground, some of which have stones at the bottom of them. It constantly amazes me that archaeologists can tell which buried stones are the foundations of a Roman villa and which ones were the walls of an iron-age hill fort. Because as far as I can see, they're all stones. At the bottom of holes.

This site hadn't been excavated, but there was a series of steps made of stones – presumably ones of no historical merit. We climbed a long, long hill, buffeted by the wind, and were a tad disappointed when we reached the top of the steps.

"There's nothing here!" said Roo.

"Well I can see the hill part, but the fort not so much."

"They should warn you about that at the bottom! I can't believe we climbed all this way for nothing."

"Yeah! When I see stairs like this, I generally expect them to go somewhere."

We stood there panting for a couple of minutes, staring in different directions to see if some other structure would reveal itself.

But it didn't.

"Let's go up there," Roo said, pointing to the crest of the hill through which the stairs ran. "If there's anything here, we'll see it from up there."

Her logic was sound, although it did involve yet more effort. *Training for The Wall*, I told myself, as I followed her up the bank.

The distance we'd come from the car park looked even more impressive from on high. The vantage point also helped to make sense of what we were looking at. "This *is* the fort," Roo said, "these hills are man-made!"

Which changed my perspective on the whole thing. Although there still wasn't much to see, the scale of the earthworks themselves was staggering. From atop them I could see that the line of ridges continued in both directions as far as the eye could see. No stone towers, no impenetrable gatehouses or cauldrons of boiling oil. Just really, *really* big hills, all around. Rows of them.

I reckon it was a fairly shrewd defensive tactic.

The first slope we'd climbed was long, rather than steep, but even following the steps up had taken us a good twenty minutes.

By the time anyone had run to the top, they'd be absolutely knackered, and in no condition to pick a fight. Not only that, but facing them would be another identical hill – with whatever fort they were trying to capture laying tantalisingly beyond it. I could almost hear the curses of the Celtic warlords as they crested the first ridge; "Oh, you have got to be f*@king kidding me! I thought that was it? Right, sod it lads, we'll try the next place over. I'm not running up another hill like that."

When we finally saw it in the light of day, the Hack Green Secret Bunker looked to be little more than a World War II radar-base. It had been re-invented several times though, and in it's current form as a museum of the Cold War it boasted the largest collection of decommissioned nuclear weapons in the world. If they were all activated, the bunker would become the world's seventh-greatest nuclear power! Entering through the canteen, Roo spotted one of the most amusing signs of the trip:

'IN THE EVENT OF A NUCLEAR ATTACK ON THE BUNKER, GET UNDER YOUR CANTEEN TABLE FOR YOUR SAFETY AND PROTECTION,' it read. Followed by, 'IMPORTANT NOTICE: FOOD IS NOT PERMITTED TO BE EATEN WHILST SHELTERING UNDER YOUR TABLE.'

I reckon the cleaners added that last part.

We descended deep into the earth, following a confusing route of corridors and stairwells. It was a huge place, designed to ensure that post-war Britain could still be governed effectively. Along with generators, radiation decontamination rooms and miles of concrete, this place was equipped with a series of old-school phone switchboards, radio monitoring rooms and a television broadcast studio.

Most of it looked like the set of a 1970's spy show, with vast arrays of fridge-sized computers, spinning reels of magnetic tape and blinking lights – which probably had the combined processing power of a *Tamagotchi*.

In the control centre, a big red strobe-light was mounted above a sign that said 'Bikini Alert'. I reckoned they'd have more use for that one on Miami beach, but I guess it's important for any military facility to maintain their dress code.

With room to house well over a hundred civil servants, Hack Green would undoubtedly be the most boring place in the world to survive a nuclear blast.

Which brings me to my thoughts on secret government bunkers.

If you think about it, if there ever is a nuclear war, what you'll have is the entire civilian population of the world wiped out, whilst the people that pushed the buttons sit safe and sound in their underground strongholds. Sealed chambers full of generals and politicians, all nursing their hatred of the politicians in the opposing bunkers... while the vast majority of people, who didn't really give a shit about who started what, get to become glow-in-the-dark skeletons. Now there's a winning scenario!

The best part is, once they decide it's safe to emerge from their bomb-proof hidey-holes, these survivors will have the unenviable task of putting the world back together. They'll be almost exclusively men, in their late 50's to early 60's, most of whom have never done a day's manual labour in their lives. They'd have impeccable personal presentation, some light computer skills and an impressive capacity to create and handle bullshit, but I doubt they'd be much good at building shelters, growing crops, hunting, foraging or animal husbandry. I can just see it: the 140kg Right Honourable Member of Parliament for East Wallop, suit-trousers rolled up to his knees, stalking his dinner through the forest with a homemade bow and arrow. And as for the process of re-populating the planet... yeah, probably best we don't go there.

We were surprised to find it was still daylight outside – the underground tour had seemed endless. Even more unexpectedly, the sun was shining brightly, so we wound Bubble's windows down and sang along to the radio as we reversed direction towards the Peak District.

During our research of Hadrian's Wall accommodation, we'd come across something known as a 'camping barn'. At first we thought these structures only existed along the line of the Wall, but it turns out they're all over the place, bridging the gap between camping and youth hostels (which are bizarrely expensive in the UK). The standard of accommodation on offer varies, but they tend to be sealed, indoor places, often with mattresses on the floor or even bunk-beds in a dormitory-type environment. With winter fast approaching this was infinitely better than camping in a muddy field, so we located one not far from Buxton and made a bee-line for it.

Driving along a boggy farmer's track, squelching up a hillside, we started to get a bit nervous – but the camping barn, when it came into view, proved to be a sturdy little stone cottage. Four walls and a roof, with a basic kitchen and a dining table on the ground floor and two rooms of bunk beds above – it was so much better than pitching our tent outside that we could hardly believe our luck. Especially as the cost difference was negligible. The cottage had power, so we cooked dinner from supplies we'd bought en route and passed a pleasant evening watching movies on my laptop.

We were inching north, slowly but surely, and had only a couple more stops to make before we reached Carlisle, on the Scottish border – and the challenge which Roo, in her infinite wisdom, had set for us.

There are definite downsides to marrying someone ambitious.

Being Mum and Dad

We woke up on the floor, because that's where we'd gone to bed, having dragged a pair of mattresses off the bunks and pushed them together in the space in between. As no-one else was in residence, we could pretty much do as we liked with the place. So we did.

We cooked a huge breakfast and cleaned the place up before we left. I always try and leave a place in better condition than when I arrived, out of some misplaced notion that this will inspire other people to do the same. It doesn't.

But with full stomachs and a pleasant, blustery day outside, we sat at the dining room table and made our plans.

Today we would continue to zigzag inexorably northwards, aiming to spend the night with my Uncle Gerard in Morecambe. It would be an easy 90-mile meander – well, easy for me, as Roo was doing the driving – and we intended to avoid Manchester at all costs (as most sensible people should). This is partly because a significant portion of Manchester's population will kill you just for looking at them funny, and also because the traffic there is pretty bad.

I'd arranged to meet an old friend on the way, which gave us a timeframe to contain our wanderings, but before all that there were some local sights to see.

First we drove past a particularly unspectacular clutch of standing stones at a place called Eyam Moor – not because we wanted to see the stones, but because I kept pronouncing the place-name as 'I-AM-MORE', and we just had to see if it was true.

It wasn't.

But that didn't stop me saying it.

Eventually, Roo stopped me saying it, by threatening to make me get out and walk. "I AM MORE than willing to co-operate," I told her.

"You are an idiot," she retaliated.

"No, that's not true," I said, "I AM MORE!"

The debate continues.

On the same flimsy premise we passed through Wormhill and Sparrowpit, Grindleford and Froggatt, Nether Padley, Youlgreave (who'll greave?) and Over Haddon. Note that we didn't pass over Haddon; we passed Over Haddon. I never found out who Haddon was, but it sounded like his day was pretty much done. The Peak District was an orgy of ridiculous nomenclature, and perhaps the finest example was our first major stop. We'd taken Bubble to the promisingly-named Castleton – to get a look up The Devil's Arse.

Now, obviously this isn't some hilariously misspelled phrase descending from Ye Olde English; this massive cave system, which was renamed 'Peak Cavern' to avoid offending Queen Victoria when she visited, was deliberately called The Devil's Arse because it makes fart noises when the water drains out of it.

Honestly! I'm not making this shit up.

It also featured the largest cave entrance in Britain, so at least we had a legitimate reason for visiting. The approach was impressive; sheer limestone cliffs dropped over a hundred feet to meet the path we were on, and the yawning gulf of the cave mouth wore the tiny ticket booth like its last remaining tooth.

The cashier on duty looked like he'd had better days.

"So, this is The Devil's Arse?" I asked him.

He just stared at me.

"So, what's the crack?"

He didn't even twitch. I guess he wasn't Irish.

Or else he'd heard that one a thousand times before, day in, day out, and was a coin-toss away from beating me to death with his Maglite.

After looking straight through me for close to a minute, he spoke two words – the abruptness of which caused me to jump a little.

"Sixteen pounds."

I gazed at him, waiting for the punch-line. Either he was the dead-pan-est of dead-pan comedians, and I'd totally missed the joke – or else he was serious.

I glanced at the Admission Price board next to me.

'One Adult – £16,' it said.

"Bollocks to that!" was what I said. "This must actually be the real, honest-to-God Devil's arse, if we've got to pay that much to climb into it!"

The cashier didn't react at all. That seemed to be his thing.

"Wow, looks like The Devil's Arse has got a stick up it," I

murmured to Roo as we walked away from the booth, "I guess he didn't appreciate my cheek!"

Much like any red-blooded male, I have a list of arses that I would happily pay £16 (or more) to see; the Devil's is not on there.

(NOTE: I have since been informed that, despite it not being specifically mentioned in my wedding vows, the marriage contract requires me to refrain from keeping such a list. Who knew?)

"Looked pretty standard, really," Roo commented as we hiked back down the approach road.

"Yeah, just a big dark hole full of rocks."

On the way out we passed a notice board advertising a Christmas carol concert to be held inside the caves. It was entitled 'The Devil's Arse Sings!' – which pretty much summed up what I felt about the place. The Devil's Arse could whistle, for all I cared, it still wasn't worth the price of two steak dinners.

Nearby were the ruins of Perevil Castle, from which the town (presumably) took its name. This presented us with an opportunity we'd been looking forward to; the chance to impersonate my parents and sneak into a National Trust monument. Yes, I know they need the money to upkeep the castles and what-knot. Or more specifically, to put iron railings everywhere with signs that say 'do not climb,' and to build gift shops that sell novelty fridge magnets and pencil-toppers.

The fact that the monuments themselves have generally stood for hundreds of years unchanged, and took an army of thousands complete with batteries of cannon to actually damage in the first place, seems completely wasted on their modern caretakers. They are a specially-bred race of sadists, who delight in repeatedly telling young children (and me) not to touch.

As for 'Do Not Climb' – oh, how I hate that sign! Why do not climb? To protect a solid stone wall designed to be indestructible from being scuffed by my trainers? No. It's to protect the National Trust from being sued by angry parents when their eight-year-old son gets a little too adventurous and twists his ankle. It's not their fault really. It's this ridiculous culture of litigation we're developing, where anyone can sue anyone for anything. It's driven health and safety standards over the top – sometimes I'm amazed we're even allowed outside without government-approved protective equipment on. One day it'll rain and someone will sue the BBC for inaccurate weather predictions resulting in damage to their none-waterproof clothing...

Whatever happened to 'climb it if you must, but don't come crying to me...'

Ah, I miss those days! Being eleven, I mean.

The National Trust could slash a fortune off their budget by moving out of their more ruined monuments and leaving a donation box at the door with a sign saying 'If you injure yourself here, call 0800-SUCK-IT-UP-CUPCAKE to hear our pre-recorded sarcastic message.'

Okay! Sorry about that. Rant over.

I guess I shouldn't moan too much – after all, I wasn't actually *paying* the entrance fee. *Or* the annual subscription…

We dug the membership cards out well in advance, so we wouldn't appear too awkward. We couldn't risk the girl at the admission counter suspecting anything.

Adrenaline was flowing as we approached the desk – the life of the criminal beckoned, ripe with promise of thrills and danger. Trembling more than was strictly necessary, I presented my (Dad's) card and managed to tell the woman half my life story in thirty seconds of rapid-fire monologue.

She ignored me. She glanced at the cards and nodded us through the turnstile – but I still felt an inexplicable urge to verify myself, to prove to her that she'd made the right decision by letting us in. I get this whenever I do anything even remotely dishonest, and it manifests in different ways each time. This time I couldn't stop talking loudly to Roo about what a great deal they were offering new join-ups, and how much I wished we weren't already members!

The woman behind the desk gave not one shit.

Roo, who can be as delightfully deceptive as she is delightfully innocent, felt no such need to prove anything. She steered me out with a firm grip on my waist before I could start praising the qualities of a monthly newsletter I'd never received.

"Why do you always do that?" she hissed once outside.

"I dunno, I can't help it. I just wanted to sound like I was a member."

Roo shook her head. "Mission accomplished. You sounded like a complete member."

Perevil Castle was spectacular for its setting, if nothing else. When the Normans chose their defensive positions, it wasn't with much care for the poor buggers that had to build the place. Climbing in switchbacks to the top of the hill, the path was so steep we had to stop and rest twice. There were frequent benches, frequently occupied by grannies who looked unlikely to survive the entire trip. They shuffled from one wooden bench to the next, accompanied by paunchy old men in raincoats. Several of the couples appeared to have harnessed small dogs to help haul them up the hill.

It was quite endearing really.

"We'll be like that one day," Roo said. "Grown old together, still adventuring, struggling to help each other up the hill."

"Again? Why would we ever want to do this twice? It's not like the castle's going to change dramatically in the next fifty years. Well, they'll probably improve the safety features and expand the gift shop. And supply an audio tour in thirty-five European languages... Couldn't we just sit at the bottom with a postcard of the place and a good book, and spend the entrance fee on a burger and a pint?"

"I thought you wanted to stay active as we get older?"

"But you said, when I have a stupid idea like that it's your job to stop me, not encourage it!"

As we clambered into a tower chamber there were two teenage lads trying to climb the crumbling masonry to the next floor. They both dropped down with matching guilty looks and scurried back out. I scowled after them, then got a leg up on the 'No Climbing' sign and had a go myself. Roo gave me that impatient look until I admitted to myself that even though it *was* possible, I was way too chicken to climb all the way up the inside of the tower. Not because I was afraid of falling, but because if I did, it would *really* piss Roo off. I muttered something about her getting a job with the National Trust as I lowered myself to the ground.

"I just don't want you to get killed," she explained. "We're meant to be together forever, remember? We've only been married for a month!"

"Yeah, alright."

Apparently, once you get married some degree of responsible behaviour is suddenly expected?

They don't warn you about that, do they!

What's that? They *do*?

Oh.

Damn it!

School Daze

Poring over the map while we planned our route north, Roo spotted a place she found very amusing. Pronounced Clith-her-ow, I grew up near there, and so never looked at it any other way. But it's spelt 'Clitheroe'. Or Clit-hero, to anyone who is actually looking for that kind of thing.

"No-one ever goes there," I told her.

"Tell me about it," she retorted.

Being of Dutch descent, Roo had also scribbled an enthusiastic circle around a place called 'Up Holland'.

"I've been there," I said, when she mentioned it.

"Great! What was it like?"

"Cool, actually. It was the best thing I ever did with school. It was at a place called Upholland Farm."

"Yeah! Farm stuff is always the best."

"Well, 'farm' was really just the name of the place."

"So what was it?"

"Um... it was a religious retreat."

"Oh."

"But it was, you know, uplifting. A bit."

"Ah."

"And we did some outward-bound sort of stuff. Like climbing in the barn."

"And that was really the best thing you did with school?"

"Yeah."

"Your school sucked."

"True."

We skirted Wigan, a place famous to everyone not from there as a bit of a shit-hole. The bleak industrial areas and sprawling council estates typified towns in Lancashire for me, supplying the truth in the phrase, 'It's grim up north'.

Wigan was also the butt of the ubiquitous 'Wigan girl' jokes, such as:

Q. How do you know when a Wigan girl has an orgasm?
A. She drops her chips.
And:
Q. Why is a Wigan girl like an old washing machine?
A. They both leak when they're f*cked.
Oh, and my personal favourite:
Q. After sex, what does a Wigan girl do with her arsehole?
A. She takes him down the pub.
I could go on all day.
But I probably shouldn't.

We were now venturing dangerously close to my old stomping grounds. By which I mean, the grounds where I used to get stomped on.

"I went to school near here," I told Roo as we approached the truck-manufacturing town of Leyland.

"Oh wow!" Her eyes shone. "Let's go see your old school!"

"Erm... nah, I don't think we need to do that. Don't want to waste time."

"Don't be silly, we've got loads of time. It won't take long. Come on, which way?"

I sighed. School had been an entirely different place for Roo – both physically and emotionally. For her it was an experience enshrined in nostalgia, full of crazy stories that she loved to tell me.

"You don't talk about school much," she observed.

"No. Not really."

Navigating through the narrow town streets brought back a flood of memories. The dog's leg crossroads at the centre of Leyland still sported an ancient stone cross, thought to be of Saxon origin – despite the fact it had been reversed into and smashed by a delivery truck while I was in my second year.

Following my reluctant directions, Roo turned through a junction barely wide enough for one car let alone two, and retraced the final leg of my morning trip to hell.

The endless black railings came into sight long before the buildings did, as they also enclosed substantial playing fields.

"It's massive!" Roo gaped. "Is all this part of it?"

"Yeah, this is all the school. It's not that big."

"We're still going past it!"

"Well, yeah, it takes up most of the road on this side. I remember it seemed pretty big when we moved up here from Primary School."

"How many of you went here?"

"I think there was about two thousand kids, all told."

"Holy *shit!* My entire school only had two hundred people in it."

"How many were in your year?"

"Ah... thirty-six."

"How many in your class?"

"That was my class. There was only one for each year."

She pulled Bubble over to the side of the road and turned his engine off. She was still getting used to this method of parking, as it's not allowed in Perth.

In my mind's eye I re-lived the throng of kids pouring in through the school gates, as the shrill shriek of the electric bell summoned us all to morning Assembly.

"Coming back here, being so close to the place, it sends shivers down my spine," I admitted. "I hated it here."

"Just the kids?"

"Yeah. The teachers were fine, for the most part. I quite liked some of them, and they all liked me. You might not believe it, but I was actually pretty good at school. The top of my class for everything except sports, which I managed to avoid almost entirely by pretending to have an ingrowing toenail for five years straight. They must have known I was lying, but it was probably easier to let me tidy up the locker room every week than it was to try teaching me how to play rugby."

"Yeah, that can be dangerous," she agreed.

"It was the kids who were dangerous," I said.

Roo pondered this for a few seconds.

"It wasn't the kids that were dangerous at my school, it was the wildlife."

"Like snakes and stuff?"

"A few times. School was in a big block of bush-land and we didn't have a playground, so we played in the forest. There were these Spitfires, like little caterpillars that would spit poisonous yellow goo. We used to find big clumps of them on branches and poke them with a stick, so they'd spray it everywhere!"

"Wow."

"But the magpies were the most dangerous. We had to walk underneath their trees to get to the car park, and in nesting season they get really aggressive – they'd swoop down and strike at us. We had to wear ice cream containers on our heads, and draw eyes on them because when the magpies swoop they usually go for your eyes..."

"Jesus! That's like something out of a horror movie."

"It was pretty freaky for a bunch of seven-year-old girls. But fun, too And in farm class, we got taken into the emu pen to look for eggs. We found the female emu sitting on her nest, but then someone started screaming 'cause the male emu had circled around behind us and started attacking! And they're big birds, like way taller than a person, and if they catch you they slice you open with these massive claws on their feet – kind of like a dinosaur. So the teacher was yelling at us to run for the gate, and everyone was screaming and trying to fling themselves over the fence… it was awesome!"

"Hm. They were a bit more safety-conscious at our school. We weren't allowed to play on the grass when it was wet. Because it was slippery."

"Really? You *did* have a rough childhood."

I stared through Bubble's windscreen at the iron railings, which had seemed like prison bars for the longest five years of my life. School, for me, had been torture.

"I was pretty unpopular, eh," I told Roo. I'd shared this with her before, something I'd only told one other person at that point. Quite why, I don't know; the spectre of shame still clawed at me, that awful, stomach-clenching fear that I was about to be recognised for what I was – a tiny, shivering, pathetic little boy whose only chance of survival was to hide and pray. It's amazing how much of that stays with you into adulthood. It had coloured my friendships and relationships – or lack thereof – right the way through college, into university and beyond.

"I guess I wasn't all that popular either," Roo said. "I never really thought about it too much, but when we finished in the pig sty and had to go back into Maths, no-one wanted to sit next to me. You could really smell the pig sty, it sort of impregnated all my uniforms after a while."

"Ouch! If you'd done that in our school you would *definitely* have had things thrown at you."

"Yeah, but because it was Roleystone, some of the kids were from farming families, or had relatives that were farmers. Farm class was the best by miles. When all the other kids were doing English, we were getting tractor driving lessons, learning how to reverse and pick up the trailer and stuff! And we bred rabbits, which is how I know that when a male rabbit ejaculates, he seizes up and falls over backwards."

I bit my tongue, not wanting to break her flow. Questions like what age she'd been when gifted with this revelation were probably best left unasked.

"So we had all these gorgeous baby rabbits, and they were all fluffy and cute, and we had to pet them and name them and feed them and look after them – right up until they were taken to the abattoir."

"WHAT?"

"Yup, they were slaughtered. It was a lesson called Animal Production and Marketing, after all."

"The bastards!"

"And that's not even the best part. Next day one of the teachers was pushing a wheelbarrow around the school full of their dead bodies – asking if anyone wanted to buy the meat! There were quite a few tears when he came into the Year 11 classroom…"

Friends and Family

An hour later we were sitting in the pub, waiting for my friend Pete to arrive.

Pete is my oldest friend – by which I mean he's my age, which is already old enough to be of concern. I generally credit him with keeping me sane during my teenage years, though most other people believe he failed miserably at this.

Pete is also the only friend I've kept in touch with from this part of my life.

Because Pete *was* my only friend.

Altogether now: Ahhhhh!

Yeah, well, bollocks to you! I took what I could get in those days, and it wasn't much. I'd agreed to meet Pete in the pub, as that's where we spent most of our free time between ages fourteen and eighteen. Acne had ravaged my face, making me look much older than I was – well, either that, or the bartenders didn't dare look at it too closely for fear of losing their lunch. Being able to get served in our local came in dead handy, as it was one place most of the other kids couldn't go.

I lost many a game of pool to Pete on their one cramped table, probably because I refused point blank to wear my prescription glasses. It wasn't like I needed something else to get teased about! Of course, I could have lost at pool because Pete – who became captain of the local team when he finally came of legal age – was a better player than me. But even if that was the case, I would never have admitted it.

Pete was also way cooler than me, but I'd never admit that, either.

I looked up as the door opened, and Pete strolled through it. I'd almost forgotten how short he was.

"Eh up, Cheery," he said with a grin.

Pete has called me 'Cheery' ever since a drunken poker night in our first week of uni. There were four of us playing poker. Three of us had actually played it before. Two of us were drunk before we started, and one of us wasn't drinking at all – which meant the three bottles of spirits we managed to get through that night were distributed fairly evenly, at about one per person. We had tequila (the good stuff, with the worm), whisky (the less good stuff, because we were students) and vodka (the cheap-as-piss stuff, because it's vodka; can anyone honestly taste the difference?). Suffice to say, the night became rather messy, but for some reason I undergo a strange transformation when drunk. Not only do I lose what few inhibitions I have, these days I rediscover the ability to speak fluent Spanish – and apparently I also become quite *funny*. According to Pete I spent the entire evening telling jokes – pausing frequently to sprint outside and vomit in the back garden, before coming back in and carrying on. He said he'd never seen anyone being so violently sick, whilst simultaneously remaining so incredibly cheerful. Hence the nickname; Cheery.

It stuck, which made me tremendously happy as the only nicknames I'd had up until that point were 'Wanker' and 'Fucking wanker' (courtesy of every other kid at my school).

I even went so far as to make a sign for the door of my room in the university halls of residence, to let people know if I was in or not. It said, 'Cheery Tony is:' and there was a blank box, into which I would BluTack a reversible IN/OUT card I made. Of course, university students are nothing if not creative, and a wide variety of things were written in that blank box over the course of the year, most of which had very little to do with my whereabouts.

Pete gave me a bear hug, and then politely shook Roo's hand – which surprised me, until I remembered that he'd never met her.

"Been a while," said Pete. Typical of Lancashire-folk, he wasn't one to waste words. 'Understated,' would perhaps be the best word to describe this trait; it had been over ten years since I'd last seen him.

"True enough," I said, reverting to type.

"Bet this place takes yer back."

"Yeah." I looked around. The pub was essentially unchanged; I even recognised a few faces in the evening crowd, which was quite surreal. I almost felt like I could wake up at any moment, and realise the last fifteen years had been an exceptionally vivid daydream.

God, what a depressing thought!

Words can't describe how glad I am that my life has moved on; that I'm not still living in the same place, drinking in the same local, with the same people around me. The walls closed in on me, causing a moment of claustrophobia. Sitting there as though in a time-capsule was terrifying. This is how it could have been, I thought. *This could have been my life.* Instead, I'd spread my wings. I'd achieved so much, been so far, seen so many new people and places…

Which is not to say that Pete hadn't achieved anything.

He could buy and sell me a dozen times over, for starters.

I hadn't seen what car he had parked outside, but I could bet it didn't have stickers of garden gnomes on it.

He'd been given a part-time job in that pub, one summer. Then he'd gone full-time, and before long he was the bar manager. When the previous owners left he'd had the opportunity to buy the place – but Pete was clever enough to know that financial hardship and the ever present threat of alcoholism went hand-in-hand with the often short life of a publican.

So he'd quit working there and got a job in a bank.

He'd taken every training course they'd thrown at him, worked his way up again, and was now one of the most respected financial advisors in the area.

It was a far cry from our somewhat rebellious youth.

"What happened?" I asked him.

Pete spread his hands. "Life happens, I suppose."

"And you're happy?"

"As happy as I could possibly be," he said.

With a wife and two young boys, a responsible job, a nice house and a mortgage, Pete was a pretty good advert for the kind of life I'd been trying so desperately to avoid.

"It'll get you eventually," he said, waving a hand towards Roo, "see!"

"Yeah. Thanks for that."

"S'all good, mate."

He showed me a picture of his sons, and it was obvious he adored them. Maybe he'd got it right? I couldn't imagine he'd want to swap his lifestyle for that of a penniless vagrant like me, anymore than I'd swap my freedom for his cage of responsibilities. Naturally, he didn't see it that way. I guess there are many 'right' ways, and everyone's path is a little different; we were climbing different sides of the same mountain, each aiming for the summit by a route the other couldn't quite see.

"So what's next for you?" I asked. "Have you got any plans for the future?"

"I'm snowed under at the moment with new training courses. They want me to get this new qualification, so that I'll pretty much be running the show. But I'm also thinking about going it alone, you know, starting my own company."

"Holy shit! That's huge!"

"Yeah. I'm also building an extension on the back of the house. Hired a mini bulldozer to clear the back garden before we get the builders in."

This caught my attention. "A mini bulldozer, you say?"

"Yeah, but don't get any ideas! Before I came out, the wife specifically told me I'm not to let you come back and play with the bulldozer!"

"Aw, what? That's a bit harsh. Doesn't she trust me?"

"Nope."

"I wonder why that is?"

"You know exactly why that is."

This was true. Pete's wife didn't trust me because every time he did anything remotely questionable, he used to blame it on me. He'd been doing it for years, way before he met her – I'd get a phone call at uni; "Hiya Cheery, it's Pete. Listen, if anyone asks, I was out with you last night. We got wasted and I crashed at your place, alright?"

"Pete, I'm in Cardiff. I'm 200 miles away!"

"S'all good mate, no-one here knows about that. Just remember, I was with you all night!"

I never received any phone calls from questioning girlfriends, but most of them gave me the cold shoulder when I finally got to meet them. Pete never batted an eyelid whilst introducing me; "Hey RandomGirl, this is Tony, who I've been telling you about."

That was usually my cue to wince, and sure enough there'd be an icy stare awaiting me from the lady of the moment – sometimes accompanied with a venom-laden "Yes, I've heard *so much* about you…"

I never got to drive Pete's bulldozer.

And no, that's not a euphemism for anything disgusting, before you ask.

For some reason, the number of people who trust me around heavy equipment seems to be diminishing. I've never figured out why.

We spent that night in Morecambe as planned, staying with Gerard and Beth another uncle and aunt of mine. They had taken a third route, and decided not to have children at all. Consequently they owned a very nice house, did lots of charity work, and had adopted a rescued greyhound that took up more room than a whole bunch of kids. He even had his own sofa, which he sprawled on full-length, looking very happy about it in the process.

I can't say I blamed him. We did a bit of route planning that evening, and described our hiking ambitions to my aunt and uncle.

Looking at what we were about to attempt, I think I'd have rather stayed on the sofa too.

Now, I've been neglecting my **Guide To A Grand Adventure** recently, so how about this one:

Do it. Even if you *think* you don't want to. Whatever the adventure is that you're afraid of, face the fear and do it anyway. Make a change in your life. Attempt something different. Let your spirit fly free! Go far, far away, and never look back.

Oh, but never, ever, admit that anyone is better than you at pool. That's just not how it's done.

Towards The Wall

The following morning we took Jack the greyhound for a run on the beach. He practically flew across the sand, covering a mile each way before we got as far as the water's edge. Gerard and Beth devoted most of their time to the greyhound rescue centre these days, saving and re-homing dogs that were no longer fit to race. It's not an industry famed for its animal welfare, and without this charity it's not hard to imagine what happens to the dogs.

Before we left, Gerard showed us an unusual burial site, perched on the edge of a cliff above Morecambe Bay. A series of graves had been carved directly out of the flat rock, in roughly human shapes. Nowhere else in the UK has anything like this been discovered, and there are no records to show who made the graves and why they went to so much effort. They're probably more famous than anything else in Morecombe, despite not being on the tourist trail – Black Sabbath used them on their 'best of' album cover.

We skirted the Lake District, which is arguably the most beautiful part of the country, and consequently the most congested. Even with the tale end of summer well and truly faded, hordes of tourists would be turning the narrow lanes around Lake Windermere and Ullswater into a giant car park. Having lived fairly close by for many years, my family know well enough not to venture into that part of the world unless some kind of natural disaster is forecast.

We very nearly visited a town called Cockermouth, but decided we'd wasted enough time already. These places were far more amusing to discover on the map than they were to drive to, and through, and around. Now we were starting to psyche ourselves up for the long walk ahead of ourselves, and we were keen to get there and get started.

We spent that night in a camping barn a couple of miles east of Carlisle.

It was another old stone building, complete with a boot-drying room and a kitchen upstairs. We dug our backpacks from the mountain of crap in the boot and dragged them up to an empty bunk room.

Piles of gear in the other room suggested it was occupied, and as we sat down to scoff some instant spag-bols, our barn-mates arrived. We heard them long before we saw them – not only because their excitement carried along with their voices, but because they *swished*. This confirmed our suspicion that they were hikers; not many other kinds of people swish as they walk. It's all that waterproof clothing; you'd never be able to sneak up on anyone whilst wearing Gore-Tex. Which is probably why ninjas didn't invent the stuff.

Four guys and two girls in their early twenties, they hiked in from the village they'd been to for dinner, a barely noticeable two-kilometre stroll each way. All six of them were armed to the teeth with branded outdoor gear; Leathermans to the belt, ponchos to the rear, and clad from neck to ankles in brand new quik-dry-sweat-wicking-wind-proof-high-visibility-base-to-shell-thermo-centric-Layering-Systems™. Which is to say, a t-shirt, a jumper and a jacket – only, ones that cost about the same as our entire adventure so far.

Roo and I greeted them politely, then withdrew into ourselves; such was the potency of their enthusiasm, their level of preparedness, that it made us feel a little embarrassed. We finished our microwave meals and hid in our dorm, before one of them could start asking us technical questions that would reveal just how amateur we were. Like which map series we were using, or how many 'clicks' per day we were aiming for. My answer to both questions would have been to wave in the general direction of our Hadrian's Wall tourist brochure and say, "Whatever it says in there really…"

These were not the kind of people who did anything on a whim. Shopping for all that outdoors gear must have taken a week by itself. They knew how far it was humanly possible to walk in a day and they were prepared to push those limits – I knew their plan was to conquer the Wall in four days, because their leader told me that in the same breath as his name.

Naturally they were on a challenge, raising money for a very specific charity – feeding disabled people to blind orphan horses or something.

They were the kind of kids that irritated me a bit, because I'd always wanted to be like them; radiating drive and motivation to succeed, powering ahead against all odds with a rucksack full of determination and self-belief.

Sadly, I was born a lazy bastard, and all that seemed too much like hard work for me. I still aspire to do many great and noble things, but I remain comforted by the knowledge that I'll never be committed enough to actually *do* them. Not so these young people; guaranteed, every one of those scrawny buggers would go on to climb Everest one day, most likely raising money to cripple starving children in the process. I wanted to loathe them, but they were doing the right thing; the only other choice was to loathe myself, and I wasn't quite there yet. So we watched *Star Wars* on the laptop instead. That counts as productive, right?

The high-tech posse were in bed by 9pm, which was about the time Roo and I tipped our backpacks out on the bottom bunk and started to sort through what we were taking with us.

And they were up at 5:30am, breakfasted (presumably on energy bars and Gatorade), and gone long before we dragged ourselves out of bed to finish the packing we'd got bored with last night.

We now had a rush-job on. Hadrian's Wall doesn't start in Carlisle, it starts on the west coast – otherwise the hordes of Scottish barbarians it was designed to contain could have just walked around it. So the first step of our journey was to reach the start, and this we would have to do by bus. Bowness-on-Solway is the setting out point for walkers heading west-east, and it's not exactly a thriving commercial hub; there were four buses a day that served the tiny village, and we'd already missed one of them. If we didn't make the 10am departure we wouldn't have a chance of hiking back into Carlisle today, as the next one was at 2pm.

We left ourselves just enough time for the drive into town, and then discovered something horrific on arrival; the parking fees! There was ample space to leave Bubble only a short walk from the bus station, but the meters would only accept coins – and as we'd be gone all day, the damn things wanted £8!

We had no time to shop around for cheaper parking, but were faced with an additional dilemma: no coins. As the bus station was nowhere near the centre of town, there weren't a whole lot of places to try for change. Leaving Roo to wait for the bus (and to prevent it from leaving, ideally), I jogged around the handful of cafés and newsagents in the area. None of them seemed keen to help me out, but finally I tricked a paper shop into changing my £20 note by buying a Mars Bar from them. I legged it back to the car park, heart already pounding from the sudden burst of exercise, and fed the coins into the meter. I pushed the button and was rewarded with the sound of my ticket printing. It was music to my ears – until I looked at it.

"You bastards!"

They'd only given me half a day. I fished around in the coin return and discovered a pound that had gone all the way through without me noticing. Now I was in real trouble. I couldn't leave the car, or we'd be facing a huge fine by the time we got back to it. But time was running out. Roo was bound to be panicking... and who the hell would give me this much change at this time of the morning? Again? I spied a workman in a fluro-vest, sitting in his car with a cup of coffee. There was nothing else for it.

"Sorry mate, I don't suppose you've got change for a tenner?"

I was in luck. Not only did he have it, he was happy enough to share it with me – possibly in exchange for the laugh he'd just got out of watching me leap around the car park, swearing and cursing and kicking the crap out of the steel base of the parking meter.

I bought another ticket, stuck it on the dashboard and ran flat out towards the bus station, only pausing to run back to Bubble when I realised I'd forgotten to lock him. Sweat was pouring off me by the time I reached Roo. The bus was already there, the driver glaring silently at Roo as she struggled to haul my bag up the steps.

"Thank God," she said, "I've been putting your rucksack on the bus for the last five minutes!"

"Sorry love, I had a few problems. But thanks for pretending!"

"Who's pretending? I can't lift the bloody thing!"

A Long Hard Walk Along A Wall

The start of Hadrian's Wall was not hard to find – it was borderline impossible. Nothing remains of this first section, although there are a suspicious number of farm outbuildings constructed of very nice quality stone. Whether this constitutes recycling or desecration is a moot point; many of the buildings are old enough to be protected by heritage law themselves. Building a wall across an entire country was always going to be a tad wasteful, and it must have presented a tempting target once the Romans gave up on it. Hell, if they'd built it across Wales, the stone would have been robbed before the mortar had dried.

The beginning of our route was meant to be a pub, where we could get a stamp in our Hadrian's Wall passports. The idea was to collect them all, proving we'd hiked through each of seven checkpoints; however, the pub was closed. Closer inspection revealed a box on the wall with a rubber stamp in it, which, while not quite as fortifying as a rubber stamp and a pint would have been, it did the job for now. And it was only 10.30 in the morning.

Finding clues to our direction in Bowness-on-Solway required a bit of detective work. I'd assumed being the start of the Wall would be the town's main claim to fame, and would be celebrated with a sign or two at the very least; this was not the case however, and we eventually came across an old bloke weeding his front garden who could point us on our way.

We found the hut that marks the official start of the walk on the outskirts of town.

'Wallsend 84 Miles', read a wooden plaque above the entrance, "Good Luck Go With You.'

We might be needing a bit of that, I thought. 84 miles! We'd planned on spending six days hiking, as the accommodation options along the Wall are quite sparse; there were precisely five of them we could afford, though details remained sketchy. I'd read somewhere that six days was a reasonable challenge for fairly fit people, and I mistakenly lumped myself and Roo into this category.

So off we trudged.

Our backpacks were incredibly heavy, as is usually the case. Since we'd be ending up back at Carlisle and the car, we didn't need to carry days worth of food and cooking gear with us; in our infinite wisdom, we'd decided to do it anyway, so as to lessen the shock of the following day — when we'd also be adding the tent.

It was a decision born of practicality, but also of arrogance; we had, after all, hiked a thousand kilometres across Australia, carrying food for over a week at a time, so we figured the extra weight would help us get back into our hiking mode.

There is a possibility that this was a mistake.

At first, we walked along a scabby beach strewn with stinking seaweed. It was about as appealing as you'd imagine a beach in Carlisle to be... or maybe slightly less. The grey of the water reflected the grey of the sky, both promising an icy-cold and thoroughly miserable soaking. Unfortunately we could only escape one of them, and whilst a swim was out of the question, the inevitable downpour was already getting started.

We hunched into our raincoats, pulled up our hoods, and trudged on.

Towards the end of the beach section we crossed over one of those dubious-looking little outlet streams, which I knew intellectually wouldn't be allowed to funnel raw sewage directly into the sea. And yet, I couldn't shake the suspicion. We stayed far away from the sluggish brown water and headed on up to a section of road.

The walking guide mentioned this bit of road, and not very favourably. Ditches either side and broken ground beyond them made the road itself the only place we could walk. It stretched off into invisibility, encompassing well over half our day's hiking, and a few hours in we could really tell the difference. Grass and earth absorb a certain amount of impact when you walk, which is kind on your knees; not so asphalt, which bounces every heavy footstep straight back up your legs, until you can feel it in your teeth. After two hours on that road, our shins were on fire. The weight of our bags forced us to stomp along, and our feet were crying out with every step. Our ankles ached; our knees were next. A couple of hours later, our hips began to share their burden of discomfort.

"We can't keep this up for the rest of the week," Roo moaned, and I echoed her sentiment with a dejected grunt.

We tried to walk alongside the road, but it varied from soggy to swampy on a step-by-step basis. We simply weren't agile enough to carry on this way; it was only a matter of time before one or the other of us fell face-first into a filthy puddle, and that would make the next ten kilometres even less fun.

It was a welcome relief when the featureless road turned into a tiny village, because that was the last we would see of it until the edge of Carlisle.

This heralded the start of the 'pasture' section of the trail, which could be more accurately described as 'mudslide', because that is what we did for the next few hours. Although technically flat, there were enough contours to the farming land we were traversing to create some truly epic bogs. We tried to creep around their edges, but frequently had to cross fences on wooden stiles – every one of which lay dead centre in the quagmire. With mud splattered up to chest-height in places, we slipped and slid and scrambled to stay upright, making painfully slow progress as a result.

"You'd have to be clinically insane to be a hiker in this country," Roo commented, as I pulled her out of yet another patch of knee-deep ooze.

Little did we know just how close to the mark she'd struck.

Finding a rare, bog-free meadow, we were finally starting to enjoy ourselves, when we spotted a pair of hikers coming towards us – the first people we'd encountered since setting off. They strode up, swishing in their waterproof jackets, and shook our mud-stained hands with their even filthier ones. Both men looked to be in their sixties, and their light daypacks were festooned with water bottles, collapsible walking poles, laminated maps and the like.

One of the men, with a gigantic binocular pouch hanging like a pregnant belly, beckoned us closer as though to impart a secret.

"I'm going to tell you something," he said, in a low voice that made it seem half like a threat. "Around those trees and down the hill, there's a bridge," he stage-whispered.

"Yes?" I said, certain some amazing discovery was about to be shared.

"In the river below there's a rock..."

"Yes?"

"That rock... has some *spoor* on it."

"Oh? Ah."

"Yes! I climbed down to get a closer look," he was hissing through his teeth by now. Both Roo and I tried to look suitably impressed.

"And you know what?" (he paused for dramatic emphasis) "It smelled like otter droppings!"

For a second I thought he was joking, but there was a strange light in his eyes, like the one Gollum gets when he mentions his *precious*...

"So, we haven't seen him yet, but keep your eyes peeled – there could be an otter around here somewhere!"

He seemed so excited with this discovery, I didn't dare ask him what in God's name had prompted him to sniff an old turd sat on a rock. Much less to climb down off a bridge for this purpose. To say nothing of how he *knew* what otter shit smelled like...

I was half afraid he was going to tell us he'd tasted it.

Utterly bereft of anything to say, Roo and I strained our fake smiles to breaking point, and nodded like we had loose springs for necks. We couldn't back away, as the ground behind us was dangerously uneven and we didn't dare take our eyes off the nutcases. And anyway, they would have followed us.

So we waited until the two men felt they had imparted enough of their secret wisdom, and let them amble away of their own accord. Only then, when we reached the Small Bridge of Potential Otters, did we allow ourselves to collapse in gales of laughter.

"Wait! There it is!" said Roo suddenly.

"What? The otter?"

"No, of course not!" She pointed to a rock in the middle of the stream. "The poo!"

I leaned over the mossy wooden handrail to get a closer look.

A squished black sausage sat atop the rock, but not one thing about it made me want to investigate further. Not even the smell.

"I wonder if it's the same temperature as other poos," I said to Roo.

"What? Why?"

"Well, I was thinking it might be a bit 'otter...'"

She sighed. "I could easily push you in, you know."

A few gentle hills later, the path turned down a particularly boggy lane. Sandwiched between two massively high hedges, we slogged our way around the next corner and came face to face – or rather, face to back-end, with the countryside's number one delight: a fully-laden muck spreader! I'm sure everyone knows the joy of following one down the road, travelling at 15mph, too wide to overtake and liberally splattering raw sewage with every jolt? It's an experience that stays with you.

Towed by a tractor at slightly-slower-than-walking-pace, this crap-encrusted tanker filled the laneway. With literally nowhere else to go, we were forced to walk behind it for over a mile. I learnt an interesting thing then – no matter how long you walk behind a truck dripping with liquid shit, you *never* get used to the smell.

"Still wish you'd married a farmer?" I asked Roo.

She shook her head mutely, not daring to open her mouth for a reply.

After escaping from Poo Truck Lane, we passed through another rural village that was little more than the junction between two farms – both of which sported large stone barns. I eyed them suspiciously; there used to be a damn big Wall around here at one time, but so far we hadn't seen a bit of it.

From here on the trail was more manicured, with wood-framed steps and cleared paths through the forest. In the next village I spotted a miniature hut, like a dog kennel on stilts, at the side of the road.

"Oh, it's one of those honesty-boxes!"

They'd been mentioned in the guidebook as being refilled by local shop owners. They operated on the honour system, and I'd kept the last of my change with me in case we spotted one.

"Please let there be a Mars Bar inside!" Roo hoped.

But there was no Mars Bar. Nothing at all in fact – not even a money jar.

Which had to make it the least-successful honesty-box in history.

Either the owners didn't trust people enough to stock the thing, or they'd been too trusting, stocked it, and some bugger had nicked the lot.

"Sorry love. We can get a Mars Bar in Carlisle?"

"We're getting more than a bloody Mars Bar in Carlisle! I need a steak pie!"

"Steak pie and a Mars Bar it is then."

Carlisle seemed to take forever. By the time we found ourselves in golf-course flat parkland we were a bit dazed, and hardly dared believe we'd made it. All in all we were glad to see the end of the first stage. Roo was limping slightly and we were both utterly exhausted. All we could think of was tomorrow's hike – just slightly longer than today's. Over slightly hillier terrain. And by then of course, we'd also be carrying the tent…

Having budgeted a sensible seven hours for the walk, it had taken us nine. I can't even remember what I ate that night, but I doubt it lasted very long. We reclaimed Bubble, drove back to the camping barn and collapsed.

"Fifteen miles down," I reminded Roo as she was drifting off to sleep, "so only sixty-nine more to go!"

I won't include her reply, because I get enough complaints about swearing as it is.

Unreadiness

You know that sensation when you've got a really bad hangover, like your whole body is pissed off at you and determined to punish you? Arms and legs feel like lead, twinges and cramps develop everywhere as though in protest...

That's what I felt like when I woke up. Only worse.

Every single part of my body ached like it had been worked over with a rubber mallet. Muscles I swear don't get involved in hiking were screaming at me for mercy – even the act of sitting up in bed was a struggle. Why did my neck ache so much? I couldn't turn my head to either side without a lance of agony piercing me from top to tail bone. Breathing was far more effort than I remembered. For a minute I thought I'd been bitten by something radioactive in my sleep and was about to begin a transformation process that could see me fighting crime in a Lycra bodysuit...

Then Roo sat up with a groan, and I could hear in the pitch of it that her pain mirrored mine. Unless we were both about to become super-heroes, there was a good chance this was real.

"I hurt!" Roo moaned.

"Where my love?"

"Everywhere!"

I was reminded of an old joke, where an Irishman goes to the doctors and says, "It hurts when I touch here. And it hurts when I touch here. And it even hurts when I touch here!"

To which the doctor replies, "That's because you've got a cut on your finger."

But no, this was the real deal. We were beaten, broken, bruised and blistering. There was a bag-strap shaped channel scored into our shoulders, lined with bits of skin that had rubbed raw. My arms were a good two-inches longer than they had been, and I'd lost about the same amount of height. My hips ached, my knees ached, my ankles ached and my spine made a crunching noise when I tried to bend over. Both of us were hungrier than we could ever remember being – and we stank like the corpse of a week-dead moose.

Breakfast was a protracted affair, because something as simple as putting a spoonful of cornflakes into your mouth requires the use of about fifty-odd muscles, and forty-nine of them were determined to take the day off. My arms shook, my hands trembled, and I ended up wearing about half the cornflakes in any given mouthful. Milk dribbled down my chin and I actually had to make a decision whether or not it was worth the effort to wipe it away. That's not normal – it's like a bird in flight debating whether he can be bothered flapping both wings.

I gave up on the cornflakes and ate toast. And more toast. And more toast. Between us we polished off half a loaf.

That's when another young couple showed themselves, emerging from the other bunkroom looking fresh and enthusiastic.

"Just starting today!" the lad informed me.

I pitied the fool.

But not as much as I pitied myself.

"Mm, toast!" he enthused. Then his brow furrowed. "Why does it smell like a dead moose?"

"Oh, that's just me," I told him. "We're too sore to cook anything other than toast. What are you guys eating?"

His face fell. He looked all of eighteen and a half at that moment, all skinny and unkempt. "We didn't really think about food... I guess I just thought... there'd be some. You know."

"Ah. So you have nothing for the journey?"

"No, but we're biking it. There'll be something on the way." He sounded hopeful, and I didn't want to crush his hopes.

"Well, you're welcome to have some toast. And cornflakes too – but watch them, they can be tricky buggers."

He took this at face value and shot his girlfriend a grin. She was equally young and equally skinny, but pretty enough to never appear unkempt. We relinquished control of the tiny kitchen and went back to the dorm to repack our bags. It was not a happy event, because today we would be carrying ALL our food – and the tent.

"We could ditch the cooking gear," I suggested half-heartedly.

"But then what would we eat? Cold beans and dry bread?"

Part of the problem was how remote this section of the Wall was. This was high moorland, and was essentially uninhabited. Towns and villages abounded further south, but that was sod all good to us. Our guidebook listed the places we would be encountering in order, and most of them were nothing more than the ruins of Roman milecastles which the National Trust were maintaining.

Along our entire day's route, there was only one village listed, and it didn't even have a pub.

"Ditch some of the chocolate?" I said.

Roo fixed me with a black gaze. "Don't. Touch. The chocolate."

The sound and smell of toast being devoured was making me hungry again. I was considering joining the couple for another slice or two, when the young guy poked his head around the door.

"Wow, that IS a lot of stuff you've got," he commented, "we haven't got half as much. I like your raincoat."

"Are you sure you've got everything you need?" I asked him. "There aren't many shops in between Carlisle and Newcastle. Not gear shops, anyway."

"Ha ha! We've made a bit of a mistake there. We haven't brought any sleeping bags."

"Really? Ouch, you'll be cold in your tent."

"Ah, yes. We haven't got a tent either. I thought we'd find places to stay, you know, along the route? We've got really nice bikes though!"

"That's good. You're into bikes then?"

"Oh, no. We just bought them for this. I quit my job you see, and we thought we'd have an adventure."

It sounded painfully familiar. I'd been a scrawny, excitable, Indiana Jones wannabe once. I still was, truth be told, though I'd done enough damage to myself in the last few years of travelling to toughen up and become slightly more cynical. This hike had beaten the snot out of me and Roo on Day One, and I was still under the impression that we were good at this sort of thing. But maybe this lad was stronger than he seemed.

"What did you work as?" I asked him.

"Me? Oh, I was an accountant."

Oh God! They were going to die.

"Here mate, take a couple of Mars Bars at least. You'll need 'em."

"Cool, thanks! We'll stop for coffee when we see somewhere, so maybe you'll catch us up."

I rolled my eyes at his naivety and gestured at the enormous shadow cast by my rucksack. It looked like a fully grown cow. "We'll be taking it slow today. Got to take it easy on the ladies! Now there's a piece of advice for you – you go at her pace, don't make her try to match yours. She won't thank you for it."

He flashed me that super-keen grin and left, clattering down the stairs to help his girlfriend unlock the bikes. She seemed quiet and shy.

If he stayed with her pace, maybe there *was* a chance we'd catch up with them – and an even greater chance of them still being in one piece when we did.

"I don't think he's got a raincoat," Roo said.

Outside a steady drizzle had set in, and from the window we could see that the sky was iron-grey from horizon to horizon.

"Poor sod! I haven't got a spare to lend him. I don't think it'll matter though. One morning of cycling in this and they'll be so miserable they'll give up before lunch. Probably check into a nice B&B somewhere and have a proper holiday."

"That's not such a bad idea," Roo said. I almost dared allow myself a glimmer of hope, but then she was all business again. "Right, let's go, before we lose the will."

"I think I dropped my will in the swamp yesterday," I said. "It was slimy and covered in mud and I didn't want to put it back in my pocket, so I just left it there."

Hitting The Wall

Leaving the sanctuary of the camping barn was hard, but we consoled ourselves with a guilty secret. The barn, which we'd chosen for its proximity to the Wall, was outside of Carlisle by a couple of miles. We'd covered those miles twice in Bubble, but we hadn't actually hiked them – and it hadn't taken much to convince us not to bother. Leaving the car at the camping barn was much safer and substantially cheaper than letting it sit in a city car park for a week, so this became our excuse; there was no way in hell we'd be walking back into Carlisle, only to turn around and walk out.

Still, it was hard to judge the effect of the missing two miles as I hadn't managed to properly calculate today's walking distance. None of our guidebooks or pamphlets were designed to plan this sort of trip – at the time, no such thing was available. The distance between places was mentioned here and there throughout the text, but mostly in terms of linking the various sites of interest along the Wall. As our start and end points fell somewhere in between, I hadn't been able to get an accurate fix on how far we'd be walking, but I had an answer ready for Roo when she asked.

"How far are we going today?"
"Too damn far!"

It started out very pleasantly though, as the rain decided to hold off and trees lined the road towards the Wall. By mid-morning, the sky had cleared up and birds were singing – it was like a scene from a Disney cartoon, only with Baloo the bear hitching a ride on my shoulders the entire time.

I'd estimated my rucksack at nineteen kilos of pure agony. Roo's couldn't have been much lighter. They constantly threatened to crush the breath out of us, their weight resting squarely on bruised hips, the straps sawing back and forth across shoulders rubbed raw the day before.

Going uphill was a struggle. Going downhill, on rain-slicked grass, was borderline suicidal. Weight x Acceleration = Velocity – I remembered that from high school physics. Strange, the things that come to you in the middle of a field, when it's angled at twenty degrees downwards and you can't seem to stop…

A lot of people tell me that an average person walks at four miles per hour. I'd LOVE to know where this common misconception comes from, but trust me – as someone who's walked a few of 'em – miles don't pass that fast. Four *kilometres* an hour is much more realistic – when happily skipping through the park on your way home from work. In thick mud, staggering uphill whilst bent double under a bag the size of a golf cart, you're lucky to manage half that.

So I wasn't too surprised to find, after four tough hours, that we weren't even halfway. It had been a monster day for sure, but we were in so much pain from the previous day's mission, and this route seemed to be nothing but hills. I was disheartened, but realistic – we had to call it a day at the next town, or we wouldn't be able to stand tomorrow, let alone hike.

We'd been walking along the top of a grassy mound which had once formed the base of Hadrian's Wall. Originally this part of the Wall had been entirely made of turf, but I guess they figured that wasn't much of a defence. The foundations had remained, but rest of the Wall had been rebuilt in sandstone – most of which now graced every building between here and Scotland. When we sighted the first chunk of honest-to-goodness Hadrian's Wall poking up out of the landscape, we decided to take a break on top of it while we figured out our options.

There was a bus service that ran up and down the Wall, following the line of the military road the Romans had built to move troops along it. Like most Roman roads, this one still existed in modern guise, and even bore the name Military Road. The bus stopped at all the main accommodation options, including the hostel I'd booked for us in Greenhead; if we were in luck, we could cheat on the last bit of today's hike, and might actually get there before midnight.

Roo studied the timetable, sitting on a chunk of ancient Roman masonry while I eased her shoes off to treat her blisters.

"We can just make it," she said, showing me the page.

The very last bus was due in about half an hour, and it stopped in the village that this chunk of Wall belonged to. I finished taping up Roo's feet and we braced ourselves for a final push.

The problem was that we'd clearly bitten off more than we could chew.

Later, when I had chance to calculate the distance properly, I discovered my error – not only had I added up figures that didn't really meet in the middle, in my head I'd been working in kilometres. Twenty-and-then-some hadn't sounded too difficult, but I'd been too tired to realise that I hadn't converted it back from the miles the book was quoting. In point of fact, we'd set out to walk a section of nearly twenty-six miles in one go – and as anyone who's ever run a marathon will tell you, it's not a good idea to do it in hiking boots.

The second problem was a distinct lack of bus stop. After being told by a local that the bus would stop "anywhere you wanted, as long as you wave at it," we hiked on even further, finally finding an official stop by a ruined watchtower about a mile away.

The third problem was that there was no bus. It wasn't listed on the stop. We checked the timetable in growing panic – only to realize at the last minute that it was last year's timetable. I dug the current one out of my rucksack and discovered it was identical except for one tiny detail; the last bus, the one we were so desperate to catch, had been axed.

This was not cool. Reaching the hostel we'd booked was now out of the question, so we'd have to accept that loss. All we could do was soldier on to the camping barn a few miles up the road, and pray they had space. As we groaned and hauled our bags onto our backs, the wind howled and it began to rain.

We stuck out our thumbs in hope, but nothing happened. We arrived dispirited, saturated, aching and so, so tired, at the camping barn – to be greeted with a notice saying 'CAMPING BARN CLOSED'. That was it. No-one around to ask and nothing else to do. Well, we did a good bit of swearing, but I don't think it helped much.

We hiked on. Roo had more blisters than toes, and the muscles and tendons in our ankles were screaming at us. Expensive cars roared past us, each one carrying a solitary, middle aged woman. None stopped to pick us up.

An hour later we arrived at the Youth Hostel at Birdoswald, ready to collapse.

Or rather, we arrived at where there should have been a youth hostel. We ditched our bags and explored the ruined Roman fort (which, had it been officially open, would have cost us almost a fiver each) – but there was no sign. Only a closed and locked building behind the visitors centre which looked like it could once have been a hostel. Not cool at all.

CAN I KISS HER YET?

It would have been time for despair, if it hadn't been for Steve and John – two awesomely helpful blokes who had also over estimated their hiking speed. They rocked up to the empty fort, decided to call it a day, phoned their wives to come get them and immediately offered us a lift. They were taking a far more attractive approach; only hiking the bits they wanted to while their wives shopped and gossiped in the nearest town, on the proviso they came to collect the fellas when they ran out of steam. It sounded like a perfect arrangement – especially for their wives, who had spent most of the afternoon reading in a coffee shop.

They drove us to a pub in Gilsland, the next town in our path. Roo and I exchanged shocked glances as the miles rolled by; Gilsland, which we'd intended to hike right through today, would have taken us hours to reach.

We thanked the ladies profusely, and they sped off to collect their husbands (who'd been kind enough to let us go first).

From here I planned to ring our hostel, in a town even further along the route, and see if they could arrange a taxi to come and get us. It was an added expense, but cheaper than staying locally – at Roo's request I asked at the pub about the price of rooms, and it was considerably more than we wanted to pay.

And that was when I discovered my phone was gone.

I'd left it in the car.

By now it would be sandwiched between Steve and John, on the way to wherever they were staying. I knew it was there because I'd pulled it out to see why it was beeping.

And it was beeping because it was about to suffer battery-death.

Which meant I wouldn't be able to call it. No-one who found it would be able to call out. Not that there were any numbers stored in the memory – I'd only bought the phone a few days before we started the Grand Adventure, to help us make accommodation bookings on the move.

Now we couldn't call for a lift, or book anything...

And I was never going to get my phone back.

I lost the plot for a bit.

Only a few minutes before, we'd been debating whether or not we could afford £60 to check in to the nearest B&B in a move born of desperation. Now all that paled into comparison. I'd lost a £150 phone, and despite the distance we'd gained, our nice cheap hostel might as well have been in Moscow. I dashed into the pub for change, and waited frantically for the payphone opposite. A bearded bloke had appeared out of nowhere and taken up permanent residence in the phone box, just as I imagined the dwindling minutes in which I could still call my own phone. I sat on the curb and put my head in my hands, close to tears. "How can this happen to us?" I asked Roo. "We're nice people! We help everyone. This morning I gave breakfast to that couple with no food. Why is Karma being so evil to me?"

Well, someone up there must have heard me and thought, 'Oops! My bad.'

Because Steve-and-John-plus-wives screeched up and handed me back my phone, in the exact same instant that it bleeped and went dead. And as we sat on the curb pondering this change in our fortunes, a random bloke in a shiny black Vauxhall stopped and asked if we needed a lift somewhere.

Amazing. He took us right to the door of our hostel, despite it being in the opposite direction to where he was headed!

We ditched our bags, said bollocks to our instant noodles, and marched into the nearest pub for some dinner. But just to stop me being too cocky, immediately after I got inside the pub, I sat in piss.

Whoever had occupied the seat before me had peed all over it – and no, it wasn't cider. I could tell this by the smell, so I luckily avoided taste-testing it. I washed my hands several times, but had no choice other than to sit and eat my lasagne in pants that someone other than me had pissed on.

And tomorrow I'd be hiking in them, too.

To round the evening out I showered in the dark (due to a busted light in the hostel bathroom), gave up trying to scrub the piss out of my pants for the same reason, and then fell in the general direction of my bed. Not at all sure that, come the 8:30am alarm, I'd be capable of climbing out of it...

Back to the Wall

As the phone alarm buzzed us awake at 8:30am, I could tell even from across the room that Roo was feeling about as enthusiastic as I was. I tried to sit up and winced – every bit of me hurt like hell.

"Are we...?" I began.

Roo just looked at me. I had the horrible feeling she was about to cry.

It was at this moment that a strategy emerged, fully formed, in my mind. I bloody love it when that happens.

"We could get the bus back to where the car is?" I suggested. "Then we could drive back here and hike the next stage without bags. Bus back here after we finish walking and collect the car again. Hell, we could do the rest of the walk like that!"

And we did.

It was the fastest we'd moved in weeks – the sudden glimmer of life without a crushing weight on our shoulders galvanized us into action. I checked the time-table – we had less than ten minutes to pack our stuff (currently scattered across the whole dorm), and get our asses down the road to the bus stop. Moving like extras in a bad zombie movie we lurched around the room, gathering up still-moist towels and struggling to don socks that had dried stiff and crusty.

In an jiffy we were out of the door, bleary-eyed, bedraggled and somewhat fragrant; the walking dead, complete with authentic sound effects.

By the time we reached the bus stop, it had become obvious that we wouldn't be hiking much further that day. Neither of us could walk like regular human beings, having pulled pretty much every muscle in both legs. Our backs were stiff, our necks ached, and Roo had a blister which was actually bigger than the toe it was attached to. It was time to admit it – this walk had kicked our sorry behinds from Day One. Perhaps we weren't as fit as we used to be?

Bubble was glad to see us, but not nearly as glad as we were to see him. Knowing that the decision was made and an end was in sight made carrying our bags from the bus stop much easier. Morning sun had warmed the inside of the car, and the seats perfectly cushioned our aching derrières. Roo fired him up and cruised leisurely back to the hostel – a journey which took all of twenty minutes. "I like this kind of hiking," Roo said, as hills we'd battled for hours flew past the window in seconds.

"Mmm," I agreed. And dozed off.

The hostel owner was happy for us to leave Bubble outside for the day, allowing us to hike as far as we were able before getting the bus back here. Roo was testing her injured ankle, seeing how much weight she could put on it before it hurt, when a thought occurred to me. "You know, we probably could have left our bags here while we went back to get the car."

She looked up at me. "Let's pretend that's not true," she said.

Hadrian's Wall accompanied us for most of the day's hike. The remains varied from a single-brick high stripe, four and a half feet wide, to a chest-height rampart of dressed stone blocks. In all cases the core of the wall was firmly-mortared rubble, so solidly built that it had resisted nearly two-thousand years of the worst weather Scotland (only a few metres away) could throw at it. Eventually, seeds falling on the Wall would sprout, forcing roots into microscopic cracks. The cracks would fill with water, which would freeze and expand in winter, forcing the cracks wider until another handful of stones collapsed into rubble. This constant process of erosion is what had allowed so much of the Wall's upper reaches to be carried away by locals. The bit that was left looked indestructible, but we passed an English Heritage bloke spraying the stones with weed-killer as part of their on-going maintenance program.

There were several forts and mile-castles on this stretch – or their foundations, at least – but there was one other thing that Roo was super-keen to see.

Scouring the guide book for points of interest, she had come across something she just *had* to photograph; somewhere on the mile of wall we had missed yesterday, some ancient Roman comedian had carved a big fat penis.

True story.

And so, bag-free, we shambled up and down this stretch of wall, enthusiastically searching for this pre-historic phallus. It wasn't easy to find. "There's no cock here," I told Roo.

"There IS," she declared. "I HAVE to see that cock!"

"You can see mine tonight," I offered.

"No. It's not ancient enough."

Such is married life. You've got to take the compliments where you can get 'em.

A group of boy scouts approached, optimistically carrying sleeping mats strapped to the side of their unfairly-small daypacks. "Any of you guys seen a big cock?" I asked the lads.

No response.

"My missis is desperate to get her hands on that cock," I tried.

Nothing.

"I think it's about yay-big…" I held my hands about a foot apart.

They must have been foreign.

By this point Roo was limping up and down, shouting "Where's the cock? I WANT the cock!" More than a few passing hikers had stopped to stare at us. But just as we decided to quit (or in fact as I attempted to drag Roo away, with her still shouting "Show me that cock!") – we *found it*.

It was spectacular.

Not.

But then, it had been carved close to two thousand years ago, and it was an amazingly accurate reproduction. I was forced to picture some unlucky legionnaire, ordered by his Centurion to flop it out in the chilly Cumbrian wind and hold it there while the sculptor chiselled a perfect likeness in limestone. On the upside, he must have one of the most famous willies in all of recorded history. And the most handled – both Roo and me had to have a sly stroke, because after all, it *is* a piece of history. With a great big pair of balls for realism, almost worn away by the passage of time. And of many, many hands.

Our partially motorised take on hiking revealed an unexpected benefit – we were first to arrive at the next camping barn. And rather than staggering up after dark, so exhausted we could barely remain upright, we cruised in, had showers, and spent an hour reading books from the crate we kept in Bubble. Carrying books while hiking was never an option, so this luxury really made a difference – as did the desk lamp I'd brought for camping. This barn had an electrical outlet, but (bizarrely) no overhead light, and I was delighted to find I had just what we needed to make things cosy. We nipped out in the car and bought fish and chips from a town a few miles down the road, another thing that would have been impossible whilst hiking. There were plenty of towns near the Wall, but none on the Wall itself. The closest were only a ten-minute drive away, but without a car that translated into a lot of extra walking miles – and they were miles that would have to be done again on the way back to the Wall.

The barn's other room seemed to be occupied. A pile of giant rucksacks, not dissimilar to our own, filled the space between the bunks. The bags had been there a while, but it wasn't until their owners hiked in (after dark, exhausted) that I realized something. Despite hiking several different bits of the Wall, we hadn't passed a single other person with a big bag. I remembered an option we'd seen advertised when we were planning this trip, and in our pride we had scoffed at it and cast it aside without a second thought. But now it made sense. Out of all the people who had dared to hike Hadrian's Wall, from the frailest old granny to the keenest Army Cadet, we were the only ones stupid enough to try to do it with nineteen kilos on our backs.

Everyone else had paid a courier.

As the new arrivals scuffled around, trying to set up their stove by the light of their head torches, I nipped over and offered them the desk lamp.

"It'll reach, I've put an extension cord on it," I told them.

They were taken aback. "Are youse hiking?" a Scouse girl asked, glancing at the tangle of electrical cables and the pile of books.

"Yeah, we're hiking."

"Which courier service did you use? Ours only takes one bag each."

"Oh, we didn't bother with a courier. We're doing it ourselves – you know, we fancied a bit of a challenge."

"Oh. Right."

I could tell she was still confused as I climbed onto my bed and fired up the laptop.

Wall's End

The next morning we left Bubble parked outside the camping barn and set off up the hill directly behind it. The scenery was spectacular right from the start, and with only a daysack full of water and snacks each, we could really appreciate it. The Wall was more complete here, perhaps on account of how remote it was; vast tracts of moorland surrounded us, the rough and essentially uninhabited country of the Scottish borders.

I spotted a tree used in one of my favourite films, Robin Hood: Prince of Thieves, with Kevin Costner. In theory Robin was walking toward Nottingham from the south coast – so he'd managed to lose his way by, oh, about three-hundred miles or so. But it made a good point; the land around here was positively medieval, with almost no visible signs of the modern world. The few man-made structures we could see were old disused shepherds' huts and dry-stone walls, and they vanished into insignificance next to the vastness of the open moors. Several hills were so steep that the Wall climbed vertically, maintaining its course in spite of the topography. To see it from on high as it unfurled across the undulating landscape was to marvel at the audacity of its creators. It only took six years for the Romans to build Hadrian's Wall – complete with eighty individual mile-castles and two observation turrets between each of them. Plus of course the fifteen or so full-sized forts they constructed for the auxiliaries that manned the Wall. And in addition to all that beautifully dressed stonework, there was a deep ditch and sloping *glacis* that ran the length of the Wall on its 'barbarian' side, and a wide, paved road on the other. It was a truly epic undertaking that almost beggars belief – when you think of the cost of building a house these days...

Ouch.

From one windswept crag we looked down on a glittering lake; from the next we gazed into the remains of Housesteads, one of the best-preserved forts on the Wall. Hiking up to it, we didn't even realise there was an entrance fee as the Wall led us straight inside. We admired the ruins, again built entirely of stone, and ate our sandwiches sitting on the edge of the latrine.

Predictably, whilst walking one way and looking the other I fell flat on my face in a ditch. Roo nearly wet herself laughing, and she wasn't alone – I stood up to find an entire school-group watching me and chortling away.

"That's why you're not allowed to hold the camera," Roo joked.

"I thought that was the point of getting a bomb-proof camera?"

"It's certainly camel-proof, but I'm still not sure if it's Slater-proof."

This time, the bus was easy to catch. This is because we knew where it would stop, and when, which I find makes things much simpler. Also, the bus actually existed, which was another point in our favour.

"This is definitely the best way to do this," Roo said. "We should really consider doing more research next time."

"Nah, that takes all the fun out of it!" I said.

We reclaimed Bubble without a hitch, and were in high spirits as we headed towards the next camping barn listed in our guidebook. This one turned out to be an actual barn, though presumably converted, on what looked like a working farm. The owner must have heard Bubble crunching up the gravel driveway, as she was waiting for us when we pulled up.

"I'm so sorry, the camping barn is fully booked," she said. She really did sound sorry. "If you had a tent…"

"We have a tent!"

"Oh! That's alright then. If you don't mind camping out?"

"No, not at all."

"And you can wee in the toilet," she said.

Which I thought was quite an odd note to finish on, until she showed us to our pitch. At the top of the field, right by the gate, stood a lonely white toilet with a low fence on two sides of it.

"It's the chemical disposal point for people with Porta-Potties," she explained.

"Ah."

"Please don't poo in it, though."

I glanced around at the unobstructed view of her house, her bedroom windows, the camping barn and the main road. "Don't worry," I told her, "we usually go inside for that."

We hadn't used the tent since cleaning it in the hallway at The International Hotel. The trade-off of comfort for privacy was welcome for a change, and after Roo cooked one of her one-pot wonders on the camping stove (I think it was a tin of ravioli and a tin of spaghetti), we snuggled up together for the night.

"I prefer this to bunk beds," she said, wriggling closer.

"Me too, actually."

"Why don't we stay here tomorrow? We planned to have a rest day, if we needed it. There's no chance of us not reaching the end now that we have the car, so…"

"Yeah. Could do, I suppose."

"We could spend all morning in bed…"

"Okay! Sold. Rest day it is."

She slid an arm around me. "I thought you'd say that."

We woke to find frost coating everything. We'd stayed snug and warm, sharing our body heat, and were quite surprised by the transformation outside. It made all the more sense to stay in bed, although Roo couldn't resist trying to photograph the effects of the frost. I lay in the tent and listened to her coo with excitement at every frozen spider-web she discovered. We clicked together so well, it was easy for me to forget the little things, like how she'd never seen snow or frost until she was in her twenties.

After an exceptionally lazy morning, we rolled into Hexham to find some lunch. Outside an impressive stone abbey with giant arched windows and turrets on the roof, there was a sign advertising free walking tours of the town.

The little clock on the sign said the tour would start at 1pm, so we sat on a bench nearby to wait for it.

1pm came and went, and we were starting to get a bit peckish, so I wandered into the church to see if anyone knew what was going on. I didn't have to go very far as there was a gift shop immediately inside. "Hi there!" I said to the two old ladies behind the counter. "Just wondering if you know anything about this walking tour? It was supposed to be at one o'clock, but no-one's shown up yet."

"What? The walking tours only run in summer."

"Oh! But there's a sign out there…"

"It's not our job to take the sign in. We don't run the tours."

"Oh. Okay then. Wait – they only run in summer?"

"Yes."

"But it's October."

"That's right. Hasn't been a tour since August."

"And no-one else has come in and asked?"

"No."

"Alright then." I thought of offering to bring the sign in for them, but if we were the only people it had fooled in the last two months, I guess it didn't really matter.

That night we cut our losses on the Wall and drove to the outskirts of Newcastle, to a cheap hotel room we booked online. The lure of a hot shower in the privacy of our own bathroom, plus the comfort of a real bed, won us over. We both felt a bit disappointed that we'd been so thoroughly defeated by the hike. We'd had a lot to focus on lately, with the weddings, the book and my emigration, and fitness really hadn't been a priority.

"As soon as we get back to Perth, let's join a gym," I said. "I want to get back in shape, and stay that way."

"I can handle that," she replied. "But I tell you what, I'm not wearing my backpack on a treadmill!"

Our Hadrian's Wall experience was completed the next day with a trip to Wallsend. We celebrated our motorised strategy by arriving on the Metro, Newcastle's underground light railway and one of only two in the UK outside of London (the other is in Glasgow). As a nod to the Roman origins of Wallsend, all the station signs were bilingual in English and Latin, but that didn't help us find the Wall's end itself. There was a museum, which we browsed, full of the usual shards of pottery and small stone carvings of large-breasted women. The Romans sure did a lot of that. But after hunting around for trail markers, and following what we thought was the right route only to end up in a dockyards, we gave up and collected our last stamp from the museum.

We planned on posting our stamped cards away to get a certificate of completion, although this did seem a bit unscrupulous, as we hadn't even come close to hiking the entire way. But when we got back to Somerset we found they'd discontinued the postal certificates – if we wanted ours, we'd have to go all the way back to Newcastle, or Carlisle, to get them.

Serves us right, I reckon.

Needless to say, we weren't *that* keen.

We killed a few hours in Gateshead MetroCentre, the largest shopping centre in the UK. We couldn't afford to buy anything bigger than an ice cream, but we had a good look around, marvelling at the volume of space inside. It took us almost as long to find the car afterwards as it had to explore the centre.

Then we drove a couple of hours down the motorway to York, a city I'd wanted to re-visit for years.

The first, and happier half of my childhood was spent in Yorkshire. I've always found the people welcoming, the countryside greener, the weather... well, that's damn awful no matter how much you like the place, but there's got to be something wrong with it. Otherwise everyone would live there.

York itself is a magnificent city, surrounded by great medieval walls that vary from many hundreds of years old to well over a thousand. We parked up and strolled through the Shambles, a ridiculously narrow street that used to house the city's butchers' shops. We had just enough time to walk the walls themselves, completing a full circuit in compensation for our slackness further north. The ancient part of the city, including fabulous gothic cathedral York Minster, was all inside the fortifications, whereas the modern city spilled out way beyond. The views from atop those walls, of magnificent old buildings in half-timber and stone, of cobbles and snickets and marketplaces, summed up what this trip had been about for me.

England had so much history you tripped over it every time you went anywhere. It was one of the things I loved most about the place – and one of the things I would miss.

"Let's celebrate with a really nice dinner in one of these old pubs," I suggested.

"Great idea," said Roo.

So I went to draw £20 out of the ATM – only to find that I couldn't.

There was nothing left in the account.

The money was all spent.

Our Grand Adventure was over.

One cheap fried chicken take-away later, we sat in Bubble and called Mum.

"We're coming home," I told her.

"No, don't!" she said.

"Eh?"

"I mean, don't try to come home in one trip. It's much too far, you'll fall asleep at the wheel."

"No I won't!"

"You say that now, but it could take you all night."

"No, I mean, I'm not driving. Roo is."

"Oh. Well she'll fall asleep at the wheel then!"

"I'll be fine," Roo said, leaning in to share the phone. "We drive long distances like this all the time in Australia."

"Still, it's a very long way," Mum warned her.

Safely out of sight of my mother, Roo rolled her eyes. "It's only England, it can't possibly be *that* far!"

It was three-hundred and thirty-six miles, as it happens. That's just over five-hundred and forty kilometres for you metric types.

It was, in fairness to my mother, a *very* long way.

Roo made it in a little under seven hours.

My parents, sick with worry, waited up until three 'o' clock in the morning for us to arrive.

"You're crazy, the pair of you," Mum said when we got back, "what on earth possessed you to drive all the way back tonight?"

"I missed my hamsters," said Roo.

Dad shook his head and went off to make a cup of tea, while Roo ran upstairs to be greeted by a frenzy of squeaking.

"She really does love those hamsters," Dad said to me, as he handed me a brew.

"Yeah. It's all she talks about these days!"

"Better not tell her that I lost one of them, then," he said, stirring his cuppa.

"Holy sh—"

"Found him again, though."

"Phew!"

"Took a couple of days, but I found him."

The End Of An Era

The Grand Adventure had only taken us three weeks.

It was true, what Dad had said; a thousand pounds doesn't go very far in a country like England. But we were back, and we were happy with what we'd achieved.

And while we were away, a few things had happened.

For starters, all the paperwork I needed to complete my Australian residency application had arrived. It was all neatly stacked together on my desk, together with a note that said I had to call my appointed Emigration Case Officer.

His name was Mr Stern, which wasn't the most encouraging of signs.

Also on my desk was a rectangular box that had been delivered courtesy of Lloyds Bank. Inside was a bottle of wine, and a printed note card that read 'We're Sorry!'

I couldn't believe it. I've had banks screw me over plenty of times, though admittedly this was the first time I'd lost any sleep over it. But I couldn't ever remember a bank admitting they'd done something wrong – much less apologise for it! What amused me most was that it was obviously a standard response, sent from their head office in London, rather than a personal apology from the lady at my branch. This meant that somewhere, high up in a glass-walled office building, someone was getting paid to spend their days printing out little 'sorry' cards and parcelling up bottles of wine to compensate for the company's cock-ups.

A professional apologiser, if you will.

Man, I know a few government departments that could use one of those!

My parents had finally finished putting all of Gramp's affairs in order. They were sick to their back teeth with legalize and pointless, repetitive bureaucracy, but there had been a silver lining to the story. Gramp had always been a modest man, living well within his means, so as well as bequeathing his flat to my parents, he had also left a tidy sum of money which was to be divvied up between us. Once the legal fees were deducted, both Gill and I had added to our initial inheritance a further sum of three-thousand pounds!

By happy coincidence, this was exactly what I needed; most of it was owed to the Australian government for my residency application, and the remainder cleared my credit card of the visa medical and two plane tickets to Perth.

It was the most money I'd ever spent in a single day — and I'm happy to say it still is!

I had to sit down for a little bit afterwards.

With my paperwork paid up and sent off, I started to think about all the other things I had to do before leaving England. These were many.

Most important of all was to pack up all the stuff we wanted to ship to Australia. My beloved books would be staying behind of course; not only were there far too many of them to ship, there would also be no place to store them once they arrived in Perth. Also, they were stacked right up to the ceiling of my bedroom in Holly Cottage, and there was a good chance they were holding the roof up.

I had a few other little items on my To Do list, like final visits to see the various friends and family members I'd be leaving behind.

Oh, and one more thing; I had to learn to drive.

I mean, I could drive already — I was bloody awful at it, but I'd been getting plenty of practice lately. The rules for new drivers in Australia are quite harsh though, and I had even less chance of passing my test over there than I did here.

So the pressure was on; I had less than a month, from start to finish.

Fortunately, I also had Bubble.

Gramp had owned the car from new, and had kept him in immaculate condition — at least until we came along. There were the inevitable car park dings and dents here and there, but in total, after twenty years of careful ownership, Gramp had put less than five thousand miles on the clock.

Over the past year, Roo and I had almost quadrupled that.

I booked a bunch of lessons with a local driving instructor, and managed to book a test on the only day still available; my last full day in the country.

So at least I had something to look forward to if I failed.

Meanwhile, Roo and I had a more glamorous chore to complete; packing.

We already knew we had far too much stuff to fit in our cases, so I ordered a 'small box' from a shipping company. They sent us a large *and* a small, 'just in case'. Those clever bastards! I suspect our story is not unusual; we quickly gave up on the small box and began filling the large. Then we placed a quick call to the shipping company, altered our quote slightly, and started filling the small as well. About the time Roo floated the question 'I wonder how much they charge for a third box...' I called time; anything that wasn't packed already was staying. Cue another frantic round of unpacking and re-packing, with Roo shoving stuff in one side and me removing it from the other. In the end our boxes were less than one kilo under the maximum allowed weight – *between them*. It truly was a feat of tessellation. The boxes would be staying with my parents until the shipping company came to collect them; until then, all we could do was pray to every God that our bathroom scales were accurate...

Our next task wasn't nearly as enjoyable. Roo had joined an online 'Hamster Fanatics Forum' almost a year ago, and if the label 'fanatic' could be applied to anyone, it was her. Now though, with our departure imminent, she had scoured the website to find suitable homes for our two remaining pets; Violet Crumble, the happiest, most inquisitive hamster on the planet, and her fat little friend Hedgehog. Slowly, sadly, Roo dismantled the Rotastak, which by this point took up more of the bedroom than all the other furniture combined. She carefully washed most of it, leaving bedding in the two central tanks we'd be using as transport cages. Roo had found two new owners, both of whom belonged to the forum, and both of whom were delighted to be adopting Roo's beloved hamsters.

And both of whom lived on the opposite side of the country, so I got five hours' straight driving practice into the bargain.

Having seen the houses where Violet and Hedgehog would be staying, Roo was satisfied that she'd done the right thing. Hedgehog had become a slow old home-body and was spending most of his time asleep, but Violet was going to achieve a dream Roo had held for her from the beginning; she was finally going to be allowed complete freedom of her new owner's house.

Free range hamster. We knew she'd love it there.

Roo cried all the way home.

As the day of my driving test approached, I was becoming increasingly nervous. I knew that age was on my side, as the examiner was likely to be more forgiving to someone he considered more mature than the average.

"Just don't let him know he's wrong," Roo told me.

She even picked my outfit for me, choosing clothes she felt would emphasise the responsibility in my appearance.

"No Star Wars t-shirt?" I asked her.

"No. No Star Wars t-shirt."

I hung my head.

"Okay then, you can take one and wear it on your way home!"

"Woohoo!"

"IF you pass."

I wanted to drive Bubble to the test centre, but nerves won out and I booked a last minute lesson just beforehand. Ian, my instructor, reckoned I'd be fine, but I couldn't help feeling that he had to say that. He reminded me not to stall the car, something I'd been achieving with alarming regularity. This was particularly impressive given that Ian's car was a diesel, and *technically* was impossible to stall. I'd rather have done the test in Bubble, too, as I felt I had the measure of him and never stalled, but I was here now.

My first and last chance.

And then, waiting for the examiner, I thought of Gramp, and wished he could see me as I drove home triumphant. My nerves evaporated as I imagined his reaction.

This one's for you, Gramp, I told him, silently.

And passed.

I drove home in a jubilant mood, but I couldn't resist mugging an unhappy face as I slouched through my parents' front door.

"Oh no," Mum said, when she saw me, "what went wrong?"

"Bloody stalled the friggin' car, didn't I? At a roundabout, on a hill. Just didn't give the damn thing enough gas."

"Oh dear! But I thought you'd get away with that. Isn't that just a minor fault?"

"Oh yeah, I mean, I passed my test and all that."

She saw my grin start to break through. "Oh, you little..."

I told Gill on Skype (as she and Chris were in France, working on a ski-field in the Alps). "You bastard," she moaned, "you got one less fault than I did!"

Of course, Gill had passed her test within a few months of her seventeenth birthday, and had been driving ever since. In fact, her first paying job had been to drive some idiot all over the country as he did a one-man shaving show sponsored by Lynx. Hm. I'll have to write about that sometime...

But for now, I had to admit, I was a tiny bit proud of myself. Okay; a lot.

Dad was also proud of me, and I liked to think that Gramp was looking down from his cloud, and that he was proud of me too.

I jumped into Bubble and drove a victory lap, celebrating my triumph along the narrow country lanes around our house.

And that was the last trip I ever made in Bubble.

I'd toyed briefly with the idea of trying to drive him all the way to Australia. Apart from a brief trip by shipping container from the southern tip of Indonesia, it was theoretically possible. We weren't likely to get much money from selling him, especially now that he was decorated with wheelie bin stickers, so if he died *en route* it wouldn't exactly be a disaster. And we were bound to need a car back in Perth, if he survived the journey. But then I did a bit of research, and discovered that the preferred route ran through Iran, Iraq, and Afghanistan. Mum was worried enough about me driving around England, so I didn't think she'd be too keen on that idea. And I know people sometimes think I'm crazy, but driving through the middle of the most violent war zone on the planet did seem like pushing the boundaries of common sense a bit too far.

So we decided not to do that.

Instead, we said tearful good-byes to my parents and boarded our plane.

Holly Cottage had been our home and our refuge for longer than any other place so far, and we were going to miss it, and its occupants, far too much. Our wedding; Gill's wedding; the splendour of Jordan, the horror of penis surgery, and the joys of hamster ownership – a lot had happened to us since Roo's troubled arrival in the country. It was hard to leave the site of so many amazing memories, but as always we'd be carrying those experiences with us as we travelled. And we were flying towards new adventures, a life filled with equal promise and potential; not heading for Perth, at least not yet, because we'd been the recipients of yet another act of astounding generosity; this time, from Roo's family.

Gerrit and the girls had clubbed together and bought us three nights in the most exclusive honeymoon resort imaginable. So as we left the grey skies of England far behind us, we were looking forward to more than just a new life, and a new beginning, in Perth; we were also looking forward to a kick-ass holiday at the Sunway Lagoon Resort in Kuala Lumpur, Malaysia.

Oh yes! Look out, five-star luxury! We were on our way...

Asia's Best Attraction

We'd never really expected to have a honeymoon. Not a proper one anyway, not like Gill and Chris on their all-inclusive Caribbean cruise. We'd chosen the backpacker lifestyle, and had long since accepted being broke as an inevitable result of it. And yet, instead of one amazing honeymoon, we were about to embark on our *third!* Well, assuming you count the Grand Adventure.

I'm still not a hundred percent sure it qualifies.

As part of the package Gerrit and the girls had bought us, we would be staying not in a room, or even a suite, but in a five-star private villa! We had two massages to look forward to, as well as dinner served on our balcony by our personal butler, cocktails and snacks served in the pavilion at sunset, and – best of all – our own private plunge pool!

It was a taste of luxury that neither of us had ever experienced, and to be honest weren't likely to again. It was the perfect antidote to our gruelling trip around England, and we could hardly wait.

It must have cost them a fortune.

Arriving at the hotel made us feel like movie stars.

The building was staggering. Twenty stories high, with turreted towers at the corners, hundreds of balconies and acres of glass. The entrance was flanked by giant columns, on top of which life-sized flying saucers were perched. Mind you, this was Malaysia; a certain degree of style-over-function was popular here, so there is a chance they were meant to be trees. The foyer was vast. In the middle of it, where some hotels might have had a water feature, they had a eight-metre tall castle with Pegasi flying out of it.

While we were gazing around like slack-jawed yokels a concierge came to take our bags. As soon as the staff realised we were staying in a villa they pulled out all the stops; they called for a car to take us through the complex, and we were led into the bar and given complimentary cocktails while we waited. Our luggage was taken on ahead, which made me laugh – a pair of impeccably-dressed bellboys staggered out of the door carrying bulging, decrepit rucksacks still liberally splattered with mud from Hadrian's Wall.

It took the car half an hour to make a journey of about two hundred metres, so bad was the traffic around the hotel, but once we passed through the gate to The Villas, all that went away. Lush green jungle closed in around the driveway, and the car slid past a handful of secluded villas snuggled into the hillside.

Our beat-up rucksacks were waiting for us in a tastefully-appointed wooden bungalow. We had a large four-poster bed covered in rose petals, a marble-tiled en-suite bathroom with an enormous sunken bath, and sliding glass doors that led out onto our private terrace. A pocket-sized infinity-edge pool, complete with waterfall, was the triumphant flourish.

"This is incredible," Roo beamed, and she was right.

We spent the next day enjoying our villa. In the afternoon we had our first massage, which had been described to us as a 'couple's massage'. Roo had never had a massage before, and was more than a little nervous. "They won't ask us to undress, will they?" she asked.

We did undress of course, donning disposable paper underwear while the masseurs waited in the next room. We wrapped ourselves in fluffy white robes and lay side by side on a pair of padded massage tables. It was a blissful experience, far removed from the brutal agony of a Thai massage, and I relaxed completely. Roo, on the other hand, found the experience quite stressful. "I don't like being touched," she explained, "unless it's by you!"

That evening we walked around a water-based theme park that was attached to the other part of the hotel. It had a lack-lustre zoo filled with sad-looking animals in tiny concrete enclosures, and the world's longest pedestrian suspension bridge. The park was billed as 'Asia's Best Attraction', with a vast neon sign stretching the length of the bridge to confirm this. But the 'e' and the 's' in 'best' had malfunctioned, leaving us with something we considered much more appropriate: 'ASIA'S B S ATTRACTION', it boasted.

Breakfast was served in our villa whenever we wanted it, which meant we could stay in bed until noon and not have to leave the place to find lunch.

"You have, ah, one more massage?" the butler reminded me.

"Oh yes! We can have that tomorrow?"

"Ah, okay. I send the girls to your villa, ah, eleven o'clock?"

Roo was a bit concerned about this. "Do we have to tidy up?" she asked later. "And where are they going to massage us? On the bed?"

That evening was a snapshot of the kind of luxury only millionaires aspire to.

It began with a phone call from our butler. He was concerned that rain was forecast, and apologised that we might have to take our dinner in the pavilion. We didn't mind at all, as we'd been planning on going there anyway for cocktails, and it was less than a hundred metres from the front door of our villa.

Then the rain started, and it hit with a fury that defied belief. In seconds our courtyard became a pond, as rain drummed against the villa hard enough to shake the walls. The phone rang again; it was the butler, apologising for the weather.

"When you want your dinner?" he asked.

"Might as well have it now," I said.

"Okay! No problem. I send a car for you."

It took me quite a while to convince him that a car wouldn't be necessary.

Bracing ourselves for a mad dash, we ducked out of our villa – and stopped dead, amazed by the rain. It was ferocious sure enough, soaking us to the skin in seconds, but it was also, rather unexpectedly, *warm*.

So we danced our way to the pavilion, giggling and cooing as sheets of lighting flashed across the sky.

Then the road became like a river, threatening to wash us off our feet, and we had to cling to the ornamental trees as we made our way down the hill.

"So sorry," said our butler, rushing to meet us with fluffy white towels. He was younger than I'd imagined, his jet black hair slicked back, his suit impeccably pressed despite the tropical heat.

We dried off, looked around the pavilion, and were bowled over. A series of tables at the far end of the hexagonal lounge were covered with plates of finger food. There must have been enough posh pastries and miniature cakes to feed ten people, but as far as I could tell we were the only ones in residence.

I looked around for the promised cocktails, expecting to see a jug of bright red liquid sitting amidst the snacks. I couldn't spot anything, so I asked our butler which cocktails were free.

"What you want?" he asked.

"Ah... whichever one is free tonight?" I glanced around for a menu, but there wasn't one in sight.

"I make now," he explained, and slowly it dawned on me — there wasn't a vat of generic 'cocktail' and a stack of plastic cups sitting behind the bar. She was going to make me any drink I asked for — *any drink* — for free. For the next hour.

"I... I don't know what to ask for," I admitted.

"Okay. I bring champagne while you decide."

When it came time for food, I thought I'd try my luck again. Not fancying any of the rather exotic dishes our butler suggested, I asked if I could just have something simple. So he sent the chef out to talk to me. "I don't suppose I could just have a burger, could I?"

His eyes lit up. "Yes sir! I make, very best burger in whole life!"

And he did.

Before we left, Roo persuaded me to clarify a few details about our upcoming massage. Our butler was happy to elaborate; "Second massage... have in your villa. Is... in bath! Is, ah... Roman Bath."

His English was broken and heavily accented, but still the words were enough to send a chill down my spine. Roman baths brought only one thing to mind.

"The girls come, ah... eleven o'clock, to your villa?"

Back at the villa, Roo was seriously uneasy. "Aren't the Romans famous for having orgies? In the baths?"

Yes, in fact they were. But I didn't say that, because the aim of this holiday was to *relax*. There was no point worrying, because this was clearly a classy place. It was also a speciality honeymoon destination; surely there could be no kind of dubious conduct involved?

But I couldn't help wandering into our bathroom to stare down into that huge, sunken tub. How the hell were they going to massage us in it? Kneeling on the tiles? With sponges on long sticks?

"What if they want to get in there with us?" Roo asked.

There wasn't much of an answer to that. Not on our honeymoon, anyway.

Roo didn't sleep at all that night. She was too scared. Next morning, after breakfast, we got the call — two girls from the spa were on their way to our villa. They arrived laden with baskets of supplies, and began their preparations in the bathroom. We spent this time trying to remain calm, sitting on the bed watching old movies on a channel called 'Star'.

"I'm keeping my swimsuit ON," Roo was adamant. "If they tell me to take it off, I'm not doing it. I'll leave."

"It'll be fine love, we're probably stressing for nothing."

But I didn't know how it could be fine. I'd take certain lengths, before the last massage, to *ensure* that I couldn't get an embarrassing erection. Even so, I'd only just gotten through it. If I ended up four in a bath with my wife and two semi-naked massage-ladies... well, let's just say there was bound to be a development.

"What if they want to do us one at a time?" Roo asked. "I'm not going in there on my own!"

The girls had been in there for almost an hour now, in their robes and sandals, running water and giggling to each other. Oh God... it was time.

"We, ah... ready for you now," one of the girls said. She lingered in the bathroom doorway, beckoning.

Roo and I shuffled forwards, hugging our dressing gowns tight around us.

"I'm *not* doing it," Roo hissed through gritted teeth.

Grimly, we approached the bathroom.

"Okay, thank-you!" one of the girls beamed at me. She smiled at Roo, too, and the pair of them withdrew to the front door and slipped out of it.

"What are they doing?" Roo demanded. "Shit! They've gone off to let us get undressed. When they come back, they'll expect us to be naked! What do we do?"

"I... I don't know!"

We stood there, robes gripped in white-knuckles, listening for the girls' return.

We heard nothing.

Roo stared suspiciously at the door. "But... what...? Are they gone?"

"I dunno?"

"Did they hear me? Do you think I scared them away?"

"Nah, surely not."

"But are they coming back?"

"I dunno!"

"Check, please," Roo begged. I shared her concern; perhaps they were waiting politely around the corner, giving us plenty of privacy while we stripped off. After all, that had happened at the last massage. Hell, maybe they were around the corner stripping off themselves!

That had NOT happened at the last massage.

But no. Both girls were gone, disappearing down the path with impressive speed, given their size. Roo and I were alone, and stressed to the point of sweating into our silken dressing gowns. As one we approached the bathroom, still half afraid there was someone waiting in there for us. This is what we saw:

The bathtub was brim-full of bubbles, steaming hot and inviting. Dozens of candles had been placed on the floor in a ring around the tub, and every surface was strewn with fresh rose petals.

It was beautiful.

I dipped a toe in, and a delicate fragrance was released from the water. It rose on the steam, filling the bathroom with the scent of exotic flowers…

And that's when I realized.

This wasn't a Roman Bath.

It was an Aromatherapy Bath.

Somewhere, lost in translation, was the truth that would have set us free from a night of sleeplessness and a morning on the borders of panic.

Aroma-bloody therapy.

Where The Heart Is

We arrived in Perth at the start of summer, and it was like coming home.

Technically, it *was* coming home.

Even though we didn't actually have a home.

Things went well for us in spite of this – in fact, they went very well.

I toyed with the idea of whether or not to tell you this because I hate to risk ruining my street cred, but I decided to include it for the sake of completion.

I had a boring year.

I know! I'm sorry.

It happens to the best of us, and it was bound to happen to me sooner or later.

I blame Roo.

Mostly because, so blissfully happy was I, that I didn't feel the need to rush headlong into inadvisable situations.

Was she making me a better man? Well, I'd like to think so.

But for a while, it meant that most of my adventures were the same, mundane adventures that we all get up to now and then.

So, without boring you all to death, this is what happened:

It was a fantastic year, and one of my personal favourites. I was a married man; my relationship with

Roo was reaching a deliciously comfortable place, where we'd managed to shake off our various insecurities and really enjoy life together as husband and wife.

We didn't get out much.
Roo got a job, cleaning for the Disability Services Commission. It wasn't what she wanted, having trained in animal care and worked previously at Perth Zoo, but beggars can't be choosers; at that point we were as close to being beggars as we've ever been.

Roo worked that job, cleaning care homes for the disabled,

mopping up sick and shit and even worse substances, for a whole year. She did all this so that I could write, and it's something I will never forget. She supported us; more to the point, she supported me, as I lounged around the house drinking copious amounts of coffee and playing at being a writer. When she dragged herself out of bed at half-past six in the morning, I either got up and helped make her breakfast – and then went back to bed – or else I couldn't get up at all. Such is the arduous lifestyle of an author! How she put up with it I'll never know, but she did, and for that she has my undying appreciation and heartfelt thanks.

By the end of the year, I'd somehow managed to finish my second book. It was rubbish, but I figured I'd better publish the thing pretty quick or else Roo might start asking me for my share of the rent. So I released 'Don't Need The Whole Dog' on an unsuspecting (and largely uncaring) public in the last few days of 2012.

It did alright.

Other things happened that year:

We bought a car, and Roo crashed it. I didn't mind; it was a damn ugly car at the best of times, and she managed to keep driving it for the rest of the year, despite it sounding like a pod-racer from *Star Wars*. The only major damage was to the air-con, which is quite important in Australia, in the middle of summer. It meant poor Roo finished every journey dripping with sweat, and after a while the inside of the car started to smell quite… interesting. Having a bonnet shaped like a question mark also seemed to attract trouble. Regularly we'd come back to where we'd parked to find several new dents, as though random passers-by thought the car looked so bad, they could get away with giving it a good kicking. And they did.

We moved into a large room in a surprisingly nice student house. It was a brand-new build with all the latest gadgets, including a flat-screen TV so wide I couldn't touch both sides of it at once! It also featured a thumb-print scanner instead of a keyhole to unlock the front door. I thought I was seeing the future. Unfortunately for Roo, the role of a cleaner takes quite a toll on the hands; by the end of her first week at work she couldn't get in, with the scanner refusing to recognize her battered and waterlogged fingerprints. Every time she got home she had to phone me from outside, and I came down to open the door for her. Eventually our landlady noticed and gave Roo a swipe-card to override the thing, but even that didn't help when the scanner batteries died; this happened roughly every two weeks, and for a day or two no bugger could get in. That was when I became most popular; all our housemates had me on speed-dial, because out of the lot of us, I was the only one that never left the house.

We joined an eye-wateringly expensive gym. All the gyms in Australia are eye-wateringly expensive, but this one just happened to be the most cornea-moistening outfit of all. Now, gyms are inherently dangerous to someone as uncoordinated as me. In a short space of time I managed to punch myself in the face hard enough to draw blood, fall off a treadmill (whilst trying to look down Roo's cleavage), and ended up exercising in one of Roo's skin-tight pink t-shirts, after forgetting to bring my own.

I got some strange looks in the changing rooms, I can tell you.

Oh, I also saw my first live scorpion – not that it stayed that way for very long. Was it on a desert safari? Or in some zoo's insect encounter experience? No. Roo's sister Sonja caught the little bugger trying to sneak into our fridge.

Ah, Australia!

Oh yes, and having sold a handful of copies of 'That Bear Ate My Pants!' to friends and family, I'd been forced to watch the trickle of sales dry up almost completely. Then Amazon, in their ultimate wisdom, unleashed a program they called 'Select'. It was an option to sell books exclusively through them (as opposed to other eBook retailers like Kobo and iTunes) – and in return, they offered the chance to make my book free for a few days at a time. I know what you're thinking – pretty crummy deal, right? Well I 'umm'ed and 'ahh'ed over it for months, and when the first success stories started rolling in I cursed my uncharacteristic caution and signed up. Having missed Christmas, I made my book free for two days on the 15th and 16th of February, figuring any women lucky enough to get a Kindle for Valentine's Day would be looking for something interesting to put on it. I spent a week preparing the sale, setting up adverts and promotions with as many websites and newsletters as I could find, then I crossed my fingers, my toes – hell, I crossed everything with an opposing appendage – and pushed the button.

Two days later, 'That Bear' had been downloaded 22,701 times. It topped the Amazon charts for free books, dropped back into the full-price charts, and within forty-eight hours was the no.1 selling travel book on both sides of the Atlantic.

So, you know, that was quite exciting.

An emotional rollercoaster ride, if ever there was one.

It very nearly paid for my gym membership.

This was also the year of the rainbow. Having dyed Roo's hair a variety of colours during our time together, we decided to step up our game. First we (by which I mean, I) bleached her entire head – then we set about turning it into a rainbow! With six different colours in vertical stripes, we managed the whole process in about four hours. Roo then got to spend a night sleeping with her head wrapped in tinfoil and plastic wrap, a look which earned her the nickname 'Condom-head'.

The next morning, as Roo stood at the sink eating chocolate sprinkles on toast,

with multi-coloured splotches staining her ears and neck and her head bristling with tinfoil spikes, it occurred to me why I married her; I collect strange things.

The dye job turned out rather well – so well in fact, that she decided to keep it. Which means I've had to do it again – and again – *and again* – every two months since then. Some days I think we spend more on hair dye than we do on food.

But she's worth it.

And... that's pretty much all I have to report. As I said: boring.

As summer came around, signalling the end of the year (I'll say it again – Australia is one weird-assed country!), both Roo and I began to get itchy feet. Either we were sharing a fungal infection, or the desire to travel was starting to reassert itself.

In case you're wondering, it was the latter.

But I bought some cream just in case.

In that strange synchronicity that sometimes happens in families, Mum got in touch to say she was thinking about booking a holiday in Australia. She wanted to bring my Aunty Margaret, Uncle Paul's wife, to get a taste of adventure.

Margaret hadn't been able to go on holiday since Paul had been diagnosed, and since losing him over a year ago, she hadn't wanted to. Mum knew this would be the perfect opportunity for her to start enjoying herself again, and so had convinced her that there was more to Australia than a breeding ground for the world's deadliest snakes and spiders.

Gill and Chris had just finished working another ski season in New Zealand, and they were keen to meet up too. It was set to be quite a gathering! We compared notes and decided that Cairns, a city in the tropical far north-east of Australia, would be the most interesting place to visit.

Can I Kiss Her Yet?

Roo and I had been trying to figure out how best to deal with our insidious wanderlust. We'd started looking at vans, wondering if we dared buy another one and try to reclaim the sense of fun and freedom we'd felt traveling around in Rusty. There was a certain type of four-wheel-drive van, a Mitsubishi Delica, that we were particularly fond of. Big enough for us to sleep in, it would allow us to reach parts of Oz that we'd never seen before – parts of Oz that regular vehicles couldn't access. Neither of us knew much about off-roading, but there was plenty of potential for practice – pretty much all of Western Australia is trackless, scrubby outback.

There was only one problem; those vans, even second hand, were damn expensive in Perth.

And then, having bought our flights to Cairns, we made the mistake of looking to see what vans were on sale over there.

And there it was: our dream machine.

Extra-long wheel-base. Fully equipped for living in. Extra fuel tanks; extra water tanks. Camping gear, fishing gear, hiking gear...

Arctic-white colour scheme. Moon roof...

There were numbers to consider.

So far to date, my book sales had managed to net us a little over eight thousand dollars. I could hardly believe it, but the proof was right there in my bank account.

Coincidentally, this van-shaped piece of perfection was on sale for just a fraction under $8,000.

It was almost too good to be true.

Of course, the van was in Cairns, on the opposite side of the country; 3,264 miles away to be exact. It would be one hell of a drive...

But that had never stopped us before.

And we'd already paid for the return half of our flights, which was a bit of a bummer.

But we'd both missed flights before. Hell, if I hadn't missed my flight home from Thailand the first time around, I might never have met Roo.

So.

It was time to do some thinking.

Holiday

Cairns, in the tropical far-north of Queensland, is every bit as exotic as it sounds.

Trapped between the mountains and the sea, surrounded by jungle, it's a tiny haven of modern life in a land still wild and primal.

Put simply, we loved it.

It had been almost a year since I'd seen Mum, and the last time I'd seen Margaret had been at my wedding. Stood together, they looked like a comedy duo; Margaret was every bit as tall as Mum was short. Gill and Chris had left England just before we had; their honeymoon tans had well and truly faded after working two back-to-back ski seasons, and they were obviously looking forward to a few days in the sun. The six of us planned to rent a car (a fairly big car!), and use it to explore as much of the area around Cairns as possible.

On our first afternoon together we wandered into the city itself, which was barely the size of a small town in the UK. There were no high-rise buildings, and none of that sense of busyness and self-importance you get in most cities. Instead, Cairns was laid back to the point of being horizontal. Wide open boulevards led past more cafés, bars and ice cream parlours than I've ever seen in one place. Great chunks of mangrove erupted from the pavements in the way that regular trees do in regular cities, proof that the entire area had been reclaimed from the swamp less than a hundred and forty years ago.

We were skirting the edge of monsoon season, so tourists were light on the ground, but the place was filled with backpackers and hippie-types – I don't think I saw a single sharp suit the entire time we were there.

It was great to have a proper holiday, as the more arduous kind of traveling I'm used to is anything but relaxing. Here, with Mum and Aunty Margaret along for the ride, we decided to take it easy and enjoy ourselves, making the most of each other's company. Of course, we still did a few bits and pieces...

We couldn't resist a trip to the jungle, for example! The Daintree, north of Cairns, is the oldest rainforest in the world; it's been growing continuously for 125 million years. We helped my Aunty Margaret cure her fear of heights by taking her zip-lining through that rainforest. She enjoyed it so much she even had a go at zip-lining upside-down. She was less keen when the guides tried to convince us to eat ants, but I had no such qualms. I bit into an ant and was rewarded with an instant explosion of lime! I've no idea how they evolved like this, but it has to be the world's worst defence mechanism. 'Don't you dare eat me, I'm... very tasty?' The poor little gits must be on the top of the menu for every creature in the forest.

I spotted more of them making a line up the curb as we sat outside the gift shop. "Mmm, lime-y ants!" I said, helping myself to a mouthful.

Even Roo looked slightly sickened. "I wish you wouldn't eat off the floor," she said. Then she noticed my expression. "Are they nice?"

"Nope. Wrong ants," I mumbled.

We went on a quad-bike safari, where both Roo and Mum nearly killed themselves. Roo's bike had no brakes, causing her to come flying off it as it careened down a hill; Mum's bike had perfectly good brakes, but being a gnome, she couldn't reach them. She also couldn't steer, making her spectacularly unsuited to riding a quad bike. She proved this by driving it up a tree stump, and managing to overturn the damn thing on top of herself! I'm happy to say that both women escaped without serious injury, though the guides led us a fair bit slower on the drive home. Honestly, I think they were glad to see us leave.

We rode horses, swam in gorges, and stayed in log cabins and posh hotels. We ate crocodile (in revenge for them not showing up on our croc-watching boat trip), we ate kangaroo (because there's too many of those damn things anyway) and we ate shark (because that's what passes for health food up in the Daintree).

We didn't eat any more ants.

We did get to visit Cathedral Tree, possibly the best example of a strangler-fig anywhere in the world. It's a vine that seeds high up in the branches of a host tree, putting down massive roots to reach the ground at the same time as it climbs skyward in search of the sun. Eventually it strangles and kills the host tree, which rots away leaving the fig vines free-standing. This one was over five-hundred years old, and we could walk right through the middle, standing inside the cavity where the host tree had once been and looking up through an insane tangle of roots and vines right to the top of the fig.

We also snorkelled the Great Barrier Reef, lazed around on a sailing catamaran for a couple of days, and generally lived it up.

One of the last things on our collective To Do list was to see a duck-billed platypus in the wild. There are only a handful of places where this is possible, and we tracked one down in the tablelands south of Cairns. At first there was nothing to see; we hiked to the edge of a muddy lake and spent a solid hour gazing in all directions with no idea of what we were even looking for. "They're shy," said the farmer who owned the land. "And it's coming into the mating season, so all the females are hiding."

"They're not keen on mating then?" I asked.

"No! See, when the male platypus finds a female, he chases her until she's exhausted. When he catches her he uses a big spur on his hind leg to inject her with a paralysing poison. Then he has his way with her, and when she wakes up she's pregnant – and he's gone!"

"Holy shit! So they're date-rapists?"

As if on cue a tiny, furry body shot to the surface for a couple of seconds. It was too far away to see the trademark duck-bill, and so tiny it was pure luck that we saw it at all. In my mind they were like furry seals with Daffy Duck's bright orange beak strapped to their faces; in reality they were about the size and shape of a king-sized Mars bar, and not far off the colour, either.

It made them pretty hard to find in a swamp the size of a soccer stadium.

As the holiday drew to a close, Roo and I realised we hadn't even thought about what we were going to do next. Taking advantage of the wireless internet in our cabin, we looked up the Mitsubishi Delica advert again. It was still for sale – and it was gorgeous.

Eight thousand dollars.

Plus whatever it cost us to drive it home.

Fuel, food, accommodation... and we were bound to stop somewhere for a bit of fun.

"I dunno. Maybe it's fate?" I said, doubtfully.

"Mm," Roo replied.

"The only thing that bothers me is, once we've bought it, we'll be broke again."

"True."

"And then we'll have this amazing van, and all we'll be able to use it for is going to and from work, until we've saved up enough money to do something with it."

"Also true."

"And then, when we've got the money, all we'll basically be doing is recreating our trip in Rusty, only without Gill."

"Yeah. When you put it like that…"

But somewhere, in the murky recesses of my brain, an idea was developing. I'd been leading up to it without even realising, talking myself into it at the same time as I was talking Roo out of buying the van.

Now, suddenly, the idea exploded into my consciousness, fully formed, dripping with promise and begging to be exposed.

It was quite an exciting one.

"I've had an idea," I said to Roo.

"Oh dear," she replied.

"No, seriously! I was just thinking, what a waste it would be to have all those thousands of dollars sitting there, invested in a van that we couldn't do much with. Or, instead…"

"Yes?" She was starting to sound excited already. I guess my mood was contagious.

"We could take that money, and go traveling! We could go some place amazing! You could jack in your job, we could give up the flat, push the car into a skip, and do one more epic adventure! That cash would only buy us one nice van, but we could have a lot of fun with it if we stuck to the cheaper countries. Like Asia, maybe?"

"Wow… That's true! We could go… Oh my God, can we please go to Mongolia?"

"I…? Er, where's Mongolia? Is that in Asia?"

"I don't know, but we could go there. I've always wanted to!"

"Since when?"

"Since… since you said we could travel around Asia!"

"Like, ten seconds ago?"

"I wanted to go *before* that."

"Yeah, right. So, Mongolia, then. And we know Thailand is cheap, but I think most of the countries around there are. Like Indonesia—"

"We could see the orang-utans! In Borneo?"

"—and Laos and Cambodia are pretty cheap—"

"That's where Angkor Watt is! We have to go there!"

"—and China can't be too bad, they make all the cheap stuff…"

"The Great Wall! We've got to see the Great Wall!"

"So, what do you think? We could just do that. Or, you know, not."

"Oh my God, we *have* to do that! Can we? Can we please?"

"So you fancy doing a bit of travelling around Asia then, do you?"

"Oh YES! We'll get to be backpackers again!"

"Well, we'll be on a small budget alright. That eight grand won't last us forever…"

"How long will it last, do you think?"

"Hard to say. Not much more than six months, I reckon."

"*SIX MONTHS?*"

And she started dancing around the cabin, causing the floor to shake quite a bit.

At moments like this I was suddenly reminded just how much I loved her, and why.

Because she was even more excited about this than I was.

And because she would far rather haul her rucksack through some tropical rainforest than invest her money in a nice car and drive it to work.

And because she hadn't spared a thought for the difficulties and dangers this decision would quite likely result in, to say nothing of the poverty we'd be reduced to once it was all over.

And because, despite years of jazz-ballet lessons, she still danced like a goon.

Crossroads

It was the end of the holiday, and we all assembled one last time before going our separate ways. Gill and Chris would be leaving first, going back to New Zealand to collect their gear, before flying on to the UK. They'd been offered jobs in a French ski resort over the winter, and were looking forward to a few more months in the snow. They'd be seeing Mum again before long, as she'd be flying straight back to England with Margaret. Roo and I, however, were an unknown quantity. We still had the room we were renting back in Perth, and I guess Roo *technically* still had a job. It was fairly obvious that she wasn't too fond of it.

We also had our return flight booked back to Perth, though until that point we hadn't actually decided whether or not we were going to take it.

"So, are you going to buy that van?" Mum asked.

I looked at Roo, and she was positively quivering with excitement. That alone told me we had made the right decision.

"Well, we thought about that. And then we thought, it *is* quite a lot of money to spend on what is essentially just a car. And then we thought, bollocks to it! So we've decided to spend six months traveling around Asia instead."

"Oh," said Mum, "right."

She doesn't surprise as easily as she used to. I guess that's mostly my fault.

"When did you decide this?" she asked.

"About five minutes ago."

"Ah! So that's what all the screaming was about. We thought someone was getting murdered."

"No, just excited."

"So where will you go?"

"Mongolia!" Roo shouted. "And Borneo!"

"And probably Cambodia and Laos," I added, "though I've always fancied visiting Nepal…"

"Wow! When are you thinking of going?" Mum asked.

I glanced at my watch out of habit. It didn't give me any clues. "Well, we'll have to do a bit of planning first."

"*Planning?*"

Now that did surprise her.

We were still talking about the possibilities when we reached the airport. This was it – time to split up. Roo and I had a flight to catch, and Mum, while waiting for hers, had a rental car to return.

"Now you make sure you look after Roo," she said, as I hugged her goodbye. "You'll have to take extra-good care of her, if you're off to all those peculiar places."

"I will, Mum," I said, squeezing her tight.

"And you be careful, too," she added. "Please don't get eaten."

That would have made me chuckle, if I wasn't already tearing up. Whether Asia happened or not, I knew it would be a long time before I'd see Mum again.

"Don't worry," I told her, "I almost never get eaten."

Mum pulled away from me, and fixed me with a look that she has perfected over many such goodbyes. It says, 'Look – *I* know you're going to get eaten, and *you* know you're going to get eaten, so don't give me any of that *don't worry* shit."

It has to be said, it's a fairly specific look.

But it gets a lot of practice.

I sighed.

"I'll be careful, Mum, I promise. But honestly, there's nothing to worry about. It's only six months around Asia. What could possibly go wrong?"

THE END.

OR IS IT...?

Your Free Ebook Is Waiting!

Hi there folks!

For a LIMITED TIME ONLY, I am offering a FREE e-copy of my first book 'That Bear Ate My Pants!' to anyone who signs up to my New Release Mailing List!

The number one question I get asked by readers is: *"When is your next book coming out?"*

Actually, that's a lie. The number one question I get is: *"How are you still alive?"*

But what if I told you there was a way to find out exactly when my next book was coming out? Personally? From me! And what if I told you I would also send you all sorts of cool stuff – *completely free?*

Well, clearly you'd knock me over the head and steal my bus money.

BUT WAIT – there is a way! I have created a special New Release Mailing List, specifically to let people know when my next book is ready to be launched. Not only will the people on it be the first to know, I'll also send (very occasionally) special offers, updates on what I'm up to and what I'm planning next…

Oh, and did I mention: a FREE BOOK?!?!

Yes, I know. I've said enough.

Follow the link below to claim your FREE COPY of the e-book that started it all; the crazy travel-comedy, 'That Bear Ate My Pants!'

You'll also be able to secure a spot on my list, which is VERY GOOD NEWS INDEED. Why? Well, because I said so! But also because I'm working on something special: a compilation of the Missing Chapters from *all* my books (you know, the ones I had to cut out because otherwise they'd be way too long…). When those puppies are ready, the only place they'll be going is to the people on this list.

So. Are you in?

Just type: **www.TonyJamesSlater.com/freebook**
into your web browser.

Hi folks! Tony here...

Seeing as how this is already quite a sappy book, I'd like to take this opportunity to express my gratitude and admiration to all my wonderful readers! Thank-you so much for your kind words, emails and Facebook messages – it really helps to keep me motivated. I love all the interaction I get with you folks, and I love making new friends all over the world. Thanks especially to those people who help me out with proof-reading, or who make suggestions like, "Hey, you should have a blacked-out chapter!" – you know who you are.

All of you lovely people are supporting me, allowing me to keep writing, keep travelling, keep feeding Roo chocolate and keep living the dream. That makes you all completely awesome, and I can't thank you enough for it.

I do hope you enjoyed this book, in spite of its oddities – rest assured, it will be back to business as usual with the next book, as Roo and I tackle our six-month adventure around Asia. There will be monkeys, there will be muggings, and of course I die at the end... :0)

Have fun until then.

Safe travels!

My earlier books, in case you're interested, are:

'That Bear Ate My Pants!' – the book that started it all, following my stint as a volunteer in an exotic animal refuge in Ecuador.

'Don't Need The Whole Dog!' is the sequel, based partially in the UK, and then following my adventures in Thailand, and

'Kamikaze Kangaroos!' is the story of my crazy road-trip around Australia in a van called Rusty.

And while you're waiting for the Asia book you can always visit my website, which features pictures of Jordan (not the model, sadly), my wedding, the Grand Adventure, and, of course, Roo's hamsters (but not of my penis surgery. I promise.) It's here:

www.TonyJamesSlater.com

Also, you can find me on Twitter:
www.Twitter.com/TonyJamesSlater
cr catch me on Facebook:
www.Facebook.com/TonyJamesSlater
cr you can always email me:
TonyJamesSlater@hotmail.com
cr check out my crazy blog:
www.AdventureWithoutEnd.com

If you enjoyed this book, please consider leaving a review on Amazon – it doesn't have to be long! Even a couple of words can help convince other readers to try it – and word of mouth is the best form of recommendation an author can get. I really appreciate my reviews, and I read every single one. Thanks in advance!

And turn the page for a pair of excellent books from my good friends…

'Free Country'
by George Mahood

The plan is simple. George and Ben have three weeks to cycle 1000 miles from the bottom of England to the top of Scotland. There is just one small problem... they have no bikes, no clothes, no food and no money. Setting off in just a pair of Union Jack boxer shorts, they attempt to rely on the generosity of the British public for everything from food to accommodation, clothes to shoes, and bikes to beer.

During the most hilarious adventure, George and Ben encounter some of Great Britain's most eccentric and extraordinary characters and find themselves in the most ridiculous situations. Free Country is guaranteed to make you laugh (you may even shed a tear). It will restore your faith in humanity and leave you with a big smile on your face and a warm feeling inside.

Check out 'Free Country' on Amazon!

'More Ketchup than Salsa' by Joe Cawley

When Joe and his girlfriend Joy decide to trade in their life on a cold Lancashire fish market to run a bar in the Tenerife sunshine, they anticipate a paradise of sea, sand and siestas. Little did they expect their foreign fantasy to turn out to be about as exotic as Bolton on a wet Monday morning.

A hilarious insight into the wild and wacky characters of an expat community in a familiar holiday destination, More Ketchup than Salsa is a must-read for anybody who has ever dreamed about jetting off to sunnier climes, finding a job abroad, or momentarily flirted with the idea of 'doing a Shirley Valentine' in these trying economic times.

Check out 'More Ketchup' on Amazon!

About the Author

Tony James Slater is a very, very strange man. He believes himself to be indestructible, despite considerable evidence to the contrary. He is often to be found making strange faces whilst pretending to be attacked by inanimate objects. And sometimes – not always, but often enough to be of concern – his testicles hang out of the holes in his trousers.

It is for this reason (amongst others) that he chooses to spend his life far from mainstream civilization, tackling ridiculous challenges and subjecting himself to constant danger. He gets hurt quite a lot.
To see pictures from his adventures, read Tony's blog, or complain about his shameless self promotion, please visit:

www.TonyJamesSlater.com

But BE WARNED! Some of the writing is in red.

Made in the USA
Middletown, DE
18 February 2022

61504643R00213